African Security Issues

Also of Interest

Military Development in Africa: The Political and Economic Risks of Arms Transfers, Bruce E. Arlinghaus

The Challenges of South-South Cooperation, edited by Breda Pavlič, Raúl R. Uranga, Boris Cizelj, and Marjan Svetličič

Communist Nations' Military Assistance, edited by John F. Copper and Daniel S. Papp

Arab Aid to Sub-Saharan Africa, Pamela M. Mertz and Robert A. Mertz

Nigeria in Search of a Stable Civil-Military System, J. 'Bayo Adekson

The Economics of Political Instability: The Nigerian-Biafran War, E. Wayne Nafziger

†*Africa's International Relations: The Diplomacy of Dependency and Change*, Ali A. Mazrui

†*The Foreign Policy Priorities of Third World States*, edited by John J. Stremlau

†*State Versus Ethnic Claims: African Policy Dilemmas*, edited by Donald Rothchild and Victor A. Olorunsola

†*Alternative Futures for Africa*, edited by Timothy M. Shaw

†*Globalism vs. Realism: International Relations' Third Debate*, edited by Ray Maghroori and Bennett Ramberg

Interdependence in a World of Unequals: African-Arab-OECD Economic Cooperation for Development, edited by Dunstan Wai

An Anatomy of Ghanaian Politics: Managing Political Recession, 1969–1982, Naomi Chazan

PROFILES OF CONTEMPORARY AFRICA:

†*Mozambique: From Colonialism to Revolution, 1900–1982*, Allen Isaacman and Barbara Isaacman

†*Tanzania: An African Experiment*, Rodger Yeager

Senegal: An African Nation Between Islam and the West, Sheldon Gellar

Swaziland: Tradition and Change in a Southern African Kingdom, Alan R. Booth

Botswana: Liberal Democracy and the Labor Reserve in Southern Africa, Jack Parson

The Comoro Islands, Malyn Newitt

†*Kenya*, Norman N. Miller

†Available in hardcover and paperback.

Westview Special Studies on Africa

African Security Issues:
Sovereignty, Stability, and Solidarity
edited by Bruce E. Arlinghaus

As African nations emerge more fully from the immediate postindependence era, there is a pressing need to examine their security concerns from both African and global perspectives. Issues of strategic access and resources, superpower and regional conflict, economic growth and internal stability, and the role of African nations as a significant bloc within the nonaligned world are examined in this collection in light of three concepts: sovereignty—the ability to achieve economic and political self-sufficiency free from foreign or domestic interference; stability—the creation and maintenance of a viable political environment in which orderly and progressive social and economic change may take place; and solidarity—the development of intraregional interdependence and cooperation to foster both sovereignty and stability as well as a more significant and beneficial role for Africa in world affairs.

Dr. Bruce E. Arlinghaus (Major, U.S. Army) has been assistant professor of anthropology in the Department of Social Sciences, U.S. Military Academy, West Point. He is currently on assignment in the Office of the Deputy Chief of Staff for Operations, Headquarters, U.S. Army, Europe. He is author of *Military Development in Africa: The Political and Economic Risks of Arms Transfers* (Westview, forthcoming) and editor of *Arms for Africa: Military Assistance and Foreign Policy in the Developing World* (1983), and (with Lee D. Olvey and Henry A. Leonard) *Industrial Capacity and Defense Planning: Sustained Conflict and Surge Capability in the 1980s* (1983).

In memory of
Raymond Joseph Arlinghaus
(1906–1975)

African Security Issues:
Sovereignty, Stability, and Solidarity

edited by Bruce E. Arlinghaus

Westview Press / Boulder, Colorado

Westview Special Studies on Africa

The views and opinions expressed in this book are those of the authors and are not intended as any official statement or interpretation of the policies of the United States Military Academy, Department of Army, Department of Defense, or of any other agency of the United States Government.

Published in 1984 in the United States of America by
  Westview Press, Inc.
  5500 Central Avenue
  Boulder, Colorado 80301
  Frederick A. Praeger, President and Publisher

Library of Congress Cataloging in Publication Data
Main entry under title:
African security issues.
  (Westview special studies on Africa)
  Based on papers presented at a panel held during the annual meetings of the African Studies Association in Washington, D.C., in November 1982.
  Includes index.
  1. Africa–Strategic aspects–Congresses. 2. National security–Congresses. I. Arlinghaus, Bruce E. II. Series.
UA855.A36 1984   355'.03306   83-14560
ISBN 0-86531-607-4

Printed and bound in the United States of America

10   9   8   7   6   5   4   3   2   1

Contents

vii

Acknowledgments

As African nations emerge more fully from the immediate postindependence era, there exists a pressing need to examine their security concerns from both a regional and a global perspective. Issues of strategic access and resources, superpower competition and regional conflict, economic growth and internal stability, and the role of African nations as a significant bloc within the nonaligned world are examined here in light of three concepts: *sovereignty*—the ability to achieve economic and political self-sufficiency free from foreign or domestic interference; *stability*—the creation and maintenance of a viable political environment in which orderly and progressive social and economic change may take place; and *solidarity*—the development of intraregional interdependence and cooperation to foster both sovereignty and stability as well as a more significant and beneficial role for Africa in world affairs.

The majority of the chapters in this volume originated in a panel on "Inter-African Security Issues" held at the annual meeting of the African Studies Association in Washington, D.C., in November 1982. I would like to thank those who participated in that panel—Mike Clough, Steve Tucker, Don Rothchild, Claude Welch, John Ostheimer, Annette Seegers, and Pauline Baker—since their efforts and cooperation have provided much of the impetus of this book. I owe a special debt to the other contributors, whose collective response to a barrage of letters and telephone calls has produced papers of equal merit, complementing those of the panelists.

Funding for my participation and research was provided by the Faculty Development and Research Fund of the Association of Graduates, United States Military Academy. I would be remiss if I failed to acknowledge the support and assistance of my colleagues in the Department of Social Sciences at West Point. I would also like to thank Lynne Rienner and Deborah Lynes of Westview Press for their good faith and patience in helping me bring this book together.

The royalties from the sale of this book are being donated to the Emergency Committee for African Refugees of the Phelps-Stokes Fund. It is the hope of the contributors that this book will assist in the peaceful resolution of the issues we discuss, but our consensus is that we also wish to assist those displaced by the conflicts that more often than not have emerged in the name of security and its pursuit.

Finally, I must advise the reader that as an employee of the U.S. government, my statements, interpretations, and recommendations are like those of my nongovernment colleagues—totally my own and in no way representative of official positions or policies of the U.S. government or any of its departments or agencies.

Bruce E. Arlinghaus

Introduction
Bruce E. Arlinghaus

As the first quarter century—more or less—of African independence draws to a close, there is a growing awareness on the part of both Africans and Africanists that the nature of political relationships in the region is changing. Despite the idealism and optimism of the independence era that somehow African states would behave in ways fundamentally different from other nations,[1] Africans and their political behavior have proved similar.

In addition to the internal instability that has characterized much of the first two decades of African statehood, there has been a growing incidence of interstate conflict and an emphasis on a military resolution of political differences. These conflicts, and African concerns with them, have provided the superpowers, as well as the former colonial powers, with opportunities for direct and indirect intervention in the region, something that African states feel powerless to prevent. Foreign military forces are now stationed on African soil,[2] and agreements permitting other forms of military access either have been reaffirmed[3] or have increased significantly as both East and West have scrambled for influence in the region.

What is most significant about these developments is that they have often occurred with African acquiescence, as individual states and leaders pursue their own political and nonpolitical goals. Although it might be argued that such agreements are merely a new military manifestation of neocolonialism, such an interpretation is both simplistic and paternalistic.[4] The situation is in fact much more complex. It is true that African states are in many ways economically and politically dependent upon the developed world, but this dependency is mutual. African leaders increasingly recognize that nations such as the United States and the Soviet Union *need them* to further their own geostrategic ends. By skillful manipulation of these needs and clever exploitation of the superpower rivalry, it is possible to further African goals at relatively low political cost. African leaders, regardless of political philosophy, are neither so naive nor so powerless that they are mere creatures of the major powers. In fact, their tendency to exploit relations with these powers is increasing rather than declining. In essence, African states may not be powerful, but they are certainly not powerless.

1

This environment provides African states with the opportunity to acquire resources and external support to deal with their own changing political scene.[5] Through arms transfers and military assistance, many African nations are developing the capability to pursue goals or influence events beyond their own boundaries. These states, in particular Nigeria, Libya, Ethiopia, and—of course—South Africa, are emerging regional powers[6] the military development of which has caused their neighbors to reconsider their own security beyond the simple requirements for maintenance of internal order.[7] Such growing regional threats, taken together with the continuing domestic instability experienced by most African states, confront them with a security situation infinitely more complex than in the immediate postindependence era. Small, lightly armed constabulary forces no longer suffice to meet their needs. Although more often than not adequate to suppress internal disorder, such forces are not capable of either deterring or repelling a neighboring state.

The increased demand for viable military forces only exacerbates the security situation for African states. Most definitions of national security include an immediate military component—the defense of national boundaries and interests—and an economic component.[8] The pursuit of national security by African states therefore presents them with a dilemma: In order to acquire the military means to preserve their national integrity, they must expend scarce resources vital for economic development. The failure to achieve economic growth in turn threatens both the overall vitality of the state and its internal stability. Although theoretically it is possible to achieve a balance between defense and development, in reality it is difficult to reach a balance without resort to outside assistance.

Many of the more economically successful African states have been able to become so through security agreements with the former colonial powers.[9] But such arrangements, no matter how pragmatic, are subject to accusations of neocolonialism and thus are often seen to be threatening to internal security. Nevertheless many African leaders, because of the tenuous nature of their regimes, have opted to mortgage their future for a modicum of security today. This may be unfortunate, but it is understandable and—more important—is *their* decision to make.[10]

There are a number of ways to examine and analyze growing African concerns with security. The first, and most obvious, method would be to examine regional conflicts occurring since independence. Even though this would provide a degree of insight into the causes of conflict and would identify principal regional actors, it would not provide a means for generalization at the regional level and an understanding of the issues confronting all African states, whether or not involved in recent conflict. Another method would be to examine security at the local or national, regional, and global levels. This method is useful, but fails to account for the overlapping nature of African conflicts, military agreements, and interventions. It could be said that every security concern has its national, regional, and international dimensions.

For these reasons a more functional approach has been taken in this volume. The chapters examine a set of security *issues* that confront *all* African states. Although many of the chapters focus on a variety of local, interstate, and global events, the emphasis is on providing the reader with an understanding of the most pressing security problems of African states. The authors who are not Africans themselves possess a depth of experience in the region that allows them to identify and examine these issues in a way that—it is to be hoped—will be useful to Africans and analysts alike. All the contributors have made a concerted effort to deal with these issues realistically and objectively, avoiding the polemic that so often surrounds them.

Recognizing the interrelated nature of the security issues, the book has been organized to deal with what appear to be the three principal areas of African concerns regarding national security:

- African *sovereignty* is threatened both internationally and regionally by the superpowers, by former colonial powers, and by neighboring states. The chapters examine in detail the growing superpower rivalry in Africa, the central role economically and militarily of former colonial powers and emerging Third World powers, and the increasingly frequent tendency of African states (especially emerging African regional powers) to intervene militarily in the affairs of their neighbors.
- African *stability* continues to be threatened by the internal forces of the 1960s and 1970s, forces caused by and acting as obstacles to economic development. The chapters analyze the persistent inability of the African state to effectively control and manage its affairs and the continued dominance of ethnic, tribal, and religious factors in domestic politics. Although military intervention in politics continues, the chapter on civil-military affairs identifies a distinctive shift in the composition and ideological orientation of military coups.
- African *solidarity*, long considered one of the great strengths of the region, especially in the immediate postindependence era, persists with limitations. Attempts at economic and defense cooperation have enjoyed only limited success, but—as indicated in the chapter on African cooperation—may yet prove useful. Another emerging regional power—Libya—is examined in light of continued attempts to promote Afro-Arab solidarity and the ambivalent relationships it causes among neighboring African states. The final chapter examines the continued utility of South African liberation as a rallying point for African solidarity and the effectiveness of that solidarity in achieving change in the region.

While these issues by no means exhaust the possible and probable security concerns of African states—as indicated in both the introductory and concluding chapters—they appear at this time to be the most compelling. Although some threats may be less probable for some states, for instance, the likelihood of African involvement in a nuclear war between the superpowers, they remain to concern and often plague African leaders.

In sum, it appears that African states, their peoples, and their leaders, despite their hopes for rapid economic development through regional cooperation and solidarity and the assistance of the industrialized nations, have discovered to their dismay that Adam Smith's dictum "that the first duty of the sovereign is to provide for national defense" applies to them as well.[11] Although subjected to external forces beyond their immediate control, Africans retain the ability, and responsibility, to preserve their own security. As the following chapters show, they are committed to doing so without sacrificing sovereignty, forgoing the idealism of Pan-African solidarity, or upsetting the delicate balance of internal stability.

Notes

1. See Dennis Austin, *Politics in Africa* (Hanover, N.H.: The University Press of New England, 1978), pp. 9–34, for a discussion of these aspirations.

2. "New Scramble for Africa," *The Economist* (September 19, 1981), p. 44. These contingents are relatively small, usually numbering in the few hundreds, with the exception of two would-be revolutionary states, Angola and Ethiopia, in which internal turbulence and radical governments have led to extensive reliance on external troops and advisors. There is an extraordinary range of variation: the overwhelming majority of independent African States do not have foreign troops stationed on their soil; a small number have foreign training missions; an even smaller number, Western military contingents; and two or three, non-Western detachments, usually of large size.

3. See *The Military Balance, 1980–1981* (London: International Institute for Strategic Studies, 1980), for a listing of these agreements.

4. An outspoken proponent of this viewpoint is Robin Luckham. See his "Militarism: Arms and the Internationalism of Capital," *IDS Bulletin* (United Kingdom) no. 8 (1977).

5. Bruce E. Arlinghaus, ed., *Arms for Africa: Military Assistance and Foreign Policy for the Developing World* (Lexington, Mass: D. C. Heath, 1983), pp. 1–7.

6. See *The Military Balance.*

7. For a more detailed analysis of this process of military development, see Bruce E. Arlinghaus, *Military Development in Africa* (Boulder, Colo.: Westview Press, forthcoming 1984).

8. Amos A. Jordan, William J. Taylor, Jr., and Associates, *American National Security: Policy and Process* (Baltimore: The Johns Hopkins University Press, 1980), pp. 1–3.

9. Again, see *The Military Balance.* Although the former French African colonies are bound most closely to their former colonial power, former colonies of the United Kingdom and even of Portugal have continued to develop and maintain formal and informal military relationships. For a recent example, see "Military Cooperation," *Africa* no. 119 (July 1981), p. 10.

10. The idealism of the independence era is not limited to Africans themselves. Many non-Africans continue to believe that security issues (and thus, by inference, military force) are both inappropriate and irrelevant in the region. Such an attitude,

though well intended, places its holders in a paternalistic position of denying African nations the means to meet genuine or at least perceived threats to their national security.

11. Adam Smith, *The Wealth of Nations*, Vol. 2 (London: Methuen, 1950), p. 186.

1. Security Problems:
An African Predicament
Francis M. Deng

The Problem

The security problem in Africa is a manifestation of yet another critical phase in the political evolution of the continent. During the 1950s and 1960s, the peoples of Africa were united by their common struggle against foreign domination. The overriding goal was total independence from colonialism, and the enemies were the foreign powers, which were seen as not only dominating the people of Africa but also exploiting the continent to their own unfair advantage. Even though the situation in Namibia and South Africa remains a painful thorn in the African flesh, the process of decolonization is nearly complete, and the challenges of nation-building are replacing the struggle for liberation. Unfortunately, the issues of nation-building are less clear-cut: the goals are not so well defined, the obstacles are less obvious, the identities of the enemies are blurred, and the whole process is much more intricate and complex.

Nkrumah had promised that once the political kingdom was attained, the rest should flow. The leaders of independent Africa soon saw that their real enemies were ignorance, poverty, and disease. Some viewed the problem in economic terms; others in cultural terms; and still others blamed these afflictions on neocolonialism and the subtleties of remote influences and continued foreign domination. While the rhetoric continued against foreign exploitation of one form or another there evolved an increasing realization that interdependency was perhaps a more accurate way of describing postindependence relations with the former colonial powers and other nations of the world. Some form of cooperation rather than confrontation became the theme. Efforts in this direction continue and despite the increasing difficulties in the North-South dialogue, the tone has been set. Emphasis is increasingly being placed on defining the mutual interests underlying international cooperation.

Originally presented as the Thirteenth Annual Hans Wolff Memorial Lecture at Indiana University, October 23, 1981. Copyright 1982, African Studies Program, Indiana University. Reprinted by permission of the author and Indiana University.

Perhaps one of the most critical developments in this evolutionary process has been the extent to which internal differences, tensions, and conflicts surfaced once the common bond of the common struggle against a common enemy was loosened by the achievement of independence. The assumption of political power by the nationals was initially viewed in collective terms, not dissimilar to economic statistics of gross national product, which do not specify who gets what from the produce. A breakdown of power has made inequities apparent, however. And just as gross-statistical affluence does not gratify the poor, collective independence that gives power to one faction does not end the liberation struggle; it only changes the identities of the conflicting parties, and internal diversities and disparities begin to manifest themselves and undermine the people's sense of unity, national identity, and common purpose in nation-building. Internal strife, expressed at various levels, follows, often resulting in frequent changes of governments through revolutions, coups, and counter-coups. Sometimes the strife extends beyond domestic confines to generate tensions between nations, exploding in violence and regional hostilities. The scope of these conflicts has unfortunately gone beyond the continental scene, entailing a new form of dependency on foreign powers, especially in the critical field of military assistance. The bonds with foreign powers may be ideological or purely pragmatic, the crucial factors being the readiness to deliver the goods or the presence of a common enemy. The more foreign intervention has increased, the greater the reaction of the African countries against foreign intervention as a matter of principle. But the reality remains a pervasive encouragement of foreign intervention.

It was at the Organization of African Unity (OAU) summit at Libreville in 1977 that the African heads of state pronounced themselves as opposing what they viewed as the grave issue of foreign intervention. Since then, far from abating, the problem has intensified as one area after another has found itself in regional conflicts that have attracted foreign intervention. The cycle between regional tension, conflict, and intervention has been reinforced, for these evils breed on one another.

The Causes

Events of this gravity and magnitude do not just occur in a senseless way, for the consequences are too severe to be taken lightly by any of those concerned. We must assume that there is some explanation somewhere, however much we may disagree on the soundness of the grounds. What are the root causes of the tensions, the turmoil, and the conflicts that plague the domestic and regional scene of independent Africa? What are the motives of the conflicting parties? What compels African nations to resort to foreign powers for military intervention even at the risk of compromising, if not endangering, their hard-won independence? And what moves foreign powers to respond positively at the grave risk of themselves becoming engulfed in armed conflict away from their boundaries?

If Africans reject dependency on foreign powers, how else do they tackle the formidable problems that compel them to resort to foreign powers?

Of course, I am not so presumptuous as to claim that I have answers to these questions, but I would like to go a little deeper into an angle that I believe is quite pertinent. I begin my analysis with the premise that issues of peace and security are domestically rooted, but that the domestic scene cannot be seen in isolation from regional and international dynamics. A cursory look at the African scene will reveal that complex trends have generated diversities and disparities that provide fertile soil for confrontation and conflict. Africa has experienced a process of fusion and fission that many consider to be part of the colonial designs of unite and divide and rule, but that the colonizers themselves defend as recognition of existing realities and protection of the weaker partners in the newly established system of nation-states. Boundaries between and within these entities were artificially conceived, severing the ties of kith and kin. New identities were fostered that maintained and even reinforced alienation and disintegration. As a result of racial, cultural, and religious manipulations, a mutually hostile view was fanned into a sophisticated political stand. During the struggle for independence, these differences were secondary and were overshadowed by the common fear, but the removal of the common enemy soon elevated them to the frontline of divisive national issues.

Colonial experience and the advent of the modern nation-state invaded the traditional African egalitarianism with European concepts of political, social, and economic stratification. New educational, economic, social, and cultural opportunities were offered, with striking consequences that deepened the new concepts of stratification. Diversities and disparities provided breeding grounds for political factionalism and power struggle. Between countries, the problem became manifest in the anomalies and sensitivities of artificial boundary demarcations. The result of these struggles and border confrontations is actual or potential hostility. To meet the challenge, the parties concerned need weapons. Weapons require financial resources and expertise that are often lacking or inadequate. So, the poor nations of Africa get into heavy debts, and experts become essential parts of the weapons. Should the exigencies demand, troops are requested and flown in. Then African nations fall back into the intractable web of dependency.

The scene is further dramatized in political, economic, and humanitarian terms by the great influx of refugees across the anomalous borders of neighboring countries, an influx that gives Africa by far the largest share of the refugee population of the world. Because of the humanitarian attitude implicit in African family and tribal values and because of the kinship ties that transcend the boundaries of the nation-states, these refugees are generally well received, treated with hospitality, and accepted into the social and economic fabric of the host countries. This favorable treatment of the African refugees contrasts with that of refugees in other parts of the world, but it also has tended to conceal their tragedy and minimize international responses to their needs. Their integration into the recipient countries, sharing the little that is there, has added to the magnitude of the problems these countries face. In political terms, the influx of refugees across the borders often implies extending the domestic problems of one country into another, especially as some of the refugees continue to harbor political ambitions against their adversaries back home. The recipient countries may happen to share the political aspirations of the refugees or at least sympathize with them and lend a helping hand in promotion of their cause. The result is a vicious cycle of complications and aggravations.

The charter of the OAU and the principles governing the organization appear to be contradictory, offering all parties some ground for justifying their conduct. The principle of self-determination appears in conflict with the principle of maintaining inherited boundaries: supporting the right of self-determination for a subject people implies interference in the affairs of others. And often the principle of peaceful solutions to problems becomes only a slogan. Before the Sudan offered a workable alternative by reconciling these principles through a negotiated settlement and the granting of autonomy to the South, the principle of maintaining the boundaries was considered so sacrosanct that even a genuine grievance of a minority people was totally disregarded. Internal suffering and subjugation were overshadowed by the principles governing the boundaries and forbidding interference in the domestic affairs of others.

While deploring foreign presence in Africa, the Organization of African Unity recognizes the right of any country to invite any power, African or foreign, to intervene and assist the inviting country with its security problems. This is viewed as falling within the sovereign right of any state, especially as foreign intervention is usually seen as a matter of necessity or survival.

Of course, the subjectivities of the states concerned are vital to their felt needs, but it would be wrong to place the motivation of all the states on par. Some are motivated by ideological missionary zeal; others have territorial ambitions in disregard of the colonial boundaries or the accepted principles of the OAU; still others are motivated by dreams of greater unity, which they believe would be facilitated by overthrowing uncooperative regimes and replacing them with more agreeable ones; and yet others are primarily reacting to the threats and dangers they see in the attitude of other states. Put in other words, some states react aggressively, others defensively.

The motivations of the aiding foreign countries also differ. Some are economically motivated to acquire or maintain access to Africa's raw materials, including the vast resourses still to be tapped and utilized; others are driven by strategic imperatives and ideological rivalry (implicit in the strategic or ideological race for military power is the accumulation of weapons that rapidly become outmoded and for which a purpose or a market must be found); others combine all these motives with the strategic move to fill a vacuum that they believe is created by the withdrawal of colonial powers. This last point is of special importance and calls for deeper reflection.

When I was ambassador to Washington, I attended a meeting between the African ambassadors and then Secretary of State Henry Kissinger. The issue for discussion was U.S. African policy. Dr. Kissinger found the meeting to be an opportunity for voicing U.S. unhappiness with the critical attitude of the Africans against the United States and their contrasting approving attitude towards the Soviet Union. According to Kissinger, whatever the United States did was viewed as wrong and whatever the Soviet Union did was accepted as right. In his own words, "It is statistically impossible for the United States to be always in the wrong." A similar complaint was often voiced to me by senators and congressmen, and I must say that I was so sympathetic to the arguments that I have often quoted them in my talks and discussions.

But I also offer my American friends an explanation that at least distributes the responsibility for this oversimplification. There is no doubt that until recently the main preoccupation of Africa was liberation from colonialism, and although the United States has been a catalyst in the decolonization process, the enemies of the liberation struggle were allies with interests viewed as inherently bound together with those of the United States. The United States found itself in something of a dilemma. On the one hand, the very foundation of the United States stood out as a conspicuous symbol of the Independence Movement, with all it implies of freedom, liberty, and equality. The motivations of the Africans' rise against colonialism were not too different from those that two hundred years ago drove the Americans to rise against Britain. Presumably this initially prompted the United States to champion the worldwide move for independence, following World War II. On the other hand, it was not easy for the Americans to take sides with their allies' adversaries and to disregard their mutual interests. The result of these paradoxes was an ambivalent relationship with Black Africa. While not vocally opposing—indeed while endorsing—the African move for independence, the United States did not actively support the liberation struggle, an attitude that the Africans identified with that of the imperial powers.

In sharp contrast to the United States and her European allies, the Soviet Union and other countries of the communist bloc took the obvious alternative, unequivocally identified themselves with the colonized peoples of Africa and worked actively to support their struggle for independence.

This complicated the picture of African-American relations and made the struggling Africans appear communist-inspired opponents of the United States. But as Africa began to score victories and liberate itself, the political strategy of the United States in the 1950s and 1960s was to strengthen those African regimes it was felt would assist in containment of communism. Cold-war political objectives and access to military facilities weighed heavily in the selection of recipient countries. But the more the United States worked to strengthen regimes against communism—with little or no regard to the interests of the masses, the more these regimes grew unpopular, the more the United States became resented, and the more the vicious circle perpetuated itself.

In the face of these deeply rooted biases, many African countries initially tended to be aligned towards the socialist bloc, even as they pronounced themselves dedicated to the principles of nonalignment. This is the attitude Henry Kissinger and congressional representatives complained about.

The picture has gradually begun to change. An increasing number of African countries have come to realize that the weapons needed for the war of liberation are not the same as the weapons needed for peacetime reconstruction and nation-building. These countries are unmasking the elements of interference, dependency, and even domination in the attitude of those foreign powers that initially appeared to have an altruistic desire to aid the African liberation struggle. Some countries have gone as far as to realize that these self-seeking motives are perhaps more dangerous in the long run than the overstated interests of the United States and the Western world against communist expansionism.

A sense of history and an explanation of past attitudes remain necessary to facilitate a better understanding and appreciation of one another and a recognition of the mutual interests at stake in the face of a more subtle, but perhaps more dangerous, threat from the opposing bloc. It does not help to resent the critical attitude of Africa, yet not to ask how such an extreme prejudice has evolved. To understand the causes of the mutual prejudices opens the door to remedying the problems.

Sudan's Experience

Now, I would like to say a word about the experience of the Sudan with respect to the issues I have raised.

Because of the domestic foundations of security problems in Africa, it is often said with justification that the best way for any government to ensure internal security is to put its house in order, serve the interests of its people to a pacifying level of satisfaction, and sustain a degree of national consensus behind government policies, programs, and actions. Sudan offers a good example of both the validity of this argument and the limitations of domestic efforts in the face of problems imposed from outside the country and the continent.

Sudan is typical of the problems of diversity and disparity that characterize many countries of Africa. The complex Afro-Arab realities of the country, which are true even of the North alone, were molded and manipulated to a point at which the country was reduced to the simplistic labels of Arab North and negroid South. (Here I must tell a favorite story of mine that illustrates this point. A southern Sudanese came to study in the United States. He had a burning desire to get into New York, and particularly to Harlem, to see the American blacks, then called Negroes, about whom he had heard a great deal. The family he lived with took him to New

York; as they drove around the streets of Harlem, he wondered where the Negroes were. His hosts drew his attention to the many people all over the area. "These!" remarked the Sudanese. "But they are Arabs." And indeed the American black looks very similar to the northern Sudanese.)

When the Sudan became independent, the South and North were almost alien parts of one country that agreed only on getting rid of colonialism but otherwise faced the dawn of independence with a political crisis that erupted into civil war. The example of the Sudan is striking—not so much because of the many problems it has in common with Africa as because of the remarkable model it offered Africa for the solution of similar problems and the unfortunate way these positive domestic achievements are being threatened by adverse external involvement. After seventeen years of an acute civil war that had devastated the country, crippled the economy, and brought the constitutional developments to a standstill, the government, under the leadership of President Nimeiry, was able to achieve peace through negotiations and dialogue, granting the South regional autonomy within the united Sudan. With this remarkable achievement, many other positive developments came in rapid succession. Sudanese were at long last able to agree on a permanent constitution. An ambitious program of social and economic development, aimed at bridging preexisting gaps between South and North and between rural centers and urban centers, soon captured the imagination of the entire country and became a constructive replacement to the psychology of conflict. Development became an ideology, a strategy for reinforcing and consolidating the achieved peace and unity. Sudan's foreign policy and diplomacy were directed towards serving the domestic purposes of soliciting foreign assistance in the monumental task of repatriating, resettling, and rehabilitating the million returnees and displaced people in the South and of promoting international cooperation for the development of Sudan's vast resources in the mutual interest of all. Trilateral cooperation with Western technology and Arab financial contributions was envisaged as turning the Sudan into the breadbasket of the Middle East.

In due course, the spirit of national reconciliation was extended to welcome back and integrate into the institutions of government those elements of the opposition abroad who had only a year before staged a bloody and costly invasion of Khartoum. Prisons were emptied of all political prisoners. Peace, unity, reconciliation, and development became the catchwords. With the success of the southern experience, Sudan extended the principle of regional autonomy to all parts of the country, thereby taking power to the people and involving them in their own government and development.

Over the years, Sudan won regional and international recognition as a country that had truly put its house in order. Bilateral agreements were concluded and joint committees established to ensure peaceful coexistence and cooperation with the neighbors. Morally strengthened by its domestic achievement, Sudan became a strong advocate of peaceful ways of resolving disputes. It took or supported regional or international initiatives towards that end, presented its own experience as a model that might be relevant to the solution of similar problems in the region, and hoped that Sudan's domestic achievements might spread in positive ripples across its extensive borders into the neighboring countries.

Unfortunately, that did not prove to be the case. As tension and conflict pervaded the surrounding areas, as refugees poured into the Sudan in unprecedented numbers, as the borders became trouble spots, and as regional and international politics began to polarize countries, Sudan increasingly became a target to adversaries operating within and abroad. The very size and composition of the country, the dualism of its ethnic and cultural identity, the multiplicity and diversity of its neighbors, and its overall geopolitical position reflect potentials for both exciting opportunities and grave difficulties. I am reminded of a conversation I recently had with a colleague from an island country. After outlining the problems his country faces, he concluded with a positive note: "At least we do not have the problem of neighbors." One only has to glance at the trouble areas surrounding the Sudan to realize the magnitude of the problems facing the country. And the danger is more than potential, for on at least two occasions the Sudan suffered severely from coup attempts that were inspired and supported by foreign powers. These past experiences, and the looming threats that have recently been the subject of wide international coverage, show the extent to which it is not enough to put one's house in order to ensure domestic security. The problem of security in Africa is local, regional, and global and should be approached as such.

The problems of the Sudan have been aggravated by the world economic crisis, especially the balance-of-payment problems resulting from the bills for oil and other imports from industrial countries dictated by the immense development activity going on in the country. The very achievements of the government—autonomy in the South, ambitious development programs, the restructure of the country's political system, broadened national reconciliation, and the more recent extension of autonomy to the other parts of the country—all imply tremendous expenditures. It is even a costly exercise to be both Arab and African and to discharge the obligations of that dual identity and the responsibilities to the international community.

Some people have chosen recently to focus on the poverty of the Sudan, wondering whether the slogans of the 1970s that promised to turn the country into the breadbasket of the Middle East have vanished. The answer may not be simple. But in reply other questions can be posed: Do not the 200 million acres of arable land and the vast animal wealth of some 60 million head on which the projections were based still exist in the Sudan? And what of the additional resources that are increasingly beginning to surface, the oil reserves, the mineral wealth, and the untapped potentials of that vast land in the heart of Africa? Short-term needs resulting from the crisis situation and the impatience of financial institutions should not overshadow long-term potentialities; otherwise, efforts to realize them might be undermined.

New Trends

Despite some of the obstacles and external threats that have confronted—and continue to face—the Sudan, the experience of ending the dispute in the South has set a positive tone towards mediation, arbitration, and conciliation that the Organization of African Unity has recently moved to reinforce and strengthen. Africans are increasingly realizing that intra-African conflicts should be peacefully resolved through the OAU or at least should be submitted to efforts at mediation by individual African leaders or groups of leaders. Committees were set up to work at resolving conflicts between a number of African countries, and in some cases leaders took their own independent initiatives while keeping the organization informed, if not directly involved. Of course, the results have not always been as gratifying as the efforts, but this trend reflects the clear desire of Africa to minimize resort to force. As a consequence of this new trend, the OAU has recently been considering ways and means for revitalizing the Commission of Mediation, Conciliation, and Arbitration provided for in the OAU Charter, which has not been active in the past.

The emphasis on peaceful solutions to problems in today's Africa also poses issues of a crosscultural conflict between the Western conceptions of power and diplomacy that Africa had adopted and assimilated and those of traditional Africa. It was Gunnar Jarring in a lecture delivered in Khartoum who told an animal story, the gist of which was to illustrate the principles of diplomacy. As the strongest animal posed the question of how they should share the prey before them, one rushed into a recklessly greedy answer and was immediately eliminated. The question was posed to the next. His answer was generous and selfless. "From where did you acquire this wisdom?" asked the master beast. The answer was "I saw what you did to the other!" Ambassador Jarring called that primitive diplomacy. Putting aside the precise meaning attached to the word "primitive," I responded by saying that it sounded to me more like what we face in our modern world, orientated as we are to concepts of power that are based on police force and military might. This is the essence of the adversary and coercive character of Western jurisprudence. It contrasts quite sharply with the emphasis that the African concept of law, and I might add diplomacy, places on persuasion and the spirit of mediation, conciliation, and arbitration. This is far from any intimidation or threat, for that would negate the value and meaning of mediation and conciliation. It is therefore not by chance that the founders of the Organization of African Unity established a special commission to discharge these precise functions. As the need has intensified, so has the call for reviewing, adapting, and activating this commission to guarantee its relevancy and effectiveness. Nor need the functions of mediation and conciliation be viewed only in the context of interstate relations, as media for harmonization: they can be exercised for the solution of domestic conflicts. Interference is the unwelcome involvement of outsiders; mediation, conciliation, and arbitration signify positive cooperation.

Issues in Perspective

I conclude with a few observations emanating from the preceding remarks. First, I would like to underline the interrelationship of all levels of the African security scene: The local, national, regional, and international levels are all involved.

This being the case, while there is a great deal of truth in the argument that putting one's house in order is the best way of guaranteeing one's security, the involvement of others—whether within Africa or outside the continent—should not be taken lightly.

In considering the domestic, continental, or international dimensions of the problem, efforts at defusing crises or conflicts through peaceful methods of dispute settlement should be the first priority, one that must be pursued with vigor and intensity.

It is particularly important that the outside world, and especially the powerful nations, view the cause of peace in global and comprehensive terms. In most cases, people hear of conflicts around the world as exciting news items, forgetting that they mean death and disaster to those involved. I recall in the sixties a world-prominent religious leader declaring, "Let there be no more wars." And Vietnam was flaming with war! To some people, the world is at peace; to others, it is at war. It is indeed telling that some of the tribes of the southern Sudan refer to the civil-war days as the time when the world was destroyed.

The global view of peace means that big powers should not continue to negotiate matters of direct relevancy to the maintenance of peace between them, while at the same time permitting and even inciting their confrontation through others on foreign soil. Peace everywhere should be the objective of negotiations anywhere.

One last, but most important, thought concerns the intellectual and scholastic tools of facilitating the cause of peace and security in Africa. Africans are now active participants on the global scene, and scholars can no longer afford to look on the African scene as an isolated frontier for field research, bearing little or no relevancy to issues of global dimensions. Even what may seem culturally remote and exotic might explain the behavior patterns of African leaders or representatives who feel they are part of the modern world and have an input that should not be ignored. Such slogans as "Negritude," "African Socialism," "Authenticity," or "Humanism," espoused by African leaders, are philosophical formulations seeking to give a sense of cultural identity and substance to the aspirations of today's Africa. It is for the intellectual and the scholar to give depth and flesh to such skeletal conceptualizations in order to facilitate the realization of the values subsumed under the slogans.

One of the most challenging intellectual and diplomatic tasks in Africa is how to reconcile principles that now appear to be in conflict. In particular, the principle of maintaining the inherited boundaries needs to be reconciled with the right of self-determination; national unity must be balanced with the aspirations of minority groups for recognition and effective participation in their own government. While it is not easy to achieve a satisfactory balance, I know it can be done because it has been done; all the same grafting a model in a different context is no mean task—but a challenging one.

2. The Soviet Union and Superpower Rivalry in Africa
Arthur Jay Klinghoffer

The Soviet role in Africa at the end of World War II was negligible; so it is certainly not surprising that it has grown subsequently. Especially evident is the dramatic upsurge of military and logistic activity during the past decade, with Cuba emerging as a significant Soviet ally on the African continent. Soviet involvement in Africa has been gathering momentum since the mid-1950s, but its scope has now been broadened to include a substantial military-strategic dimension. Does this expansion therefore mean that Soviet foreign-policy priorities have been adjusted, thereby attaching greater importance to Africa? Not necessarily. It appears more likely that the Soviets have not altered priorities but have been taking advantage of increased opportunities. Subsaharan Africa remains a low-priority region, and North Africa ranks only somewhat higher.[1]

The Soviet Union has many attributes that enhance its image among African states. It is perceived as a valuable source of arms, economic assistance, and student scholarships, and it provides a relevant developmental model based on elite-fostered rapid modernization, socialist economic principles, and centralized one-party rule. The Soviet Union does not have the stigma of having been a colonial power in Africa, and its dearth of historic contacts has largely obviated the possible charge of racism. The Soviets, as exemplified by their assistance to the Popular Movement for the Liberation of Angola (MPLA) in Angola, are commonly viewed as strong supporters of African liberation movements, and the polycentric tendencies within the communist world make Africans less fearful that close ties will lead to subjugation. In contrast to Western states, the Soviet Union does not have to protect access to African raw materials or sea routes, nor does it view revolutionary change as a threat to its influence or ideological goals. Therefore, the Soviet Union is often perceived by the West as favoring destabilization, while Soviet analysts at the same time accuse the United States, Britain, and France of fostering neocolonialism and economic imperialism through a policy of maintaining the political status quo in Africa. Western ties to South Africa are seen as consistent with this pattern.

Conor Cruise O'Brien, an international political observer and former Irish diplomat, has discussed "the counterrevolutionary reflex" that has haunted American foreign policy; his comments bear relevance to the positions of other Western states as well. O'Brien argued that major social changes are taking place in the Third World and that they are inevitably accompanied by political revolution. Communists naturally encourage social and political revolution, and the United States, dreading eventual communist influence, seeks to bolster counterrevolutionary forces.[2] O'Brien presented this analytic scenario in 1966, but his views retain much of their validity today. Central America is an obvious case in point, and superpower activities in Africa also retain many cold-war overtones. While the Soviets aid southern African liberation movements, such as the African National Congress (ANC) in South Africa, the United States (especially during the Reagan administration) has been maintaining a working relationship with the white-minority government of that state. Anticommunism (combined with democratic proclivities) usually prevents the United States from supporting movements that use violence to further their goal of social revolution, but advocacy of evolutionary change is usually ineffectual where counterrevolutionary governments are solidly entrenched through the force of arms. When peaceful social revolution is not possible (as in Zaire), the United States generally opts for the preservation of the existing regime.

Socioeconomic trends in the Third World seem to favor the Soviet Union as traditional and colonial systems of rule give way to the forces of social and political change. Nevertheless, the Soviet Union has displayed limited ability to capitalize on its advantage in the African context—several factors have produced a deleterious impact. The Soviet economic model has been seriously tarnished by mismanagement, production shortfalls, shoddy goods, and the need to import grain and technology from the West. Even most communist-ruled states are attempting to modify substantially their application of Soviet economic mechanisms. In Africa, Marxist economic programs have rarely been successful, but capitalism has clearly fostered growth (despite costs in terms of self-sufficiency and societal inequality) in the Ivory Coast and Kenya. The economic reality is therefore at odds with the socialist, anticolonial psychology.

Although the Soviet Union would prefer to be viewed as revolutionary and attuned to Third World needs, it is actually rather revisionist and part of the industrialized "North." During the 1960s and early 1970s, China was able to outradicalize the Soviets on the left, but its post-Mao shift to the right and alignment with the United States on many African issues has facilitated Soviet political entree in Africa. However, African nationalism is a powerful force that has so far been able to withstand even the most ardent hugs from the Russian bear. Soviet military personnel have been expelled from Egypt, Sudan, and Somalia, and friendship treaties with Egypt and Somalia have been unilaterally abrogated by those states. As Alexander Dallin pertinently averred two decades ago: "African nationalists may adapt Communism, but they will not adopt it. Communism could perhaps become 'nativized' in Africa, but Communism africanized would not yield a Muscovite Africa. The prospect therefore seems to be: Soviet appeal, yes; Soviet control, no."[3]

When evaluating superpower competition in Africa, one must recognize that African states are not merely passive actors. Major crises have usually grown from indigenous roots, and outside states have been encouraged to intervene by sovereign governments or liberation movements. The Soviet involvement in Ethiopia and Angola was based on invitations from the Dergue and MPLA, and Soviet arms and advisors were provided upon request. Similarly, Qaddafi in Libya and Amin in Uganda contributed to the Soviet role in their states by actively seeking weapons. Therefore, to a great degree, Soviet tactics must be viewed as reactive rather than primary.

Africa is frequently the scene of external involvement, as its own armies are often weak, its governments unstable, and its fragile political orders exacerbated by ethnic and boundary problems that derive from the colonial territorial legacy. Former colonial powers retain considerable influence and the Organization of African Unity (OAU) has been unable to resolve most African disputes. The Soviet Union acted decisively in Nigeria in 1967, Angola in 1975, and Ethiopia in 1977 only after the OAU had displayed its ineffectiveness.

The Soviet Union and United States have reciprocal perceptions of supposed imperialist and communist plots in Africa, but direct superpower military conflict has always been avoided. Nevertheless, competition is becoming increasingly military oriented as arms deliveries and the securing of logistic facilities are emphasized. Economic assistance and the activities of the U.S. Peace Corps have been downgraded in importance, and both states have extended their ideological flexibility. The Soviet Union has developed a significant trade relationship with monarchist Morocco, whereas the United States has moved toward strategic alignment with professedly Marxist-Leninist Somalia.

The Evolution of Soviet Policy

The Communist International, founded in 1919 as an organization dedicated to the goals of Soviet foreign policy and the furtherance of socialist revolutions, established an affiliate in 1930 known as the Negro International. Contacts were developed with African (as well as West Indian and American) Marxists, but they bore little fruit as communist influence in Africa failed to grow. After World War II, the Communist parties of France and Britain tried to spread their doctrines in the African colonies, and they met with some success. The major umbrella organization of black political parties in Francophone Africa, the Rassemblement Démocratique Africain (RDA), forged close ties to the French Communist and Socialist parties, but this relationship foundered in 1950 as RDA leader Félix Houphouët-Boigny moved to the right and became a dedicated anticommunist. The British communists tried to influence the primarily English-speaking Pan-African movement. Some of its members, such as Kwame Nkrumah, were decidedly Marxist, but most rejected entreaties from the British communists.

Stalin, who died in 1953, depicted Africa in simplistic cold-war terms. African colonies were considered appendages of the capitalist states, and middle-class African nationalists were labeled "the national bourgeoisie" and deemed proto-capitalist. According to the Soviet interpretation, only the African proletariat under Communist party leadership could effect the true liberation of the colonies. Of course, the African proletariat was miniscule and the sole substantial Communist party in Subsaharan Africa was in South Africa, where whites formed a major membership component. The Soviets therefore missed an opportunity to cater to the good will of African nationalists, who were organizing movements against their colonial rulers.

Soviet attitudes became more flexible during the post-Stalin period. The year 1955 marked a significant turning point in Soviet policy. Under the leadership of First Secretary Nikita Khrushchev, the Soviet Union made a concerted effort to seek political accommodation with Third World nationalist leaders. The neutralism espoused by these men was seen as a "progressive" step away from colonial subservience and as an indication of the weakening of Western capitalist control. Consequently, the national bourgeoisie was viewed more positively, and the Soviet Union praised the convening of the first Third World nonaligned summit in Bandung, Indonesia, in April 1955. Prime Minister Nehru of India visited Moscow in June, and Khrushchev, accompanied by Prime Minister Nikolai Bulganin, traveled to India, Burma, and Afghanistan in November. The Third World diplomatic offensive was underway.

In Africa, the Soviet Union developed close relations with Gamal Abdel Nasser of Egypt, and it welcomed the attainment of independence by the first decolonized black state, Ghana, in 1957. Many African governments espoused socialist ideologies, and the Soviets made a special effort to further contacts with them. Delegates from the ruling parties of Guinea, Ghana, and Mali were invited to the Twenty-second Congress of the Communist Party of the Soviet Union in October 1961, even though these parties were clearly not communist. Lenin Peace Prizes were also awarded to the rulers of these states: Sékou Touré received one in 1961, Kwame Nkrumah in 1962, and Modibo Keita in 1963.

The Soviets maintained that African nationalists could indeed embark on socialist reforms, and this perception was formalized in the adoption of the new ideological concept of "national democracy" in 1960. Modeled on the transformation of Fidel Castro in Cuba, national democracy emphasized the "progressive" role that could be played by Third World nationalists. They could evolve into socialists, convert their parties into socialist parties, and initiate socialist programs of development. Although national democrats were not deemed "communists," they were clearly anti-imperialist and useful allies against the West (Castro was later accepted as a communist in 1962). As a practical consequence of this new ideological interpretation, the Soviet Union no longer endorsed the organization of Communist parties in Africa. Instead, it called upon African communists and other leftists to join the dominant nationalist parties in order to help steer them further in the direction of socialism.

After Nikita Khrushchev was removed from power in 1964, the Brezhnev regime was soon faced with numerous problems in Africa. Three of the leaders most favored by the Soviets for their socialist orientations were overthrown: Ahmed Ben Bella of Algeria in 1965, Kwame Nkrumah of Ghana in 1966, and Modibo Keita of Mali in 1968. At the same time, most African socialist economic programs were beset with mismanagement and inefficiency, and the military seized power from civilian political leaders in approximately half the states in Africa.

The Soviet response was clearly pragmatic. No longer would ideological compatibility serve as an important precondition to diplomatic relationships; economic aid would be allocated sparingly and would be based on careful cost-benefit analysis; ties to military governments would be developed, as the more "progressive" members of the armed forces could be considered "revolutionary democrats." Consequently, the Soviet Union emphasized logistics, trade, and diplomatic tradeoffs and downplayed ideology. Close relations were established with Libya after Muammar Qaddafi overthrew the monarchy in 1969 and with Uganda after Idi Amin toppled A. Milton Obote in 1971. By no stretch of the imagination could either Qaddafi or Amin be considered a Marxist, and neither man organized his political or economic system along Soviet lines.

Soviet pragmatism was particularly evident in Nigeria. When war erupted in 1967 between the Federal Military Government and the secessionist state of Biafra, the Soviet Union at first did not know which side to favor. Neither party to the conflict had warm relations with the Soviet Union, and neither had Marxist proclivities. The Soviets were therefore free to choose sides, and they based their decision on some very practical factors. The central government had seized the early military advantage, and both Britain and the United States, Nigeria's closest Western friends, had announced that they would not provide arms to either combatant. The Organization of African Unity had shown its inability to resolve the conflict, but it was evident that almost all OAU members condemned the Biafran secession and called for maintenance of Nigeria's territorial integrity. The Soviet Union therefore jumped into a power vacuum at little risk as it supplied aricraft and arms, as well as technicians who assembled and tested the aircraft, to the Federal Military Government. The Soviet Union probably hoped to displace Britain and the United States from their influential positions in Nigeria, and it had little to lose even if Biafra won the war. There would still be a central Nigerian government that would possibly be indebted to the Soviet Union for its assistance. As events turned out, Britain shifted its stance and provided some arms and ammunition for Nigeria, Biafra was defeated and reintegrated into Nigeria, and the Soviets were not able to bring about any reorientation of Nigeria's relationship with the superpowers.

The Extension of Soviet Power

Strategic considerations became increasingly significant for the Soviets as a result of the extension of fleet operations, the growing and allied Cuban military role in Africa, the opportunity afforded to replace the North Atlantic Treaty Organization (NATO) as the prime logistic presence in Portugal's African territories, and the anti-Western turn of the Ethiopian revolution. The Suez Canal was closed during the 1967 Arab-Israeli war, and it did not reopen until 1975. In the meantime, the Soviet Union had to redirect its trade with African states toward a circum-African route from the Black Sea through the Mediterranean Sea and the Atlantic and Indian oceans. The Soviet naval fleet therefore began operating further afield in order to secure commercial sea routes and at the same time to expand Soviet military potential vis-à-vis the United States and to show the flag as a means of acquiring greater political influence in Third World states. The Soviet Mediterranean fleet was enlarged, and ships from the Pacific fleet were frequently assigned to the Indian Ocean. In this latter region, geopolitical considerations related to the Sino-Soviet conflict were especially pertinent. In order to sustain its fleet, the Soviet Union needed facilities for refueling, repairs, and shore leave; agreements were worked out with many African states. The situation has surely been fluid, but at one time or another since the mid-1960s, the Soviets have had port rights in Egypt, Sudan, Ethiopia, Somalia, Mozambique, Mauritius, Angola, Congo, Equatorial Guinea, Nigeria, Benin, Guinea-Bissau, Guinea, Algeria, and Libya.

Cuba became an important arm of Soviet strategic policy in Africa. After the Cuban missile crisis of 1962, the fear of a U.S. invasion was considerably alleviated, and cabinet ministries began to replace the armed forces in most aspects of economic administration. Cuba therefore had less need for the maintenance of a large army for domestic purposes, and this freed troops for overseas assignments. Furthermore, Cuba wanted to project the image of a revolutionary power that would assist Third World liberation movements, and it became particularly active in Latin America and Africa. It provided arms, training, and in many cases troops.

Members of a Cuban tank brigade fought on behalf of Algeria against Morocco in 1963, and Che Guevara led an ill-fated insurrection in the Congo-Léopoldville (now Zaire) in 1965. He then established close ties to the MPLA movement in Angola, and training facilities were set up in the Congo (Brazzaville). Cuba also began to assist the Partido Africano da Independência da Guiné e Cabo Verde (PAIGC) in its struggle against Portugal, and Cuban military advisors served in the field in Guinea-Bissau. Cuba was basically acting on its own initiative and was presenting a model of revolutionary communist guerrilla warfare that provided a challenge to the more static and revisionist Soviet model. This was most evident in Latin America, where Castroite movements did not cooperate with the pro-Soviet Communist parties (Che Guevara had little regard for the Bolivian communists during his attempted revolution there in the mid-

1960s), and, in effect, offered a more militant alternative to their existence. The Cubans were not close allies of the Soviets at this time, but beginning with the Cuban endorsement of Soviet intervention in Czechoslovakia in 1968, the relationship changed into one of Cuban support for Soviet foreign-policy ventures.

The Cuban military presence in Angola and Ethiopia reached twenty-six thousand and sixteen thousand respectively, and Cuban military personnel have also served in advisory capacities in Mozambique, Tanzania, Zambia, Somalia, Libya, Congo, and other states. The Soviet Union arms the Cubans for their African adventures and helps transport the troops. However, Cuba pays the salaries, and the host countries provide the housing and food. The Soviet Union has increased economic subsidies to Cuba at times when Cuba has been militarily active in Africa, but any direct causality is difficult to substantiate.

The Soviet Union is viewed warily by many Africans because it is a "white" state that has turned from a bastion of revolution against colonialism and imperialism into a traditional geopolitical competitor for world power. The Cubans present a much more favorable image and are therefore useful adjuncts of Soviet policy. They are Third World revolutionaries from a small country that does not have strategic designs on Africa. They are more willing than the Soviets to mix with the local population, live at a lower standard, and engage in physical labor such as road or bridge construction. In addition, about one-quarter of the Cubans are black.

Cuban military personnel in Africa certainly act in accordance with Soviet foreign-policy interests, but they are not mercenaries: The soldiers do not receive any extra payment for their services in Africa, and the mercenary hypothesis overlooks Cuba's own motivation in sending members of its armed forces to Africa. In addition, the Soviets and Cubans have had some policy differences. They disagreed about the merits of an attempted coup in Angola in May 1977, and the Cubans balked over a major combat role in the Eritrean region of Ethiopia. Overall, the Cubans have strongly assisted Soviet efforts in Africa, especially in Angola and Ethiopia. They are trained in the use of Soviet weapons and can go into battle immediately. Had they not been present in Angola and Ethiopia, a lengthy period would have been needed for the training of Soviet-supported African forces, and the entry of heavy Soviet weaponry into the wars would have been seriously delayed.

Soviet arms and Cuban troops proved decisive in the Angolan war of 1975–1976 and the Ethiopia-Somalia war of 1977–1978. Logistic rights were extremely important: The Soviets transferred arms to Angola through the ports of Pointe Noire (Congo), Dar es Salaam (Tanzania), and Conakry (Guinea); used the airspace of Algeria, Mali, Guinea, and the Congo; and refueled aircraft in Mali, Guinea, and the Congo. In the Ethiopian situation, South Yemen provided the most essential logistics. The direct Soviet-Cuban military role escalated from the Angolan conflict to the one on the Horn of Africa. Soviet arms supplied to the MPLA totaled only $300 million, while over $2 billion in arms went to Ethiopia. Approximately two hundred Soviet military advisors served in Angola, but about two thousand were present in Ethiopia. In the latter case, Soviet generals even conducted field operations of Ethiopian troops. Air power was not used during the Angolan war, but Cuban pilots flew Soviet aircraft on behalf of the Ethiopian cause. In both Angola and Ethiopia, the Soviets were surprised by the events that led to instability: the Portuguese and Ethiopian revolutions of 1974. However, they then reacted to the opportunities afforded them and moved to replace Western states in their positions of influence.

Current Soviet policy toward Africa is more ideological than it had been during the period from the mid-1960s to the mid-1970s in one fundamental area: alliance strategy. The Soviets suffered major setbacks in states such as Egypt and Sudan where the governments had little ideological proclivity toward Marxism-Leninism. Consequently, the Soviet leadership has embarked on a new path emphasizing common ideology as the cornerstone of long-term political relationships. Cadre development has been stressed as the Soviet Union has encouraged the efforts of Angola and Mozambique to organize political parties on the basis of Marxist-Leninist principles. The Soviets have been trying to push Ethiopia in the same direction, but have met with strong resistance from the military leaders of the Dergue. Linked to this neo-ideological approach is the conclusion of friendship treaties with like-minded African states; treaties are now in effect with Angola, Mozambique, Ethiopia, and the Congo.

Prior to the Angolan war, China was actively competing with the Soviet Union for influence in Africa and was meeting with considerable success, especially in southern Africa. However, China was in no position to match the Soviet-Cuban stake in Angola (it was trying to rebound from the economic mismanagement evident during the Cultural Revolution), and it played a minimal role there. The victory of the MPLA provided the Soviets with extensive diplomatic momentum, as African states and liberation movements perceived the Soviet Union as a reliable ally that could supply large quantities of arms. China became largely discredited and has ceased to be a significant factor in the superpower competition. Adding to China's problem was the fact that it aided two Angolan movements, the Frente Nacional de Libertação de Angola (FNLA) and the União Nacional para a Independência Total de Angola (UNITA), that were simultaneously being backed by South Africa.

Zambia, Tanzania, and Mozambique, which had leaned toward China, shifted toward the Soviets, and the Southwest Africa People's Organization (SWAPO) became almost exclusively reliant on the Soviets as a source of arms and training. Even Robert Mugabe's Zimbabwe African National Union (ZANU), which had been aligned with the Chinese, sought Soviet arms, but they were not forthcoming. The Soviets continued to concentrate their largess on Joshua Nkomo's Zimbabwe African People's Union (ZAPU). The Congo, which had fostered close relations with both the Soviet Union and China, swung into the Soviet orbit with the signing of a friendship treaty. Soviet influence is now strong in southern Africa as the superpowers jockey for position in expectation of a major showdown over South Africa's apartheid system. A military confrontation would find the Soviet Union placed advantageously with logistic facilities and training bases in neighboring states (such as Angola and Mozambique) and a firm relationship with the leading black nationalist movement, the African National Congress.

Soviet Objectives

Soviet objectives in Africa appear to include: (1) extension of Soviet logistic facilities, including the prepositioning of equipment and possibly military personnel; (2) reduction of Western political influence and strategic rights; (3) extension of the type of political influence that can lead to stronger African backing for Soviet international policies and to the granting of logistic rights to the Soviet Union; (4) receipt of diplomatic support on basic world issues and the establishment of close ties to the most politically compatible states through the device of friendship treaties; (5) weakening of Chinese influence; (6) facilitation of the advent to power of liberation movements opposed to colonialism or white-minority rule; (7) development of an image as a strong proponent of Third World efforts directed against colonialism and neocolonialism; (8) establishment of African political systems based on Marxist-Leninist ideology and Leninist party structure; and (9) the extension of the type of political influence that can give the Soviet Union some control over domestic African policy and personnel decisions.[4] The establishment of communist-ruled systems does not appear to be a major objective, and the Soviet Union has done little to foster the growth of African Communist parties. David Morison, veteran British observer of the Soviet role in Africa, aptly averred: "Preoccupation with a 'front' against the West is the constant in Soviet policy; concern for the future of Communism often seems to be a variable, despite the most earnest asseverations by Party leaders."[5]

Some potential Soviet acts have been cited as objectives by Western analysts, but there is, as yet, no clear indication that they are indeed Soviet objectives. In this category should be included the interdiction of oil-tanker transport, exploitation of African natural resources, obstruction of the flow of raw materials to the West, and the sharp reduction of African trade with the West. This latter aim could be achieved by the strengthening of African trade relations with the Soviet Union and members of the Council for Mutual Economic Assistance (CMEA).

Objectives may be categorized according to goal orientation, priority, time scale, and difficulty of attainability. Additional nuances that lend greater sophistication to understanding of objectives have been contributed by Dan Papp, a Georgia Tech political scientist, and Morton Halperin, former foreign-policy specialist in the Nixon administration. Papp makes a useful distinction between three possible policy postures associated with a state's objectives, and Halperin delineates different operational modes.[6]

Table 2.1. Typology of Soviet Objectives in Africa

Attributes	Examples
Goal orientation	
Positive	Secure logistic rights
Negative	Secure the removal of French troops from African states
Priority	
High	Reduce Western strategic presence
Low	Gain additional fishing rights
Time scale	
Short-term	Secure the independence of Namibia
Long-term	Establish communist-ruled systems
Difficulty of attainability	
Minimum	Decolonization
Maximum	Removal of Western influence
Policy of posture	
Declared	Opposition to colonialism and neocolonialism
Undeclared	Desire to contain Chinese influence
Denied	Secure military bases
Operational mode	
Foreign policy	Solidify ties to liberation movements
Battlefield	Prevent the secession of Eritrea from Ethiopia
Political effects (propaganda)	Link the United States to the South African system

Source: Dan Papp, "The Soviet Union and Southern Africa," in Robert H. Donaldson, ed., *The Soviet Union in the Third World* (Boulder, Colo.: Westview Press, 1981), p. 70; Morton Halperin, *Limited War in the Nuclear Age* (New York: John Wiley, 1963), pp. 3–4.

All of these attributes may be applied to Soviet objectives in Africa as shown in Table 2.1. Of course, the typology of a particular objective can change. Countering Chinese influence in Africa has a lower priority than it did prior to the Angolan war, and decolonization was converted from a maximum to a minimum objective once it became more easily realized, beginning in the late 1950s.

Any objective may be analyzed in terms of all six attributes, as the latter are definitely not mutually exclusive. For example, look at the objective of securing access to a port facility in Ethiopia. The goal orientation would be positive; the priority, high (due to the expulsion of the Soviets from Berbera, Somalia); the time scale, short-term; the difficulty of attainability, minimum; the policy posture, undeclared; and the operational mode, foreign policy.

A further refinement of the typology of objectives would be the introduction of policy levels to the discussion of objectives. Soviet policy obviously operates at several levels, and objectives vary on the basis of which level is being emphasized. Taking Soviet involvement in Angola during the 1975–1976 war as a case in point, one can distinguish between Soviet objectives at different levels of the conflict. In terms of the MPLA itself, the Soviets tried (after August 1974) to buttress the position of Agostinho Neto against rebellious party factions. In regard to internal Angolan politics, the objective was to install the MPLA in power and, in a regional context, to establish a base of operations for expected conflicts against white-minority rule in Zimbabwe, Namibia, and South Africa. Viewed in a continental perspective, a major Soviet objective was to encourage a majority of the members of the Organization of African Unity to recognize the government declared by the MPLA; in terms of international superpower competition, the Soviets hoped for the defeat of forces supported by the United States and China. Therefore, the Soviet Union had many objectives in Angola, just as it has in almost all comparable situations. Simplistic unicausal analysis should thus be eschewed.

Soviet Strategy and Tactics

Some aspects of Soviet strategy, the means used over the long run to achieve objectives, are fairly consistent and somewhat predictable. The Soviet Union lends military and diplomatic support to African liberation movements, votes with the majority of African states on most Third World issues at the United Nations, and provides advisors on economic planning and on party and security-service organization to socialistic African governments. Nevertheless, some fundamental changes in basic strategy do take place, and it appears that the military dimension of strategy in Africa is now being advanced at the expense of the economic dimension.

As discussed previously, the Soviet Union has become increasingly concerned about the logistic potential of Africa, and it has also turned toward the use of military power and Cuban troops as a means of resolving African conflicts. In analyzing these developments, one must be careful to distinguish between power projection and the extension of influence. To take an extreme but illuminating example, the U.S. base at Guantanamo projects U.S. power into the Caribbean, but in no way gives the United States any influence over the government of Cuba. Looking at Soviet policy in this context, Angola may be cited as a country in which the projection of power has produced considerable Soviet influence. Egypt, on the other hand, presents a case in which the projection of power was at one time extensive, but influence rested on a shaky foundation. Egypt was in a strong enough position to expel Soviet military personnel, effect a rapprochement with the United States, and eventually sign a peace treaty with Israel. In fact, power projection can sometimes serve as an obstacle to influence. An African state can threaten to reduce Soviet logistic rights in order to ease the application of Soviet political pressure.

The Soviet Union usually has developed little influence where Soviet power has not been projected. Certain African states where there is little Soviet power, such as Benin and the Malagasy Republic, have tended to align with the Soviet Union on most issues, but this is probably due to a common outlook rather than to the exertion of Soviet influence. In fact, Soviet influence in Africa is not too extensive, so that it is the accelerated projection of power that should more critically concern the West. Power can be projected in the absence of influence (witness the Soviet port rights in Lagos, Nigeria), but influence generally evolves from a power base.

Soviet strategy is based less on economic competition with the West than it was a decade ago. Formerly, the Soviet Union hoped to reduce Western trade and investment in Africa, activities seen as instruments of continued neocolonial control. Perhaps the Soviets also wanted eventually to cut off the flow of natural resources to the West in order to undermine capitalist economies. Now friendship-treaty states, such as Angola and Ethiopia, still trade extensively with the West, with no Soviet pressure to alter this pattern. Mozambique, which sought to direct its trade more toward the communist-ruled states, was denied full membership in CMEA! The United States is still the major recipient of Angolan oil, and at the end of the Angolan war, the Soviet media condemned "ultra-leftists" who wanted to nationalize the American-owned Gulf Oil Corporation and praised the decision of the Angolan government to permit Gulf to renew operations.[7]

The Soviet Union is not in a position to replace Western economic interests in Africa. The Soviet economy is hard pressed domestically and burdened by huge expenditures in Afghanistan, Cuba, and Poland. Soviet financial assistance (as opposed to military aid) to African states is minimal, and so is Soviet-African trade. The Soviets realize that African states will have to rely on the West for many years to come (even the Soviet Union itself is dependent on Western credits, grain, and technology). As discussed by Elizabeth Kridl Valkenier of Columbia University's Russian Institute, the Soviets no longer seek to undermine the Western economic role in the Third World, as the "traditional Manichaean view of world economies, in which the socialist and the capitalist camps compete for the exclusive control of Third World resources, is being questioned. Indeed, it is increasingly being seen by many Soviets as not applicable to the present-day world in which advances in science and technology are militating toward global interdependence."[8]

Evidence belies the suggestion that Soviet strategy toward Africa is based on some master plan. Objectives have maintained a certain consistency, but the Soviet strategy for achieving them has been highly reactive to events and subject to many fluctuations. It is true that the Soviets have taken advantage of many targets of opportunity, but they have also experienced great confusion, such as in their response to events on the Horn of Africa in 1977. They tried to extricate themselves by proposing a regional federation, including Somalia and Ethiopia, but were singularly unsuccessful. A major strategic shift then took place as Soviet allegiance was transferred from Somalia to Ethiopia. A move with similar strategic impact was carried out in the early 1970s as a foothold was lost in Egypt but gained in Libya. In this case, however, the Soviets were pushed into action by increased Egyptian coolness toward the Soviet Union.

Soviet tactics in Africa are applied on a multifaceted basis. Some tactics are related to government-to-government contacts in areas such as diplomacy, aid, trade, or logistic agreements, and others evolve out of ties between the Communist party of the Soviet Union and socialistic African political parties. Military tactics may pertain to government-to-government or government-to-party relations. The latter would include military assistance to nonruling parties such as SWAPO in Namibia. Of course, another tactical area is that of covert operations.

The Soviet Union tries to appeal to Africans in nonofficial ways through the media (such as Radio Moscow) and through front organizations for journalists, students, writers, and others. It also tries to influence African trade unions through the Soviet-affiliated World Federation of Trade Unions. Some Soviet programs aimed at the masses are established through government-to-government agreements. They include cultural exchanges and the educating of African students in the Soviet Union and East European communist-ruled states. Approximately seventeen thousand Africans are now studying in the Soviet Union and another fourteen thousand in Eastern Europe.

African states are not mere objects subjected to Soviet tactical moves. Although the Soviets surely seek benefits from their policies, African states may gain simultaneously. The Soviets may try to indoctrinate African students at Lumumba University near Moscow, but these students are learning useful skills as well. The Soviets may purchase African commodities to foster political good will, as was the case of Egyptian cotton sales during the 1950s when the Soviet Union had no need for cotton. However, Egypt certainly found a market for its cotton and avoided economic calamity. African states may grant the Soviets use of port facilities, but they may receive needed armaments in return.

Tactics aimed at furthering Soviet objectives may have a detrimental effect on African communist parties. Since the mid-1950s (except for a brief interlude in 1959–1960), the Soviet Union has attached little importance to these parties or to the Marxist doctrine of proletarian revolution. Instead, collaboration with African nationalist governments has been the keynote. As a consequence, Egyptian communists were often arrested during the period of Nasser's rule when the Soviet Union desired close state-to-state relations, and many of the smaller communist parties in Subsaharan Africa have fallen by the wayside altogether. However, an outwardly correct posture toward an African government does not preclude the possibility that the Soviet Union is covertly trying to undermine it. For instance, diplomatic relations with Somalia are still in effect, and Soviet officials have made overtures regarding an improved political atmosphere. Simultaneously, however, efforts have been underway to topple Siad Barre's government through collaboration with the Ethiopians and the Somali Democratic Salvation Front.

The Soviet Union has capabilities commensurate with its objectives in Africa: It has an ample supply of arms, suitable logistic facilities, a diplomatic presence throughout the continent (South Africa being the only notable exception), front organizations and East European allies willing to further its foreign-policy aims, and Cuban troops and advisors who contribute substantially to Soviet military potential on the continent. Nevertheless, several constraints on Soviet behavior are readily apparent. Economic resources are limited, and logistic overextension may be setting in. The Soviets are bogged down in Afghanistan and Ethiopia and must be prepared to take action in Poland. Embarking on further military adventures in Africa at this time would probably overburden the Soviet support capability. The Soviet Union also needs the concurrence of Cuba for certain military actions in Africa, and it must stop short of provoking a direct military confrontation with Western states. Public opinion also acts as a constraint on Soviet policy. Intervening to maintain Idi Amin in power would have been unpopular in many black African states, and the Soviets did nothing to assist him. Broad cooperation with South Africa in the marketing of gold would make sense economically, but contacts have remained limited and unpublicized.

Soviet Aid and Trade

As discussed earlier, Soviet economic assistance to African states is not substantial, trade is not well developed, and military assistance has increased dramatically over the past decade due to events in Angola and Ethiopia. A more detailed exposition on these facets of Soviet external economic relations is essential to an overall understanding of the Soviet Union's role in Africa.

Soviet economic aid to Third World states is less than that of the major Western states, either in pure quantitative terms or as a percentage of gross national product (GNP). It also tends to be distributed in a more concentrated fashion, so the Soviet aid role is minimal in most states.[9] The Soviets rarely provide grants; instead they emphasize low-interest credits that must be repaid (the rates went up and the repayment period was shortened after Khrushchev's removal in 1964). These credits serve to increase purchases of Soviet goods, spread political good will, and help states produce goods that were formerly supplied by Western firms. Soviet credits are never advanced for private enterprises, therefore their entry into the state sector furthers socialist construction. They may also contribute to Soviet logistics through port, airport, or highway construction.

During the years 1955 (when the Soviet aid offensive began) through 1979, the Soviet Union extended slightly over $1.2 billion in aid (credits plus grants) to Subsaharan African states and just under $3 billion to North Africa (excluding Egypt).[10] Since aid to all Third World states totaled over $18 billion, Africa obviously did not have a high priority. Also, the aid for North Africa is somewhat misleading, as two-thirds of it is accounted for by 1978 credits extended to Morocco. It is interesting to note the periodic fluctuation in aid. Less was extended during the period 1965–1974 than during 1955–1964, but there has been a noticeable increase since 1975.[11] Over the complete time framework beginning in 1955, Ethiopia and Guinea have received the greatest assistance, but Morocco will surely surpass them as it draws upon the Soviet credits extended in 1978.

East European states have extended only half the Soviet Union's quantity of economic aid to the Third World, but they have concentrated on Subsaharan Africa and have surpassed the Soviet total of assistance to that region. About two-thirds of their aid has been extended since 1975.[12] Chinese aid to Subsaharan Africa has been about double that of the Soviet Union, but little has been provided to North African states. Total Chinese aid to the Third World is only slightly more than a quarter of Soviet aid, so China has surely lavished particular attention on Black Africa, especially southern African states. However, Chinese assistance has been dropping off considerably since 1975.[13]

The number of Soviet nonmilitary technicians in Africa has been rising constantly, especially in North Africa. A similar increase applies to the technicians in Africa as a percentage of those assigned throughout the Third World, and the total in Africa stood at over thirteen thousand in 1979. China has lagged behind the Soviet Union in this area, with the notable exception of the early 1970s when it furnished more technicians to the Third World than did the Soviet Union. This was due to the extensive Chinese involvement in the Tazara railway from Zambia to Tanzania. In fact, there have always been more Chinese than Soviet technicians in Subsaharan Africa, and this remains the case despite the decline in Chinese economic assistance since 1975.[14]

Soviet military deliveries to Third World states have been increasing, and African states were receiving about 40 percent of the total before the huge infusion of arms into Afghanistan began in December 1979. North Africa has always received more than Subsaharan Africa, despite the flow of arms into Angola and Ethiopia, but more Subsaharan military personnel have received Soviet training and more Soviet military technicians now serve in Subsaharan Africa.[15] Libya is a major recipient of Soviet arms, and it propositions some of them for Soviet use elsewhere, such as Ethiopia. Libya has also introduced Soviet arms into Chad, Uganda, Burundi, and other states and has assisted the POLISARIO (Popular Front for the Liberation of Saguia el Hamra and Rio de Oro) movement in the Western Sahara and the Somali Democratic Salvation Front.

Soviet arms sometimes provide a balance to U.S. arms. This was the case in the Congo-Léopoldville (now Zaire) during the early 1960s, and later in Libya and Somalia, as the Soviets countered U.S. assistance to Egypt and Ethiopia. However, Soviet arms sent to Angola far exceeded those supplied by the United States, and the same holds true in regard to the current Ethiopia-Somalia conflict—the Soviet flip-flop has led to huge military deliveries to Ethiopia. U.S. arms were not sent to Somalia until 1982, but Ethiopia started to receive Soviet arms in 1977.

The Soviet Union is not exploiting Africa economically, as it has ample supplies of most natural resources except phosphates (imported from Morocco). About the only commodities imported on a large scale are coffee (from Ethiopia and Angola) and cocoa (from Ghana and the Ivory Coast), so perhaps the Soviets are bent on cornering the world's beverage supply! Angola and Ethiopia purchase much more from the Soviet Union than they sell, so the Soviets have really found markets for their goods rather than sources of raw materials. Actually, total Soviet trade with Angola is exceeded by trade with states not enjoying close political ties to the Soviet Union such as Egypt, Morocco, and Nigeria. In addition, the first two states have a greater trade turnover with the Soviets than does Ethiopia. Libya and Algeria, which have warm relations with the Soviet Union, are also major trading partners, but the Congo, Mozambique, Benin, Tanzania, and Zambia are not.[16] Surely economic bedfellows make strange politics!

Looking more closely at the Angolan situation, one can see that 6.9 percent of the country's exports went to CMEA states in 1979 and only 6.3 percent in 1980. Meanwhile, the figures for Western Europe were 28.5 percent and 22.2 percent; they were 21.4 percent and 31.8 percent for North America. Angolan exports to the United States rose from $348 million in 1979 to $559 million in 1980.

In the area of imports, Angola does have greater dependence on CMEA states, but it is still mainly reliant on Western Europe. In 1980, Angola purchased 16.9 percent of its goods from CMEA members, 7.1 percent from North America, but a whopping 51.6 percent from Western Europe. Imports from the United States totaled $111 million, having risen from $32 million in 1978 and $93 million in 1979.[17] Angola's economy is clearly not directed eastward, indicating that a major Soviet military role in an African state need not lead to the weakening of that state's economic ties to the West. In fact, Angola's burgeoning trade with the United States, its acceptance of private U.S. investment, and its receipt of Export-Import Bank credits are all taking place in the absence of diplomatic relations.

The Balance Sheet

Soviet gains in Africa have been considerable, but not at all surprising considering the Soviet Union started from such a weak position and has been favored by ideological and revolutionary trends on the continent. However, the Soviets have surely had their share of setbacks and miscalculations, which their military victories in Angola and Ethiopia have been unable to obscure. Leaders of friendly governments have been overthrown, several expulsions of Soviet military personnel have taken place, and the Soviet image has been tarnished by close relationships with tyrants such as Idi Amin in Uganda and Macias Nguema in Equatorial Guinea. Libya may serve partially as a Soviet military proxy, but its radical actions threaten many Arab and black African states and tend to push them away from any Soviet embrace.

The Soviet Union failed completely in its efforts to counter the United States in the Congo-Léopoldville (now Zaire) during the early sixties, and it was unable to maintain its links to Somalia while developing ties to Ethiopia. Sadat's expulsion of the Soviet military in 1972 was a devastating blow, compounded by Egypt's swing into the Western camp, its receipt of U.S. arms, and its conclusion of a peace treaty with Israel. In Zimbabwe, the Soviets gave considerable support to Joshua Nkomo and ZAPU, only to see Mugabe and ZANU rise to power. Soviet relations with Mugabe have been chilly, and he has cooperated closely with Western states.

In terms of superpower competition, the Soviets have clearly gained the ascendancy over the Chinese. The British have withdrawn as a strategic force, but they are still important diplomatically, as demonstrated during the Zimbabwe and Namibia negotiations. The French retain their strong military presence in Senegal, Ivory Coast, Gabon, Central African Republic, Djibouti, and the Comoro Islands, and they have acted against Soviet interests in Zaire, Chad, and Mauritania.

The major superpower competitor is certainly the United States, as a new version of the cold war has come to Africa. Soviet actions in Angola led to a U.S. effort to counter the Soviets in Africa, and it is not surprising that Kissinger was dispatched on a trip to Subsaharan states in April-May 1976, just after the conclusion of the war in Angola. In the seven years he had already served in the Nixon and Ford administrations, he had never visited this region, but this was to be the first of several missions. In June 1976, Donald Rumsfeld followed suit. This was the initial visit by a U.S. secretary of defense to Subsaharan Africa. UN representative William Scranton led another delegation the same month.

Basically the United States feared that the Soviets and Cubans had seized the military initiative in southern Africa and that they would possibly enter the fray in Zimbabwe. The United States therefore tried to eliminate the conditions that could produce such a move by acting forcefully on the diplomatic front. The principle of a peaceful transition to black-majority rule was endorsed, and the United States, along with Britain, was able to conclude successful negotiations toward that end. Any aggressive Soviet intentions were thereby blunted, as military force was not the determining factor in ending the Zimbabwean political morass.

U.S. arms sales to African states increased substantially, and the United States advanced its logistic capabilities in Egypt, Kenya, and Somalia. A rapid deployment force was organized, and air and sea facilities were developed on Diego Garcia in the Indian Ocean. These moves served as response to the Iranian revolution and the Soviet intervention in Afghanistan, but they were actually initiated earlier in order to protect Gulf oil and to counter the Soviet role in Ethiopia.

The United States has been trying to balance Soviet military involvement through its own provision of arms. Zaire, which borders Angola, has long been a U.S. recipient, and Egypt serves as the U.S. antidote to Libya. U.S. deliveries to Morocco are matched against Soviet assistance (via Algeria) to the Polisario movement, but the quantity of arms sent to Somalia pales in comparison with those supplied by the Soviets to Ethiopia. In this latter situation, the United States is committed to the defense of Somalia, but it does not want its weapons to be used by the Somalis in order to further claims to the Ogaden district of Ethiopia.

U.S. policy since 1976 has been rather pragmatic and nonideological. It is true that the Reagan administration is "tilting" somewhat toward South Africa as part of its "constructive engagement" approach, but this has not significantly altered the course for the rest of the continent, which was developed by the Ford and Carter administrations. The United States is willing to collaborate with governments that declare themselves "Marxist-Leninist" (Somalia) or "Marxist" (Zimbabwe), and it even has an extensive economic relationship with "Marxist-Leninist" Angola. In fact, supercap-italist David Rockefeller, chairman of the Chase Manhattan Bank, has endorsed this economic approach to Angola and has called for the estab-lishment of diplomatic relations. Although the Soviet position may be strong in Angola, Ethiopia, and Mozambique, the United States has maintained contacts in all three cases with the hope that these governments will eventually turn away from the Soviet Union. The United States has not used punitive actions against them, except for the lack of diplomatic recognition of Angola, but this policy is largely a function of Cuban-American relations and the ongoing Namibia negotiations rather than an effort to penalize Angola. U.S. diplomats visit Luanda, and Export-Import Bank credits have been extended.

U.S. strategy in Africa is based primarily on the recognition of a power rivalry with the Soviet Union, rather than on the need to protect economic interests. U.S. dependence on African raw materials and the scale of U.S. trade and investment in Africa are not substantial when compared to those of West European states. In addition, there is as yet no evidence that African states, no matter how radical their ideologies nor how close their ties are to the Soviet Union, will attempt to harm U.S. economic interests. One has only to look at Libya, Algeria, and Angola. Robert Price has written, "The conventional notion that radical solutions necessarily mean a threat to the United States has a variety of unfortunate effects: it locks the United States into an antagonistic, or extremely tentative, posture toward movements of oppressed groups; it produces a supportive posture toward admittedly unsavory political regimes; and it has often led to an interventionist stance in situations in which no national interests are at stake."[18] The U.S. government no longer adheres to this "conventional notion," and it has adjusted its policies accordingly.

Both the United States and Soviet Union view Africa within a competitive superpower framework. They are particularly concerned about global strategic relationships and logistic rights, and these take precedence over ideological or economic considerations. Military factors have come to the fore, but the U.S. negotiating advantage is an extremely valuable asset and must not be overlooked. As demonstrated at Camp David and in Zimbabwe, this advantage tends to freeze the Soviet Union out of the process while furthering American good will. The United States (along with Britain, France, West Germany, and Canada) is now attempting to do the same thing in Namibia.

The major issue confronting the Soviet Union and the United States is the future course to be taken by South Africa. The Soviet Union has adjacent military staging areas and close ties to the ANC, while the United States has a diplomatic edge emanating from its official relations with the South African government and contacts with the Inkatha and other moderate African movements. Diplomatic skill in effecting a peaceful transition to black-majority rule will surely serve the U.S. cause, whereas a destructive civil war will abet Soviet interests and confront the United States with a moral dilemma regarding possible support for the white South African government. So far, the ANC and the Botha regime have not entered into negotiations, and violent acts against the authorities are increasing in frequency. The task faced by the United States and other Western states may therefore prove to be herculean.

Notes

1. See David Albright, "Moscow's African Policy of the 1970s," in David Albright, ed., *Communism in Africa* (Bloomington: Indiana University Press, 1980), p. 49.

2. Conor Cruise O'Brien, "The Counterrevolutionary Reflex," *The Columbia University Forum* 9, no. 2 (Spring 1966):21–23.

3. Alexander Dallin, "The Soviet Union: Political Activity," in Zbigniew Brzezinski, ed., *Africa and the Communist World* (Stanford, Calif.: Stanford University Press, 1963), p. 47.

4. For other listings of Soviet objectives in Africa, see Albright, "Moscow's African Policy," p. 7; and Michael Samuels, Chester Crocker, Roger Fontaine, Dimitri Simes, and Robert Henderson, *Implications of Soviet and Cuban Activities in Africa for U.S. Policy*, Significant Issues Series, 1, no. 5, (Washington, D.C.: Center for Strategic and International Studies, 1979), pp. 35–37.

5. David Morison, *The U.S.S.R. and Africa* (London: Oxford University Press, 1964), p. 7.

6. Dan Papp, "The Soviet Union and Southern Africa," in Robert H. Donaldson, ed., *The Soviet Union in the Third World* (Boulder, Colo.: Westview Press, 1981), p. 70; and Morton Halperin, *Limited War in the Nuclear Age* (New York: John Wiley, 1963), pp. 3–4.

7. Valery Volkov, "Angola at Work," *New Times* no. 21 (May 1976):23; and Valery Volkov, "Angola: First Spring of Freedom," *New Times* no. 41 (October 1976):7.

8. Elizabeth Kridl Valkenier, "The USSR, the Third World and the Global Economy," *Problems of Communism* 28, no. 4 (July–August 1979):17.

9. For an analysis of these issues, see Roger Kanet, "Soviet Policy Toward the Developing World: The Role of Economic Assistance and Trade," in Donaldson, *The Soviet Union in the Third World*, pp. 331–357.

10. All of the following statistics for Africa exclude Egypt, which is listed in Central Intelligence Agency (CIA) statistical tables as a Middle Eastern state.

11. Central Intelligence Agency, National Foreign Assessment Center, *Communist Aid Activities in Non-Communist Less Developed Countries, 1979 and 1954–1979*, ER 80-10318U (Washington, D.C.: Central Intelligence Agency, 1980).

12. Ibid., pp. 18 and 39.

13. Ibid., p. 39; and Central Intelligence Agency, National Foreign Assessment Center, *Communist Aid to Less Developed Countries of the Free World*, ER 76-10372U (Washington, D.C.: Central Intelligence Agency, 1976), pp. 32–33.

14. Central Intelligence Agency, National Foreign Assessment Center, "Communist Aid Activities," p. 10.

15. Ibid., pp. 14–16.

16. See Ministerstvo Vneshnei Torgovli, *Vneshniaia torgovlia SSSR v 1980 g: statisticheskii sbornik* (Moscow: Financy i statistika, 1981).

17. Banco Nacional de Angola statistics released in March 1982. *Facts and Reports* 2, no. 50 (June 12, 1982):13.

18. Robert Price, *U.S. Foreign Policy in Sub-Saharan Africa: National Interest and Global Strategy*, Policy Papers in International Affairs, no. 8 (Berkeley: University of California, 1978), p. 29.

3. Africa and the West: The French Connection

I. William Zartman

Introduction

As a result of the waning applicability of such terms as *cold war* and out of respect for African feelings about independence, anticolonialism, and nonalignment, it has not been fashionable over the past decade to talk of Africa as part of the West. Yet the reality of relations indicates that such is the case. The political values for which Africans have struggled, the unfulfilled aspirations they entertain, and the ties they have maintained after achieving independence show the continent to be very much part of the Western world, even if nonaligned in terms of military capabilities and security alliances. There are many nuances to this attitude, both in the West and in Africa, but as a fact and as a basis of perceptions, it represents a starting point with serious implications.[1]

Specific interests may tie individual African and North Atlantic countries together, but a recognition of Africa's place in the free world provides the soundest basis for understanding the shared sense of common destiny and Western sense of responsibility for helping African states with their problems (within the limits imposed on both sides by capabilities, sensitivities, and sovereignties). Since African economic and political development crises can be expected to draw in Western powers at times and places not of their choosing and not necessarily to their advantage, if only because of a need to counter Communist states' preying on African targets, it is in the Western interest to help prevent the conditions of unrest and instability from which such crises arise. Unlike the nonsequitur analysis in one U.S. official's recent comment about another continent—"Their economy is weak and we can help them with some training for their police"[2]—the view taken in this chapter emphasizes the need to understand the relation between the needs and nature of African states and the role of Europe, particularly France, and the United States in defending free world interests.

French African Policy

In its African policy, France has a very different concept of its role than have the other former metropoles. This different attitude is reflected in

39

the nature of economic relations between France and some of its former colonies, and in particular, in the fact that the French view of things African goes far beyond a handful of economic ties. Most Western states base their African policies on varying interpretations of risk, opportunity, and interest, having had no—or very limited—colonial responsibilities on the continent or else considering the colonial era ended with no residual special responsibilities. France, however, continues to express an attitude of postcolonial commitment, feeling that it has a special role to play in assisting the destiny of countries that it created.

There are at least four ingredients to this commitment: a cultural element that emphasizes the common heritage of French-speaking societies; a moral element that translates the experience gained during the colonial years into a sense of ongoing responsibility; an economic element that seeks sure sources for crucial raw materials and growing markets for goods and investments; and a power element that recognizes that a large following within the Third World makes France a more important state. All but the economic element are absent from the attitudes of other European countries— including Great Britain, which might have been expected to hold similar views. The French view is perhaps most closely approximated by the attitudes of communist countries toward the Afro-Marxist regimes in Ethiopia, Angola, and Mozambique.

The official French attitude has undergone some change as a result of the 1981 elections, but the change has not affected the basic postcolonial theme. The Socialist government in France continues to reinforce its relations with socialist-oriented and even Marxist-oriented governments within and outside the French-speaking area; pay greater attention to poor-country needs as a basis for internal stability; give an important place to other moral considerations, such as concern over poverty, injustice, and apartheid; and develop new forms of international assistance to bring in other Western sources to supplement French efforts. France is not likely to change views on the importance of Africa, on the need for a broad approach to African issues that covers security as well as economic measures, on the obligation to intervene under extreme conditions, or on the need to deal with African states regardless of the ideology of their regimes. All of these are Gaullist ideas that may take on a socialist form but are deeply rooted in French-African policy attitudes.

France, as well as other European states, sees Africa as a continent of limited means, with growing problems of domestic stability and interstate frictions related to economic weaknesses and differences. The presence of Communist states is regarded as foreign, unnecessary, and unhelpful, but a situation that can be prevented only by removing the causes, not by direct confrontation. France's attitude is that once installed, such Communist regimes are hard to remove in the short run, but in the long run will show their inability to meet Africa's real needs and can gradually be replaced. Therefore, it is above all important to keep access open to Europeans, so that they may help maintain stability in African states, meet

European requirements for trade and investment, and assure European security against hostility and disorder on the southern Mediterranean and Atlantic flank. Subregional groups of states are important, because sharp differences within a subregion can lead to political conflict, whereas subregional cooperation can lead to larger markets and economic stability. Access and stability are thus more important than control and ideology.

Extension of French ties beyond the immediate French-speaking club of former colonies does put strains on French resources and attitudes and encourages an evolution of basic French policy. The more France expands its area of interest, the more assistance it requires from other Western states in providing technical personnel, overseas-development assistance, and investment capital. Conversely, the more basic poverty appears as the prime characteristic of Sahelian and other states of Africa, most of which are French speaking, the more help France needs within its own area of immediate interest if it is to maintain its position of responsibility and commitment. (Recently, for the first time in its twenty-five-year history, the Central Bank of West African States [BCEAO] was in deficit to the French treasury.) Thus both maintenance and expansion of traditional French positions require greater Western cooperation, and such cooperation brings with it strains on traditional French attitudes toward France's place in Africa. This dilemma helps explain French emphasis on multilateral institutions, which reduce competition. The policy of sharing France's burden in Africa was begun as early as 1956, when the rest of the then six nations of the European Community were obliged to include part 4 of the Treaty of Rome, a provision effectively requiring multilateral contributions to French (and other European) colonies in Africa without diluting French preeminence there. A quarter of a century later, the pressures to provide multilateral assistance continue, providing an opportunity for shared benefits and complementary roles in Africa.

Another implication of extended French presence is that France becomes more susceptible to African pressures for African interests. The more the Western presence spreads in Africa, the more its effects are diluted by the need to talk and listen to a larger number of African voices, often raised in concert to increase the volume. As the decolonization process became multilateral in Namibia through the inclusion of the Front-Line States and Nigeria and in the Franco-African summits through the inclusion of non–French-speaking states, greater French and Western activity in Africa brought greater African influence on the Western states. In the 1979 Franco-African summit, a discussion of military cooperation could have taken place, as the French wanted, had it not been for the presence and opposition of a group of leftist states (Benin, Burundi, Congo, Mali).

French-speaking states tend to regard France with the ambiguity born of familiarity, seeing a sometimes overly heavy and colonialist presence in expatriate, business, economic, and governmental relations. This ambiguity is a normal concomitant of postcolonial relations and has not in the past prevented mutually frank speaking between Africans and French.

As the generations of African leaders succeed each other, however, the basis of close personal relations enjoyed by previous leaders changes. Benin, Upper Volta, Chad, and Mauritania are countries in which a younger generation of leaders—mostly military men—without the French ties and experiences of their predecessors brought attitudes of distance and suspicion with them to power. Not all younger-generation leaders bring such a change, as the experiences in Senegal, Togo, and even Congo show. Much has to do with the degree to which the new leaders' coming to power is a reaction to their predecessors, from whom the new leaders must be distinguished. Thus, a Camerounian- or Senegalese-like succession in such crucial states as Ivory Coast and Gabon would bring a change in degree, but not in nature, in relations with France. A Chadian- or Mauritanian-like change would bring a cooling of political relations. Yet both examples show that French commercial and other economic presence can remain as long as security conditions are amenable.

English-speaking African states, on the other hand, tend to regard France with suspicion and misunderstanding, a strong heritage from different colonial pasts. This feeling is accentuated in West Africa, where English-speaking states are each surrounded by an area that France considers as its primary zone of interest and activity. A sense of vocation can then evolve, particularly in Ghana and Nigeria, to free neighboring countries from neocolonialism and to substitute their own legitimate African assistance for France's illegitimate postcolonial interference. In this context, other Western countries' cooperation with the French is open to misconception. It can be seen as providing alternative—and therefore less suspect—assistance to reduce French presence or as another form of neocolonial collusion. Since this ambiguity is inherent in any Western cooperation or competition, it can be minimized by presenting cooperation as a collection of alternative roles within an overarching Western unity. But it can never be eliminated, and it must be counted as simply a cost of operating effectively in Africa.

A Geopolitical Analysis of French Policy

French views and activities in Africa cannot be divided merely into relations with former colonies and with others' former colonies, any more than they can be divided into relations with moderates who frequently cooperate with France and with radicals who often oppose French policies. Neither of these dichotomies, although accurate, are dominant. Here a different categorization is proposed as being more meaningful—a geographic breakdown into the *Active Zone* (from Senegal to Zaire), the *Passive Zone* (south and east of Zaire), and the *Mixed Zone* of the Mediterranean and Red Sea shores that is at the same time African, Mideastern, and Indian Oceanic or Mediterranean. This breakdown is first of all an organizing device, but it is not absent from French thinking. Such geopolitical categories were found in the Socialist party program on Africa, and they are dominant over other ideopolitical categories.³ Nor is it a static typology, for the zones change—Zaire was added to the Active Zone in the late 1960s and Angola may be added in the 1980s. In addition, relations between English-speaking West Africa and the responsible French ministry shift—just as policies within the zones can change and roles adopted by France and other Western allies will vary. Nonetheless, a geopolitical portrayal is unusual and provides insights and an organizational framework not found in a single French/non-French or other dichotomy. (Additionally, it is a true reflection of the Caesaro-Cartesian tripartite division of things French.)

The Active Zone

The western arc of Africa from Senegal to Zaire is the zone of active French concern. The level of French interest varies considerably from state to state, but because the states are located together, with geopolitical effects on each other, additional interests and tensions are created. In most of the former French colonies of this zone, French capital and personnel dominate foreign commerce, banking, and investments. This dominance becomes a basic element in French interests in the area, and the French role becomes one of protecting these interests, intervening in a number of forms against external invasion and internal collapse.

In other states of the region—primarily English-speaking—direct French interests do not predominate, and yet the states cannot be ignored because of their location among states of primary French interest. To this situation, there are a number of responses. France has been quietly expanding its commercial and banking interests in English-speaking countries, although investments and aid are likely to continue to remain far behind those of the United States and Great Britain. In exceptional cases, such as Gambia and—to a lesser extent—Sierra Leone, an active role of intervention has been assumed by a French-speaking African neighbor with French support. At the other extreme, a major element of Nigerian policy is active opposition to the French role. This element cannot be stressed too much: Nigeria views France with hostility and suspicion and sees as a justification of its own role the need to replace French influence with African influence in the states around it.⁴ Even when there is common interest and momentary cooperation, as in Chad in 1979, the situation is likely to turn sour and even lead to worsened perceptions between the two countries because of their suspicions, as in Chad by 1980.

In the Active Zone, other European countries have a minor or passive role, with the partial exception of Belgium in Zaire. Great Britain and Germany have important economic interests in some countries, but have no place for an active, or security, role in their policy regarding those countries. In this way, European policy in the French Active Zone resembles French policy in the Passive Zone (discussed below).

The Active Zone contains all nine of the French-dependent states in Africa (Ivory Coast, Upper Volta, Senegal, Niger, Chad, Central African Republic—CAR, Congo, Mauritania, and Gabon). It is made up of the four core states (Senegal, Ivory Coast, Cameroun, Gabon), a protective buffer of French-speaking states around them, and others that are mainly English-speaking. Technical assistants in the core states number from 700 (Cameroun) to 4,000 (Ivory Coast); of these, over 500 to over 3,000 are in education. In the buffer area, former French colonies all have from 200 to 450 technical assistants from France, except Benin (140) and Chad (almost none) for the moment; French-speaking former Belgian colonies have between 100 and 200 French technical assistants. French bases are located in the core states of Senegal, Ivory Coast, and Gabon and in the part of CAR next door to Cameroun. There are military technical-assistance teams in all the core and buffer states (including Zaire) except Guinea, Mali, and Benin.

The core states constitute the major second-level investment sites in Africa (between $350 million and $800 million), immediately after the top-level sites (Liberia, Zaire, and Nigeria, each with foreign investments at about $1.2 billion). Although precise and current figures are hard to obtain, the French sector is still dominant in all former French states. In fact, it is increasing in absolute figures although declining proportionally. For example, France held 80 percent of direct foreign investment in Ivory Coast in 1967 and 60 percent in 1980, representing more than half of total capital in Ivory Coast at the end of the 1960s and less than a third in 1980. The situation is similar in all other former French colonies, where France held 75–95 percent of all direct foreign investments in 1967 (except for Guinea, where the French share was 25 percent, and for Benin and Togo, where it was 55 percent). French investment is very low in Zaire—less than 1 percent of the $7 billion Belgian investment.

Investment trade levels are more important for French interests than specific product dependencies. France takes major imports of uranium from Niger, CAR, and Gabon; manganese and oil from Gabon; bauxite from Guinea; and iron ore from Mauritania. Other than petroleum, these imports create long-term supply relationships rather than short-term dependencies.

When all is well, French positions and relations in the Active Zone prosper. In time of conflict and crisis, France may deem a more active policy necessary in the Active Zone, rather than simply the maintenance of access. Three types of intervention have been used in the Active Zone of Africa: intervention against external invasion, intervention against internal collapse, and intervention for cooling conflicts.

External Invasion. During the past decade, Western states have intervened in Zaire (twice: in 1977 and 1978), in Mauritania (1977), and in Chad (1979 and 1983). The United States, France, and Belgium were involved in handling the Shaba invasions in Zaire; France was alone in supporting Mauritania against the POLISARIO (Popular Front for the Liberation of Saguia el Hamra and Rio de Oro) attacks and Chad against FROLINAT (Front de Libération National du Tchad) advances. The U.S. role was limited to providing an airlift for French and Belgian troops. France supplied troops and military advisors in all four cases, as did Belgium in the second Shaba invasion. The troops came from continental Europe in the case of Zaire and from Senegal in the case of Mauritania.

Focusing on the French role, one finds a number of constant elements in these cases—all occurred (except for Chad in 1983) during the advisorship of Rene Journiac (1976–1980) and may be seen as hallmarks of his approach to African affairs. If that were the only characteristic, one might not expect intervention against external invasion to reoccur, especially under a different French administration. However, Journiac is not the only French policymaker who found such intervention to his liking; others have done so and may do so again, even if in different form or frequency.

The four cases of intervention against external invasion have other common characteristics. First, French intervention was invited by the government under attack. It should be noted that a formal treaty for interventions is not a common requirement. France had military technical-assistance agreements with Mauritania and Zaire, but they did not provide for bilateral defense or military intervention. There is much hue and cry about this point, although it does not seem very important as long as there is a government invitation to intervene. It is worth noting that public opinion in Cameroun is that the French would intervene if necessary, although there is no such military agreement.

Second, all states receiving assistance were French-speaking and part of the Active Zone. Two are members of the Franco-African Summit Group (Zaire and Mauritania), albeit in somewhat special status: Zaire is not a former French colony and therefore requires special attention, and Mauritania is a restive and independent-minded ally. Third, French personnel as well as friendly regimes were in danger, although the case is not so obvious in Chad. In Zaire and Mauritania, the armed intervention specifically sought to protect expatriate investment and the French (and other) citizens working there. In Chad, there were not many French people in the combat zone, but French personnel and economic activities are important in Chad in general.

Fourth, in all cases the enemy was an irregular force of political dissidents attacking its home regime rather than a sovereign state, although in each case the irregular force did have the support of a sovereign neighbor (Angola was behind the Congolese National Liberation Front—FLNC, Algeria behind the POLISARIO, Libya behind the FROLINAT). As it worked out, French intervention did not put it in direct conflict with another African state. Fifth, all cases were important to French credibility among its Black African associates, although each case drew heavy criticism from other African states. To many Africans, the justification for the interventions is not convincing, but moderate African states found much to applaud. African states were associated with the Mauritanian and Zairois interventions in different ways: Morocco supported Mauritania; Morocco, and then a six-state Inter-African Force, supported Zaire. Even in Chad, the French intervention in 1977–1978 was succeeded by an uneasy pairing of French and Nigerian troops in 1979–1980 and then by an Inter-African force in 1980–1981. Nonetheless, it cannot be said that these cases were absolutely crucial to French credibility in Africa, and indeed two of the supported governments (the Ould Daddah and Malloum regimes) fell within a year of the original French intervention without triggering a French reaction.

The intervention in Chad in August 1983 finally occurred because of pressure from the presidents of Senegal, Niger, Togo, and especially Ivory Coast, and due to the demonstration effect of a radical camp in Upper Volta.

Sixth, France had a clear and demonstrable military capability in each case. French aircraft—Jaguars in Mauritania and Transalls in Zaire—had a nice demonstration effect, and the ability to deliver Foreign Legionnaires (albeit in U.S. carriers) made a useful show in Zaire. Seventh, the interventions were most successful when they were *surgical strikes*, designed to defeat the enemy and retire, leaving the local forces to handle the aftermath, as in Zaire and Tunisia. They were least successful when the surgery became a continuing treatment, as in Mauritania and, worst, in Chad. The intervenor seeks to end the intervention as rapidly as possible, not to prolong it.

In the future, occasions for intervention against external invasion are bound to occur. Although the locations cannot be predicted with certainty, some realistic hypothetical cases can be posited: a Moroccan or POLISARIO invasion of Mauritania, a Libyan or national-liberation-movement invasion of Niger or Mali, a Nigerian-Camerounian war, and another "second independence" invasion of Zaire.

In the case of a Libyan-supported national liberation movement's invasion of Mauritania, Niger, or even Mali, French intervention would be likely if it were invited and if French installations or expatriates were threatened; its likelihood would decrease to the extent that these conditions did not exist. Intervention could take the form of stationing and then using troops or perhaps planes. A Moroccan invasion of Mauritania or a Libyan invasion of Niger also would bring French intervention if invited, although it would likely be preceded by diplomatic warnings in an attempt to avoid actual confrontation of military forces if possible. Similarly, in a Nigerian-Camerounian war, France could be expected to support Cameroun, first with arms supplies (as actually occurred in 1981) and then possibly with troops or planes, in order to maintain a regional counterweight to Nigeria (France feels that Cameroun is the only Nigerian neighbor that has stood up to it). Finally, invasion of Zaire by a "second independence" national liberation movement, again if accompanied by an invitation from the government and a threat to expatriate interests and personnel, could trigger a French and Belgian intervention, even though there would be an effort to avoid making it look like "more of the same" and less alacrity in appearing to "pull Mobutu's fat out of the fire."

Internal Collapse. The case for shoring up a collapsing regime or political system is more complex and less clear, but the occasion is increasingly likely to present itself in the coming years. Past instances are hotly debated as exceptional measures: French intervention to remove an embarrassing regime in the Central African Empire (CAE)—like Tanzanian intervention to remove an embarrassing regime in Uganda and Russo-Vietnamese intervention to remove an embarrassing regime in Cambodia—is presented as a unique necessity, not a precedent. Other French interventions to support a collapsing regime—in Chad in 1969 and 1980—have failed. Intervention to thwart a coup occurred only in the previous decade, in Gabon in 1964 and preemptively in four equatorial states and Mauritania in the early 1960s.

Because of the disparity and uniqueness of the cases, it is hard to find common, guiding characteristics. The sites of French intervention in the 1970s are all part of the interior buffer part of the Active Zone that protects more important coastal core states (of which Gabon, the state involved in the 1960s intervention, is one). CAR and Gabon have bilateral defense agreements that cover intervention; Chad has only military assistance agreements with France. No other members of the Franco-African Summit Group have faced the same collapse of a political system as Chad, although Mauritania and CAR come close, and Guinea, Mali, and Zaire may be future candidates. France has responded to invitations to intervene but has withdrawn more or less whenever the invitation is withdrawn. However, in a number of cases in the 1970s and 1980s—Mauritania in 1978, CAR in 1981, Upper Volta in 1980, and Chad in 1975—France, whether invited or not, did not intervene to prevent the overthrow of a historic figure who was becoming a troublesome partner.

The line between thwarting coups and preventing collapse is not always clear; one is a short-term incident and the other is a longer process. The cases involved show that a steady supply and a reasonably fair distribution of natural resources is more important for the stability of a political system than even a successful intervention and that intervention only makes the need for resources more urgent for the restoration of stability. By this measure, a number of states face collapse and threats of internal coup: Guinea, Zaire, CAR, Mali, Benin, Mauritania, Togo, and Senegal, particularly as incumbent leaders face problems of succession; only CAR, Senegal, and perhaps Togo have a treaty provision for intervention (as do Gabon and Ivory Coast). Although the circumstances would have a large role to play in determining the type of response, it is most likely that any French regime would take measures to maintain incumbent stability in the core states where resources are available, that is, to restore Diouf, Houphouët (or his immediate successor), or Bongo if they happened to be overthrown by a lucky military coup that indigenous efforts were not able to handle. (The same can be said of Djibouti, to be discussed below.) In all three of these states (Senegal, Ivory Coast, and Gabon), the deterrent effect of the small (four-hundred to six-hundred man) French contingents is much more important than their actual use. As the 1981 CAR coup illustrates, no intervention is likely elsewhere (including Shaba or Kinshasa in Zaire). In these cases, any justification for exceptional intervention would depend on circumstances, of which the most important are whether French citizens are in danger and whether a Libyan hand could be seen in the coup.

The possibility of intervention raises further questions about African reactions, postintervention policies, preventive policies, and alternative security arrangements. African reactions to French or other Western interventions are likely to be considered beforehand and may inhibit such interventions. French military presence in Niger, Mali, or Mauritania may be viewed no more positively in the abstract by Algeria and Nigeria than by Libya itself, although a French presence may appear slightly preferable to Algeria and Nigeria if it is the only alternative to Libyan intervention. As a rule, a country can be expected to prefer intervention by a distant power to that by a neighbor, but in this region the presence of a number of potential intervenors (Libya, Algeria, Nigeria, and Morocco in addition to France) means that any move can serve as a justification for a spiral of interventions that undermine rather than protect central authority and may eventually raise the specter of partition. One can easily imagine an evolution of events in which African and other criticism of the Inter-African Force (IAF) as an African agent of the French is both accurate and facile. If properly functioning, the IAF performs the stabilizing role formerly exercised by French intervention, and it does this in the name of the African community of states rather than as one power offering its protection. It is inevitable that if the collective response does not occur, the individual one will, since political as well as physical nature abhors a vacuum.

Postintervention policies in case of collapse are such difficult and delicate matters as to deter intervention even if it were feasible in the short run. Increasingly France, along with other Western and African states, will have to ask itself how to put a state back together when it falls apart; the question will have to be faced whether there is intervention or not, but the burden of providing the answer is not taken on lightly by a country that has just recently pulled out of the colonial business. France has only twice tried to engineer a new African regime—in Chad in 1978 when it imposed Hissène Habré on General Malloum, with no success in the longer run, and in CAR in 1979 when it restored David Dacko, with no better success. This record (again from the Journiac era) argues in favor of working with whoever is in power rather than taking on the responsibility of choosing a replacement—the policy in fact followed toward Goukouni and then Habré in Chad and Mobutu in Zaire. Beyond the question of choosing a candidate, an intervention in the case of collapse must restore security, provide massive technical assistance and budgetary aid, and maintain a low profile. These three contradictory requirements work to inhibit intervention. The same requirements have been faced, with no more success, by Libya in Chad and by Tanzania in Uganda.

Cooling Conflicts. Preventive policies are therefore most important, if most difficult. Their importance is on the increase as weak states increasingly become the prey of stronger ones and as weak governments become the victims of violent frustration. Increasingly the security threat appears as the consequence of internal weakness and not as an independent variable.

It therefore becomes important to make intervention unnecessary. When intervention was a purely military response to a security threat, it could be obviated by stationing troops in a country as a deterrent; that is no longer very acceptable, nor is it an answer to the larger question. Economic intervention is now needed.

Continued economic support has been the French policy toward a number of states in chronic difficulty in recent years; economic intervention has returned to a level that was characteristic of the later preindependence years and that was hoped to be unnecessary after independence. Niger, Mali, Senegal, Togo, and CAR are cases where low per capita income and low economic growth create a context that can threaten political stability and where France has responded helpfully. Few common elements or clearly distinguishable characteristics determine the choice of these countries rather than others as recipients of French economic support. Although they share some or all of such characteristics as a sizable group of French expatriates, a strategic position, products important to France, and a special historic relationship, these elements can be found in other countries as well. What stands out, besides an initial membership in French-colonial Africa, is first, the country's willingness to enter into a close relationship of reliance on France and, second, a magnitude of need such that France can remain the dominant developed partner in that relationship. The latter is important, but is probably causing problems to French thinking (even if these problems are not faced consciously): since its initiative in the Rome Treaty of 1957, France has tried to involve other Western countries in the task of bailing out African economies while at the same time retaining a dominant position. Such a pair of goals can only be noncontradictory if the associated Western states are willing to support an essentially French effort. It is as if France wished to retain a controlling interest in the enterprise, while benefiting from other countries' minority capital participation.

In Niger in 1980–1981, France provided budget support of over $40 million and product support by the year-end purchase of uranium at a beneficial price. Western partners in the uranium consortium complained of hidden foreign aid to Niger. In CAR, the same sum of about a third of the state budget was provided in the year following the reinstallation of Dacko—more than the amount that was cut in 1979, the cut that led Bokassa to run to Libya for support.

In the case of Togo, France used its position as the chair of the Paris group to reschedule the debt on terms favorable to Togo in early 1981. For Senegal, with an economy in deep trouble, France produced a major injection of financial support in late 1980–early 1981, accompanied by similar support from the European Economic Community (EEC) and the International Bank for Reconstruction and Development (IBRD).

In Mali, France supported the return to the West African Monetary Union (UMOA). This measure involves further heavy costs for France, including possible partial debt forgiveness, and additional burdens on the

BCEAO, which for the first time is in debt to the French treasury. Yet without such a measure, the buffer belt in the Active Zone running from Mauritania to CAR would have a serious gap in it, which could attract greater attention from the USSR (Mali's arms supplier) and Algeria (Mali's ideological as well as geographic neighbor). French support for Malian reentry into UMOA is one of the most important and most costly actions France has taken recently to exercise preventive policies against international collapse within the Active Zone.

This set of policies in the Active Zone—involving intervention against domestic and inter-African causes of instability, use of an Inter-African Force, and preventive economic support—represents a coherent array of means to maintain stable conditions (rather than simply friendly regimes) that enhance French interests and security in the area. Not only is it a set of mutually supporting policies, but also it is one that represents a continuity from the policies of DeGaulle to the present Socialist regime. There are no radical departures, and if there are changes in emphasis, they only reinforce essentially Gaullist approaches in an evolving context.

But this is not the only policy mix possible. If there has been a departure in French-African policy with special regard to the Active Zone, or at least a rather different set of emphases, it was during the Giscard-Journiac era. During these years, intervention was less narrowly circumscribed, domestic engineering was more directly attempted, the Inter-African Force idea was inaugurated (the one departure that has developed further in the Mitterrand era), and preventive economic support was seriously reduced. (Since this survey is not a history of French African policies, and since the first three items have already been mentioned, only the last item will be discussed further).

In 1979–1980, France cut budgetary support to a number of states, oblivious of the security role that economic stability played. In Mali, the budgetary aid reduction in 1980 brought Mali to return to the UMOA and to set its finances in order (assuming the scenario is played out in coming years). But in CAR, the elimination of budgetary aid in 1979 led "Emperor" Bokassa to turn to Libya for his financial fixes (which in turn led to his overthrow). In Benin, budgetary aid ended in 1975 was probably replaced to some extent by Libya. Other cases of cutbacks may exist as well. In this regard, the Socialist policy is different. The question remains, however, in this regard more than in the other differences, what happens to the policies of a freely spending Socialist regime when the money runs out? Part of the answer again is that France will feel compelled to bring in other donors in support of its political aims and will be subject to the pressures for conflict and cooperation among donors that such a situation brings.

The Passive Zone

The area of fourteen countries south and east of Zaire, on the south Atlantic Ocean and Indian Ocean coasts of the continent, is France's African

Passive Zone. There France—and other European countries as well—sees no security role, there is little Western presence, Western interests are primarily commercial, and the French role is reduced to the level of the British and other European countries. Under the present system of relations, which is not likely to change in the near future (even though changes may not be totally inconceivable), there is no likelihood of French intervention in this zone. Specifically, intervention could occur only in the event of a South African war and that is a long way off. Western intervention in the recent past in this area has been associated with decolonization, notably in Angola, Zimbabwe, and Namibia, of which only the last remains an open case. Current intervention forces in the southern zone are Cubo-Soviet and South African, both of which are beyond Western control and influence. Despite the threats and promises that are addressed toward these forces, there seems little possibility of removing them in the near future; at best, Cubo-Soviet forces in Angola may be reduced as part of a Namibian settlement.

European policy therefore seeks to maintain access to the area for commercial and strategic reasons and to prepare targets of opportunity (to borrow a phrase) so that Western countries may be in a position to pick up functions in currently Cubo-Soviet–influenced countries as they might appear. French and other European policy in this area is limited by the availability of policy means—aid monies, investment capital, trade interests, and technical personnel. Resources are small, both because of limitations at the source and because France and most other EEC countries have other baskets of greater importance in which to put their eggs. In this zone, the French position seems to be to play the role it expects others to play in the Active Zone, that of a supplement to others' more important roles. However, the French—and sometimes the German—policy also is aimed at providing alternative forms of Western presence and policy, a position that France does not welcome in its Active Zone.

Zambia, Zimbabwe, Angola, Namibia, and South Africa are typical examples of Passive Zone countries. In Zambia, there is little French activity, and in exchange, little sympathy on the part of Zambians for French positions on Africa. In Zimbabwe, France is fifth-largest and the EEC the fourth-largest contributor to the Zimbabwe Conference for Reconstruction and Development (ZimCORD). Other elements of French policy are small, and even in ZimCORD the French contribution ($140 million) is only a tenth of the total and is mainly in soft loans. Yet it does represent a significant contribution to a Western effort in a country outside the active French-interest area, in which the only French concern is directed toward keeping the country within the Western zone of influence. French companies benefit from the business access and contracts that these loans represent, but they are contributing to an area where the interests of the United States and Great Britain are much stronger. Zimbabwe's socialist government, however, makes it more attractive to the current French regime.

In Angola, France is leading a small effort to increase the West's presence in order to be in a position to compete with and eventually replace the

Cubo-Soviets. France already has two hundred technical assistants there (as many as in Togo and more than in Benin), and these French technical assistants and small investment sums are scheduled to increase over the coming years. Other Western countries are scarcely in a better position.

In Namibia and South Africa, the human-rights position of the Mitterrand regime has given France a more liberal role within the Western Five, shifting it from the right flank to the left flank of the group. Much like the U.S. position in Chad vis-à-vis the French position, the French policy on South Africa is to act as an outrider on the common Western position, presumably strengthening it while preserving the integrity of France's own position by playing the tough-cop–soft-cop routine. The South African position is an integral part of French policy in another way: If the French policy is one of divorcing access from issues in Black Africa and speaking frankly about policy differences to African states despite French presence, interests, and ties to the country, the same operates in regard to South Africa. There France has a product dependency on coal, and yet does not hesitate to cross the South African government on political issues. By the same token, France had no interest in leaving the Group of Five, despite tactical threats to the contrary, when it had no more effective position to take, since effectiveness is its criterion of criticism against the Contact Group. As the moment of truth is played out, France will doubtless remain an active—even if not crucial—member of the Contact Group as long as the group's proposals have a chance of Front-Line acceptance and will doubtless jump ship if it appears that they do not. Jumping ship is not likely to take the form of supporting full sanctions, but it might appear as a vote for a ban on further investment or withdrawal from the Koeburg atomic plant and would certainly be expressed as a strong verbal attack on U.S. policies.[5]

The Mixed Zone

The third area of Africa is the region of the Red Sea and Mediterranean coasts that belongs in part to other geographical and policy arenas related to the Middle East and therefore falls under mixed policy criteria. In addition, the French physical positions in the region are a combination of its positions in the Active and Passive zones, so that its constraints, interests, and opportunities are mixed as well. This second consideration does not obtain for other European countries, although the first does; because of the complexity of policy criteria, the discussion that follows will focus on the French situation, with incidental mention of other EEC countries only as specifically relevant.

The French position in the Red Sea part of Africa is centered about its relations with its former colony of Djibouti and is contained within its broader concerns about the Indian Ocean. France's Indian Ocean interests derive from its view of the French global great-power role, its perceived need to watch over the oil stream out of the Gulf, its territorial position as an Indian Ocean country through the possession of Reunion, its sense of postcolonial duty to defend the security of Djibouti, and its perception of a unique contribution that it can make to easing tensions in the Horn of Africa. In the African role that follows from these bases (leaving aside the other aspects of France's Indian Ocean role), France begins with its military contingent of about four thousand troops stationed in Djibouti, the single most important element in the continuing independence of this fragile state under the covetous glare of its two neighbors. In a historical view, there was a momentary lapse in this French commitment in 1978–1979, as France planned a gradual reduction of its troops on the assumption that Ethiopia and Somalia would slowly get used to Djibouti and would each generally come to accept its independent existence as long as the other showed a willingness not to challenge it. The Iranian hostage crisis and the Iran-Iraq war in 1980 led France to revise its plans and extend the military guarantee for five years, with a mutual expectation stretching into the 1990s. The possibility of Djibouti joining a Marxist Bab al-Mandab confederation with Libyan support, as the only alternative means of securing the external financial and military support that it requires, has led France to reaffirm its protection and presence. This commitment has been maintained by the Socialist government.

Djibouti has nearly five hundred French technicians, the fifth-largest number in Africa and by far the largest per capita figure; most of them are in education, as usual. France supplies over $2 billion in annual subsidies, a huge figure by any count and by far the largest figure per capita. France is the sole military supplier, and French military technicians control military material through maintenance, refusing to keep up non-French military material. Indeed, French presence in Djibouti has changed less with independence than has the name of the country. In return, France gets very little from Djibouti except a major Indian Ocean naval base. Its interest in the country is purely strategic.

But unlike the situation in the Active Zone, there is no other country in the region to buffer or reinforce the French enclave nor does it have all the attractions of a core state. France therefore must create a political buffer rather than a territorial one, by making its position in Djibouti so useful to neighboring countries that they will want (or at least accept) its continuing presence. Here the tactics have changed with the new French government, because both the sympathies and the opportunities have changed. But the strategy remains the same. Until the Ogaden war of 1977–1978, Ethiopia was entirely equipped by U.S. military material and Somalia by Russian; French policy was to pose as the mediator in the conflictual situation by means of a proposal of a conference of the parties in the region, an invitation that France continues to issue from time to time. When Somalia lost its arms supplier in 1978, France entered the scene; however, when the French government changed and France saw an opportunity for developing a Western relationship with the government of Ethiopia—with which the new French regime has both past contacts and present sympathies—France dropped its arms-supply role to Somalia.

French policy toward Ethiopia in the 1980s is similar to its policy toward Angola: to serve as the African Marxist regime's door to the West and to put itself in a position to lead a greater Western presence when the opportunity arises through Soviet default. Through its contacts with the Ethiopian left, before and after the revolution, France is in a good position to play this role, again offering an alternative among Western policies, as the United States concentrates on Somalian relations.

Again, the difference between "taking opposite sides" and "maintaining Western communications open to both parties" is entirely a function of the tightness with which one interprets Franco-American ties at the source. France has no special role or entree into Somalia or Sudan and is viewed with suspicion by the latter. Despite a strong history of presence and influence in Egypt, where its cultural presence is still important and its commercial presence growing, France has little role to play. Thus, except for Djibouti and Ethiopia, northeast Africa is treated as a Passive Zone in French relations.

The other part of the Mixed Zone is North Africa. France's positions are strong in the former territory and protectorates of the Maghreb, but its opposition to the non-French-speaking state of Libya is nearly as pronounced as that of the United States. The maturity of the North African polities means that the French influence and presence cannot be the same as in Black Africa, and the traditional French policy—enforced by geographical contiguity—of playing off one Maghrebi state against another in their relations with Paris means that Active Zone type of relations cannot obtain in North Africa. One might expect this policy to be attenuated to simply a policy of equilibrium and access as the intensity of Franco-Maghrebi ties diminishes with time, but that time has not yet arrived, and the influence of the past pattern is too strong to be ignored by French policymakers.

France has a high level of ties with Morocco in a number of fields: forty-eight thousand French people live in Morocco and many Moroccans work in France; France is the first trading partner with Morocco in both directions; France has supplied quantities of food aid to Morocco during the current Moroccan drought and is to play an important role in financing the Moroccan Five-Year Plan; and France is a major arms supplier to Morocco. Hassan II's relations with Giscard d'Estaing were close, and a number of members of Mitterrand's entourage, as well as the president himself, have had close ties with Morocco.

On every count the picture is different in regard to Algeria. Fewer French people live there, and the question of Algerian workers has been a burning issue only settled formally in 1980; France buys little from Algeria except some energy supplies, but sells heavily in Algeria; Algeria is armed by Russia, and the Algerians regard Mitterrand with suspicion for his past. However, other members of the Socialist government, notably Claude Cheysson (who has shared North African policy neither with presidential advisor Guy Penne nor with former cooperation minister Jean

Pierre Cot), have had close relations with Algeria and seek closer ones. The Saharan war, in which Socialist party sympathies lie strongly with the POLISARIO Front, provides a major issue of contention and suspicion with Morocco and of sympathy with Algeria, but it is only an issue, not a basic cause in French relations.

Two elements appear to constitute the axes of Franco-Maghrebi relations with particular reference to Africa, happily (for consistency's sake) running parallel to each other. One is the ideopolitical disposition of the current Socialist government toward the two states. Monarchial Morocco with its Socialist party in opposition and in jail is an unattractive ally in Africa for a Socialist France, whereas Socialist Algeria with its continued, if tempered, aspirations of Third World leadership is a much more presentable partner. Furthermore, Morocco seems to be moving closer to the United States, whereas Algeria presents an image of responsible radicalism.

The other element is geopolitical disposition of the two countries with regard to the main opponent of France in the region and the continent: Libya. Reliance on Morocco against Libya would polarize Africa into moderate and radical camps and run the risk of shoving Algeria into the latter, in accordance with its 1975 alliance with Libya. Reliance on Algeria reinforces a barrier to Libyan expansionism, neutralizes a potential opponent by coopting its support, bets on the strongest state in the region (rather than playing a regional balance of power), and leaves Morocco unhappy but with no place to go in opposition. Thus Cheysson's visit to Algeria secured agreement to a leading French role in Chad. This may have paved the way for French support of a greater Algerian role elsewhere in the Sahel and prevented either an Algero-Libyan or an Algero-Nigerian alliance against French predominance in the Active Zone.

There are other ingredients—Mediterranean and Mideastern—to Franco-Maghrebi relations, but they are outside the scope of this review. It should be noted that in both cases the United States is the other most important Western power, leaving it an ambiguity of roles in both Morocco and Algeria: backstop or rival, competitor or supporter to the French.

Finally, in regard to Libya, the Mitterrand regime came to power determined to overcome the ambivalence of the Giscard regime toward Qadhdhafi. The French see in Libyan policies a dangerous source of destabilization in Africa and a serious challenge to French predominance in the Active Zone and in Qadhdhafi a potentially disruptive actor who refused to play by the rules. The response soon decided upon was one of containment, as opposed to the previous policy of contest-and-cooperation, by coopting and strengthening the governments of the buffer states in the Active Zone and by engaging the cooperation of Algeria in the Maghreb. However, this variation on a basic policy also shifted with time back to the ambivalent pulls of contest-and-cooperation, as seen in the political versus commercial ingredients of French policy toward Libya in the 1983 Chad crisis.

Managing Conflicts

One activity—conflict management—cuts across all the zones. In addition to intervening in support of one side in inter-African conflicts, France and other Western states have acted in various ways to reduce conflict between Morocco and Algeria (1978, 1980, 1981), Nigeria and Cameroun (1981), Kenya and Somalia (1979–1980), Somalia and Ethiopia (1978), the Horn in general (1977 on), Zaire and Angola (1978), and South Africa and the Front-Line States over Namibia (1977 on), among others. France facilitated contacts between Moroccans and Algerians over the western Sahara but without tangible results; in the aftermath of the Mauritanian coup, the French appear to have attempted some substantive input by floating federal solutions, but in the 1980–1981 efforts their role was purely procedural. France alerted and was joined by the United States, Great Britain, and West Germany in urging calm and restraint on the Nigerians in the flare-up with Cameroun. In the Horn of Africa, Great Britain and the United States attempted to reduce Kenya-Somali tensions. The United States obtained a commitment from both sides to respect the Somali-Ethiopian border at the end of the Ogaden war, and France has tabled a proposal for a conference of states in the region to discuss outstanding problems. At the end of the second Shaba invasion, the United States and other Western states arranged for the mutual elimination of grievances between Angola and Zaire, notably the withdrawal of support for national liberation movements operating on their territory against the other party. Namibia has been discussed above. There have doubtless been other demarches as well over the past decade in other inter-African conflicts.

French efforts at conflict management are less distinctive than French responses to external invasion or internal collapse. One procedural characteristic seems to be a repeated presentation of good offices, or more precisely of "good places," through the proposal of a French venue for a conference as in regard to the Horn, or smaller and more discreet contacts as in regard to the Sahara. A second, substantive characteristic is the call for mutual restraint and respect for established boundaries. The mutual nature of conflicts and the existence of African norms on boundaries lend themselves to this type of appeal, but such an approach is useless in the more serious type of conflict where boundaries are in dispute (in the Horn and western Sahara, for example). A third characteristic is that French attempts at conflict resolution always appear to carry with them a major purpose of raising the prestige of France or of its associates. Its conflict-managing interventions are not disinterested; when there are no side effects, mediation is less active.

In the future, African conflicts that require external help in management are bound to appear, ranging from a new Ogaden war to a new Nigerian border alarm. In general, France can be expected to have little interest in conflict management in these cases, except where it can enlist other parties' help in protecting its associates (on the Nigeria-Cameroun model). Characteristically it will seek to ride out the conflict without taking any noticeable part, much as did the United States in the Saharan conflict during the Carter administration, but without the moralizing rhetoric. However, diplomatic initiatives such as those in Namibia, Rhodesia, and Shaba under the Carter administration are not likely to be part of French policy (although France would continue to join in some initiatives that others initiate, as in Namibia). In sum, it is unlikely that even if asked, France would be interested in a direct peacemaking role in a major African conflict, for example, more than a procedural role of hosting a conference to redraw the map of western Sahara. Such a role would be seen as too much of a colonial-type interference in matters for which Africans should now take the responsibility.

Conclusion

English speakers who do not know the French language nonetheless know two contradictory stock phrases that are always evoked to characterize the French people: *Plus ça change, plus c'est la meme chose* and *Vive la différence!* In examining French African policy under the first Socialist government since World War II, it is the first rather than the second that applies. French African policy is constant, Gaullist, analyzable, evolving, and committed, a strong element in Western relations with the African part of the free world. In the words of President Mitterrand while visiting Libreville, "France does not compete with anyone. There is enough room here for others. Simply, France wants to remain number one in the heart and the economy of Congo."[6]

Notes

1. I am grateful for the support of the Department of State's External Research Division for the preparation of this chapter, although, of course, no official responsibility is engaged in the views here expressed. Much of the information contained in this chapter can be found in news reports and studies of the individual incidents, rather than in a more general treatment of French policy. References have not been given in these cases. However, for other treatments of French policy in Africa (not including the European Community relation with the Lomé Conventions, which is not covered here), see:

Edward M. Corbett, *The French Presence in Black Africa* (Washington, D.C.: Black Orpheus, 1972).

Lawrence Franko, "The European Connection," in Richard Bissell and Chester Crocker, eds., *South Africa into the 1980s* (Boulder, Colo.: Westview Press, 1979).

Helge Hveem, "The Extent and Type of Direct Foreign Investment in Africa," United Nations Institute of Economic Development and Planning Conference, Dakar, 1974.

Edward Kolodziej, *French International Policy Under DeGaulle and Pompidu* (Ithaca, N.Y.: Cornell University Press, 1974).

"French Arms Control and Disarmament Policy," *Journal of International Relations* 4, 3 (1980):4–42.

"France and the Arms Trade," *International Affairs* 1 (1980):55–72.

"Europe: The Partial Partner," *International Security* 4, 1(1980–1981):104–131.

"Determinants of French Arms Sales," in Patrick McGowan and Charles Kegley, eds., *Threats, Weapons and Foreign Policy* (Beverly Hills, Calif.: Sage, 1980).

Colin Legum, *African Contemporary Record* (New York: Holmes & Meier, annual); especially annual articles by varying authors on "France's Year in Africa."

Pierre Lellouche and Dominique Moisie, "French Policy in Africa," *International Security* 3, 4 (1979):108–133.

Bruce D. Marshall, "Recent Developments in French Strategic Doctrine," in James Roherty, *Defense Policy Formation* (Durham, N.C.: Carolina Academic Press, 1980).

Lynn Mytelka, "Business in Ivory Coast," in I. William Zartman, ed., *The Political Economy of Ivory Coast* (New York: Praeger, forthcoming 1984).

William Raiford, *The European Role in Africa and U.S. Interests*, Congressional Research Service Report 81-202F (Washington, D.C.: Library of Congress, 1981).

John Ravenhill, "The Future of Eurafrica," in Timothy M. Shaw, ed., *Africa Projected* (London: Macmillan, 1983).

Alex Rondos, "France/Africa, A Widening Role," *Africa Report* 24, 5 (Sept.–Oct. 1979):4–8.

U.S. State Department, Conference on European-African Relations and U.S. Policy, Washington, D.C., 20–21 April 1981.

I. William Zartman, "Europe and Africa: Decolonization or Dependency?" *Foreign Affairs* 34, 2 (1976):325–343, updated and revised in Timothy M. Shaw, ed., *Alternative Futures for Africa* (Boulder, Colo.: Westview Press, 1982).

2. Jeanne Kirkpatrick, *New York Times*, 19 December 1981.

3. See Louis De Guiringaud, "La Politique Africaine de la France," *Politique Etrangere* 47, 2 (June 1982):441–457; "La Partie Socialiste en Afrique," *Le Mois en Afrique* 16, 186–187 (1982):16–42; and Jacques Guillemin, "L'Intervention Exterieur dans le Politique-Militaire de la France en Afrique Noire Francophone et Madagascar," *Le Mois en Afrique* 16, 186–187 (1982):43–58.

4. For a very typical Nigerian perception, see Joseph Wayas, *Nigeria's Leadership Role in Africa* (London: Macmillan, 1979).

5. Foreign Minister Claude Cheysson announced that the linkage of Cuban withdrawal from Angola and South African withdrawal from Namibia was "not acceptable," but France did not withdraw from the Contact Group, until the end of 1983, nor from the Koeburg nuclear project. See *New York Times*, 13 October 1982 and *Washington Post*, 8 and 9 December 1983.

6. *Washington Post*, 25 October 1982.

4. Brazil-Africa Relations: Third World Alternatives for Development and Security

Wayne A. Selcher

Brazil's African Thrust

Without rejecting ties with the North and with a minimum of stridency, in the mid-1970s Brazil set about making greater use of the Third World elements in its mixed identity with a twofold purpose: to advance its own development and to further its plans to become a leader of the capitalist Third World (rather than simply to aspire to a formal position in the ranks of the industrial West).[1] Brazil has used the concept of South-South relations to project a cooperative image to other LDCs (less developed countries), and Subsaharan Africa has been the location of its greatest recent initiatives outside South America. Activities like this, in which Brazil is the major partner and motivating force, reveal Brazil's participationist Third World stance and provide insight into the viability of closer relationships between more developed and less developed Third World states.

The progress of Brazil's relations with Africa over the last decade has been remarkable, with broadening areas of cooperation and complementarity. It may well be the most diverse cross-continental relationship among LDCs; yet it has proceeded without any long-range planning or coordination. Most surveys of the topic are still optimistic that this cooperation will continue to grow. However, as relations since 1975 have passed from the rhetorical stage to the project-realization stage, from occasional surges to steady amplification, both sides need to appreciate more clearly what the other can or cannot contribute. Choices have to be made and some risks taken. From the African perspective, Brazil must produce contributions to Africa to satisfactorily strengthen the ties; from the Brazilian side the attention paid to Africa must carry a tangible economic payload. Unintended consequences may arise, as each side relates to the other from different sets of national circumstances, priorities, and global perspectives. Some disappointments and points of attrition have already arisen as the Brazil-Africa relationship intensified in 1980 and 1981 but was then beset with economic reverses in 1982.

Brazil's chief goals in Africa are economic, but political considerations abound. Among Brazil's disadvantages in dealing with Africa are its inability to make the level of economic commitment Africa would like, its conservative government, its reluctance to get involved in African political or security issues, its competition with established powers, and its problems delivering financing for projects. Also, Brazil's racial system has come under increasingly critical African scrutiny as Africans visit that country, and beyond rhetoric, Brazil has only very gradually weakened ties with South Africa and carries on a significant level of trade with the republic.

On the other hand, Brazil has largely overcome earlier criticism caused by its support for Portuguese colonialism and has developed closer relations with Angola and Mozambique. Some of its foreign-policy spokesmen are expressing support for the concept of a "peaceful South Atlantic," in contradistinction to rumors about Brazilian interest in a hypothetical South Atlantic Treaty Organization. African receptivity to Brazil is good, but the problem of consolidation or sustained follow-through on initiatives continues to hinder real progress on a broad front. Most importantly, it is not yet clear what the effects on the political relationship will be of the economic constrictions starting in 1982 that stemmed from a more competitive world petroleum market and the African and Brazilian economic recessions and debt crises.

Third World Political Credentials and Capitalist Economic Interests

The dilemmas and contradictions of Brazil's position between First and Third worlds clearly impinge on relations with Africa in advantageous and disadvantageous ways. It requires considerable deliberate effort for Brazil to assert bona fide Third World membership while maintaining favorable bilateral relationships with key countries of the First World. Africans who see Brasilia, Rio de Janeiro, or São Paulo for the first time find a largely capitalist model, widespread foreign investment, and a level of technological development so far beyond that of their continent that doubts set in about whether Brazil is typical of the Third World or is of the Third World at all. A visit to Bahia, with its African cultural components, modifies this first impression somewhat, as does the argument that Brazil's recent success in modernization under tropical conditions is more relevant to the experience of Africa than are the models of Northern Hemisphere states. Even after this attempt at cultural-technological balance, Africans see Brazil as large and powerful, while Brazilians describe their nation as poor, weak, and much more limited in potential to cooperate with Africa than the major states already involved.

Ironically, vis-à-vis the North, Brazil has been resisting formal institutionalization of the economic categories of advanced developing countries and newly industrializing countries, with the conviction that its inclusion in such divisive groupings would carry more hindrances than privileges.

A probable negative consequence for Brazil of such a restrictive categorization (a supposed "promotion") would be to have its Third World credentials threatened to an extent damaging to its successful commercial policy. Further, it would be expected to grant concessions to—and to give up preferences in favor of—those Third (or Fourth) World countries lower on the development scale, including almost all of Africa. This it is not prepared to do. (Current Brazilian policy defends the validity of the Third World category even while acknowledging the heterogeneity of the countries composing that group.)

The conservative character of Brazil's government and its "born again" anticolonialism, after steady support for Portugal, caused frictions with Africa up to the end of the 1970s. Brasilia saw fit to compensate for those doubts with diplomatic plays to win African confidence, such as rapid recognition of the Popular Movement for the Liberation of Angola—MPLA (1975), condemnation of Zionism as "racism" in the UN General Assembly (1975), and initiation of visits to Brazil by revolutionary leaders of continental stature, such as Kenneth Kaunda (1979), Luis Cabral (1980), and Sékou Touré (1980). Of special effectiveness was a well-timed, heavily political tour of Brazilian Foreign Minister Saraiva Guerreiro in June 1980 during which he spoke to the chiefs of government of the Front-Line States—Tanzania, Zambia, Mozambique, Zimbabwe, and Angola. The tone of this visit was certainly not radical by African standards. However, it contrasted strongly with that of the 1972 trip to eight African countries of former Foreign Minister Gibson Barbosa, who represented a harsher Brazilian regime that supported Portuguese colonialism and was caught up in the euphoria of the "economic miracle." Barbosa dealt heavily in commercial and cultural affinity matters, avoided discussions about liberation movements, and announced in Nairobi that Brazil did not recognize the existence of a Third World.

The success of these diplomatic moves during the late 1970s was interpreted by the foreign ministry as a "green light" of acceptance for further approximation to Africa. Still, the political distance involved in accommodation regularly provides some interesting incongruities, as in the offer of the domestically conservative Brazilian government to provide humanitarian aid (but not arms) to black liberation movements,[2] or the assistance of Brazilian companies in parts of Mozambique's land reform and state collective-farm projects.[3]

Whereas Africa's foreign-policy style tends to be highly political, symbolic, and rhetorical, Brazil's is marked by caution, restraint, nonideological pragmatism, nonconfrontation, and a clear reluctance to take unambiguous positions on controversial issues not directly affecting Brazil. Even though political interests may eventually accrue with the development of commercial involvement in Africa, Brazil resists new entanglements in the Third World now that it has set itself free from the former system of political obligations to Washington.[4] Policy on Africa can serve as proof of Brazil's political independence, but the African image of Brazil as a country still largely in the U.S. sphere of influence has not died. Thus, to gain favor with Africa, Brazil has had to be more outspoken on issues affecting that continent than on those elsewhere in the Third World (with the partial exception of Arab-Israeli questions). That posture has evolved only gradually and with constant African prodding. Although Brazil is not a member of the nonaligned movement, it wants to project a measure of independence congenial to those who are. Therefore it usually adopts most of the essentials of the Organization of African Unity's (OAU) consensus as its own, with sufficient differences from typical Western positions to fall clearly within the moderate Third World group rather than the liberal Western one.

Brazil's official position is that the country is not out to replace any of the established powers in Africa or to duplicate their practices, which would merely implant a variant of neocolonialism. In order to present itself competitively as a new option and to overcome the advantages enjoyed by powers currently active in Africa, Brazil has emphasized affinities growing from cultural, climatological, and geographical similarities. The image-conscious vocabulary used includes "cooperation," "mutuality of interests," "balance of advantages," "horizontal relations," and "South-South relations" in an attempt to develop a new terminology and style for what is in fact a pioneering operation among LDCs. Although Brazil is willing in principle to lend modest disaster or refugee aid (so far done almost completely through the United Nations), it does not wish to be cast in the role of a donor nation or one with large-scale capabilities for foreign aid. Words such as "assistance" and "help" are therefore carefully avoided, in favor of a phraseology of mutual advantage in which Africans are said to request Brazilian products, services, and expertise, and both sides benefit. Africans do perceive a positive difference relative to the West in Brazilians' more relaxed and cordial style, their adaptability to African culture, and their lower level of condescension and paternalism, but the commercial promotion and the priority of the profit motive remain similar. Unlike the major powers of East or West, Brazil does not export ideology or social planning, nor does cooperation with Brazil bring sovereignty concerns or implications for either East-West or African politics. Unlike India, Pakistan, and South Korea, Brazil does not involve large numbers of Brazilian laborers in its projects, leaving some of them behind as potentially unwelcome by-products of a construction job.

Trade and Economic Relations

In addition to touting its medium level of development, to which Africans can relate easily, Brazil is willing to take greater risks than those run by the United States or European powers, to barter, and to extend more favorable benefits. For the time being, subsidizing the African venture is an investment in what for Brazil is a sizable future market, a market that established powers see as of marginal importance. Lower prices on simpler, but more durable ("tropicalized"), goods are combined with technical assistance and training on the more sophisticated purchases to establish competitiveness against existing sources of supply or consumer preferences. Brazilian sales personnel stress willingness to transfer intermediate or appropriate technology to Africa without mystification and to train local skilled labor, but some Africans comment that in practice such transfer is neither as rapid nor as complete as they would like and that it is a lower priority for Brazil than is trade. Further, Brazil's reluctance to make investments—stemming from lack of experience in the practice, capital shortages, or concerns about instability—is criticized by Africans as ignoring an important area of contribution. Commercial relations with Africa in the recent past have suffered from Brazil's overconcentration on what it could sell, as opposed to concern about what it could buy. Within its limits, Brazil has been generous in granting lines of supplier's credits, but it is unable to compete with larger powers. Even so, some loans may have to be renegotiated or become de facto write-offs.

Only recently have Africans come to consider some of the limitations on Brazil's cooperation. Earlier they tended to regard Brazil as in the same league with members of the Organization for Economic Cooperation and Development (OECD), or "Club of Paris." Brazil was seen as a well-advanced country, a useful but previously unknown alternative for such countries as Nigeria and Guinea that wished to diversify their foreign relations. Now African countries must concede that the extensiveness of Brazil's activities and the number and choice of countries with which it will become deeply involved are restricted by its domestic demands and priorities; its status as a major debtor, a large petroleum importer, and a technology importer; and its insistence on ultimate profitability.

Brazilian technology and products are suitable for any African application and are competitive. But as contracts have multiplied and initial dabbling has yielded to major projects, there has been an irony of success for the foreign ministry. Once political transit had finally been gained through painstakingly patient efforts, economic feasibilities became much more pressing because of African and Brazilian domestic difficulties. Brazil's lending capacity slackened just when Africa required easier loan terms. Joint ventures with third countries would be one solution to this problem, along with association with the larger local companies. Beyond maintaining its own agencies in several capitals, for example, the Bank of Brazil is associated with the International Bank of West Africa, a French concern that is a major financial force in the region. In order to render economically feasible what is politically desirable, Brazil is trying to arrange triangular deals with African initiative, Brazilian expertise, and third-party hard-currency finance. Cooperation with Portugal in the Lusophone states has been discussed but is unlikely, since Brazil prefers to serve its own purposes and not to become enmeshed in any residual disagreements from the colonial period.

Present multilateral schemes, such as those of the World Bank, the United Nations Development Program, and the European Development

Fund, are designed to operate in a North-South direction and to rely on existing systems. Ironically, even the Organization of Petroleum Exporting Countries' (OPEC) finance channeled to Africa through Western Europe has tended to reinforce the hegemonic position of the established powers. To offset these disadvantages, Brazil is trying to establish the technological-assistance principle that—in the cause of South-South relations—preference in execution should be given to other LDCs when multilateral funds design projects. Intergovernmental organizations have sponsored several conferences on technical cooperation among developing countries (TCDC), but in a practical way do not act as if they are aware of—and responsive to—the capabilities and institutions of the more advanced LDCs to meet the needs of poorer ones.

Cooperation with OPECs development fund would be an asset for Brazil, which is already sensitive to the need to defuse the charge that its African venture is largely a front to channel activity of multinational corporations under a false South-South label. Brazil must be careful not to appear to be a tropical surrogate for the economic or political interests of a major power, a sort of "commercial Cuba" in Africa. It desires a major role with at least the appearance of autonomy in any multilateral operation. Yet if the established powers have been reluctant to yield position to a newcomer, the Arabs have proven just as cautious with their finances and, until late 1980, slow to help Brazil with petrodollars. In the name of South-South cooperation, however, partnership with OPEC in the Third World began in 1982 in a coking-coal exploration and extraction project in Mozambique, backed by Arab money and Brazilian expertise and shipping. Such cooperation facilitates commercial exchange by giving Mozambique something to trade for Brazilian products without the need for financing. Brazilians would like to extend this type of cooperation to oil exploration and railroad construction, among other projects, but the disunity within OPEC and an uncertain cash flow for oil producers now make such agreements unlikely in the near future.

Brazilian Commercial and African Security Interests

Most African governments appear to regard Brazil as friendly to their interests, even though they would prefer more militance and action on matters concerning anticolonialism and national liberation movements in southern Africa. They have been somewhat satisfied with the symbolism of a change in pronouncements, although Brazil's declaratory allegiance is seen as largely exemplary. Brazil is not yet in the problem-solving stage in Africa, although it is an official observer at OAU meetings. At this point African diplomats value Brazil's votes and its consideration of their points of view in policy formation, but reserve their greatest efforts for attempts to change the behavior of the great powers and Cuba, which have some political impact on the continent. Should Brazil continue to expand its interest in Africa, however, it is not inconceivable that it could be pressured into assuming more assertive actions than heretofore. Countries that are pivotal in Brazil's African relations, such as Nigeria and Angola, would be in the best position to exert influence. Brazil is susceptible to such influence because it is trying to make an impression on Africa, rather than the reverse.

Both African and Western governments are starting to ascribe some significance to Brazil's stands on African matters. Brazil, in turn, sees value in its Africa policy for the image of its emerging global role. It is therefore paying more attention to articulating positions on African questions in talks with a wider range of countries; yet it is not allowing itself to be drawn out, to take responsibilities as a mediator, or to endanger the good will it has carefully managed to build up in Africa. As one example, some U.S. officials, after initial strong disapproval, came to see Brazil's presence in Marxist Angola as a Western influence for moderation, and consultations on African matters between the two governments occur with some frequency. Yet Brazil definitely does not interpret its actions in Angola as having political significance as a Western presence. As another example, during Saraiva Guerreiro's trip both Chancellor Helmut Schmidt of West Germany and an unspecified African leader were cited in the Brazilian press as having suggested that Brazil mediate in some fashion in the dispute over Namibian independence. The government declined on the basis of insufficient political dialogue with the South African government and made no claim to an entree with Pretoria lacked by the West.

Declarations aside, in 1982 the economic limits of effective Brazilian participation—beyond rhetoric—in the solution of African problems were indicated when the United Nations invited Brazil to become part of a multilateral peace force to act in Namibia during the transition to independence. Brazilian participation would have been a useful image booster in relations with Africa and a start toward a voice, however restricted, in continental security matters. Brazil turned down the request for contribution of two air force observation and transportation squadrons, largely on the grounds that domestic operations and costs would not allow a diversion abroad of personnel and equipment. The need to cover the expenses while waiting for reimbursement from the UN was also cited as a factor in the decision.[5]

Beyond the cognizance of the country's political and economic weaknesses and vulnerabilities in Africa, and a sense of how counterproductive political involvement beyond symbolism is for its own purposes, Brazilian policy reflects the fact that its political relations are used primarily to break ground and establish a climate of confidence and a framework for commercial relations. Thus, African receptivity to Brazil varies between the pragmatists, who are interested primarily in economic contributions, and the ideologues or militants, who place political or security considerations foremost and criticize Brazilian Third Worldism as insincere and opportunistic. Although Brazilian actions are tailored to appeal to the first group, which has predominated in official circles, a superficial type of attention is paid to the claims of the more vociferous purists, mainly intellectuals and radical leaders, who usually are not assuaged. Because of the Brazilian government's sensitivity to this skepticism, it considers the state of relations with Angola and particularly with Mozambique as the litmus test of acceptance by socialist or radical regimes. Brazil courted both capitals persistently. Rapprochement with Angola was gained with relative ease and speed, but only with the successful September 1981 visit of Mozambique's Foreign Minister Chissano to Brazil were political relations with Maputo really thawed. (Diplomatic relations have been established since 1975, but neither country has yet established an embassy in Brasilia, ostensibly for financial reasons.)

Commercial opportunities, more than any other factor, determine the priority accorded by Brasilia to ties with various countries. Those with markets for exports (particularly manufactures), projects for Brazilian participation, and resources to sell (particularly petroleum) rank highest on the list. Greatest activity has been carried on with Nigeria, Angola, Gabon, the Ivory Coast, and (recently) the Congo and Mozambique, with a lower level of interaction with Senegal, Ghana, Zaire, and Zambia. Brazil maintains formal diplomatic relations with nearly every African country, but dealings with most of them (for instance, Tanzania and Guinea) have been relatively sporadic and minimal, often largely for the symbolic political content involved. Brazil's connections with East Africa are especially weak. In future practice, those stable countries that can pay their way will receive the bulk of the attention, while poorer countries or those with less trade complementarity will be limited to "political relations." Portuguese-speaking Guinea-Bissau and São Tomé fit in as special Fourth World exceptions, the only ones in which the relationship is heavily donative on Brazil's part.

As a matter of strategy, foreign ministry officials dealing with Africa first set about firming up the ties with the generally more moderate West African governments (the linkage of longest standing), then turned to thorough consolidation of deeper relations with the socialist Lusophone states. Building upon experiences with Angola and Mozambique, they intended to extend some attention to the other countries of southern Africa and the East Coast. In practice, however, there has been some overlapping of stages as opportunities presented themselves and some postponing of plans because of higher priorities elsewhere.

Arms Sales and Military Aid

If Brazil has found it difficult in Africa to maintain its preferred separation of economics from politics, a new dimension of its presence there has the potential for carrying clear political and security connotations. Brazil is now the sixth-largest exporter of arms, and although the exact size of the trade is difficult to determine, about $1 billion worth of a wide variety of military equipment was exported to dozens of countries in 1980 and again in 1981, with sales in rapid expansion.[6] Most of Brazil's arms trade is carried out with the Middle East and Latin America, but Africa is now being approached in hopes of cutting into French, British, Belgian, Italian, and Soviet markets.

No stable supply relationships have been worked out yet. Togo purchased six Xavante jet fighter trainers, and Gabon bought four transport aircraft for official and military use and over a dozen patrol boats for coastal surveillance. Greatest hopes were placed on armored-car sales to Nigeria, but in spite of several military missions to Brazil, Lagos continues to prefer the traditional suppliers from whom it obtains better terms of finance and higher technology. Similar disappointing results were obtained after Zambian and Zimbabwean inquiries. Brazil is willing to sell to Angola and Mozambique, but they still rely on socialist and—lately—Portuguese arrangements.

Weapons-sales contracts are made largely from government to government, with the Brazilian military attaché serving as an initial contact point. For this reason, Brazil is considering creation of military-attaché positions in more key African embassies. Military-cooperation agreements, such as those for training and technical advisors, perhaps related to sales, cannot be ruled out, but more significant military ties do not appear imminent. Possible levels of interaction that have been mentioned include enrollment of a few African students in Brazilian military academies and technical missions of Brazilian air traffic controllers (an air force function).

Brazil's military sales policy is attractive to Africa because of appropriate technology, effectiveness, price competitiveness, and lack of political preconditions. The government provides export credits for military equipment, as with other exports, but is unable to match the financing conditions of the major powers in large purchases. Unlike the major suppliers, Brazil does not use arms sales as a tool for influence, nor does it appear likely to do so in the near future. Its market position is too small and uncertain to allow such policy even should the government desire it.

The National Security Council rules on all sales, with rather little coming to light on its political standards. The only countries certain to be vetoed appear to be national liberation movements, Cuba, and South Africa. (Both the USSR and China have shown definite interest.) At least three political vetoes have been reported: the case of Somalia, which wanted to pay cash for twenty Xavante jet fighters to use against Ethiopia in 1978; Ian Smith's Rhodesia, which wanted Xavantes to use against black guerrillas; and South Africa, which wanted a Bandeirante military transport.[7] Brazil's public policy is to avoid shipping arms to countries at war, a principle it flagrantly violated, however, in supplying Iraq in its war with Iran.

Brazil is a major supplier of armored vehicles to Libyan ground forces, and its weapons saw combat in impressive numbers in Libyan hands during the brief 1977 Libya-Egypt border skirmish and during Libya's invasion of Chad in late 1980. The latter action created considerable concern in Lagos, but no repercussions on relations with Nigeria could be detected.

The case nevertheless could be indicative of potential political embar-
rassments for Brazil because of the uses to which its weapons may be
put. In the short run the sale of the armored cars used has only been
enhanced by descriptions of their battlefield performance.

Brazilian Policy Toward Southern Africa

The most problematic region of Africa for Brazilian diplomacy has been
southern Africa, where Brasilia's previous support for Portuguese colonialism
and its unwillingness to follow fully the African line toward South Africa,
as well as Marxist governments in Luanda and Maputo, have given rise
to uncomfortable incidents, internal political disputes, attempts at molli-
fication, and delayed accomplishments. It is in policy toward this region
that strains between Brazil's Third World ties and its First World ties have
been most pronounced.

In the cases of Angola and Mozambique, Brazil would like to see the
emergence in the longer run of a Portuguese-speaking community of nations
with Brazil as major partner, but because of the pre-1974 connotation of
the Afro-Luso-Brazilian Community as a prop for Portuguese colonialism,
it is still too early to float the idea. Timing is crucial. Brazil's political
acceptance in Lusophone Africa is still too recent and too hard won to
bear the creation of such a multilateral cooperation scheme, because the
Africans involved might well take Brazil's support for the idea as indication
of sphere-of-influence ambitions. Brasilia regards with favor the modest
steps already taken since 1979 by the five Lusophone states to exchange
ideas and coordinate international action, without the participation of
Portugal and therefore in contradistinction to the neocolonialist implications
of the British and French systems. Brazil would prefer to see the gradual
development of a "community of equals" on African initiative, with Brazil
invited to join only when African confidence in its intentions is higher.

Meanwhile, Brazil has become one of the most significant trade, aid,
and investment partners of Angola and Mozambique. Achievement of this
status has been aided by the initial low level of attention paid by Portugal
to its ex-colonies and by the recent interest of these countries in diversifying
away from heavy reliance on the Soviets and Cubans. Brazilian Africanists
are convinced that Brazil stands in good stead to take advantage of the
growing African perception that Soviet help remains attractive only during
the period of struggle and immediate postindependence, but proves ineffective and meager in building a sound economy. Although Brazil is
uncomfortable with the Cuban presence in Angola (it has not maintained
relations with Havana since 1964), the foreign ministry is gambling on
the stability of the MPLA government and is reluctant to irritate it. So
Brazil supports the questionable MPLA contention that the Cuban soldiers
are present only as a counter to the South African threat. To date, there
is no evidence suggesting that the Soviet or Cuban presence per se has
been a major factor impeding Brazilian rapproachement with Angola and

Mozambique; to the contrary, Brazil may well have benefited from the initial limitation of Western competition. The instability caused by Angola's internal fighting and attacks from South Africa, however, has delayed the realization of as much progress as Brazil and Angola have already agreed upon. Even so, the continued pace of the relationship in spite of Agostinho Neto's death indicates momentum and some institutionalization on Luanda's part. Absence of Angolan and Mozambican representation in Brazil has also proved a hindrance to rapprochement, but diplomats of the three countries work together rather closely at the UN.

Brazil has been vehement and rhetorical in condemning South African attacks (and even rumored preparations for attack) on Angola and Mozambique. It recognizes the Southwest Africa People's Organization (SWAPO) as the representative of the people of Namibia, supports the outlines of the approach of the Western Contact Group, and prefers a Zimbabwe-type settlement in Namibia, but resists the establishment in Brazil of a SWAPO office. Regularly criticizing apartheid, Brazil has gone so far in the UN (mid-1981) as to propose compulsory and mandatory sanctions against South Africa and a cutoff of military sales and cooperation, petroleum, transportation links, and cultural ties, as well as a general retraction of commerce, credit and investments.

In actual practice, however, Brazil has only very gradually weakened its own ties—refusing to break relations with South Africa—and carries on a significant level of trade with the republic. Varig still maintains a Rio-Johannesburg air route. South African companies have investments in the mining and explosives industries in Brazil. Official relations with South African diplomats in Brasilia are correct but aloof. In deference to enhanced harmony in the Third World policy, the foreign ministry does not invite representatives from the South African embassy to occasions with a Third World component. South African diplomats have considerable difficulty in being received in the ministries. (The South African consulates in Rio de Janeiro and São Paulo, dealing with businessmen and travelers, are noticeably busier.) Brazil maintains only a chargé d'affaires with the rank of second secretary in its legation in Pretoria and has no trade-promotion activities in South Africa. Yet South Africa is too large a factor in the world minerals market for Brazil to shun it.

Black African radicalization toward South Africa has made less acceptable Brazil's contention that during negotiations on Namibia a thread of representation is needed in order to maintain access to information, opposition elements, and official communication. African demands for total isolation of South Africa, persistently articulated during Saraiva Guerreiro's tour of Front Line States and reinforced by the ties with Angola and Mozambique, are causing greater pressure on Brasilia, which continues to vacillate with occasional small concessions timed to garner some political value. Fully aware of the touchstone quality of this issue in African solidarity, the Foreign Ministry still finds it incongruous and unprofitable to yield to the severance demands of African states that in many cases maintain their own economic relations with South Africa.

The U.S. turn of policy toward southern Africa with the Reagan government's East-West orientation under Secretary of State Haig initially caused apprehension in Brasilia, which took pains publicly to place some distance between itself and Washington on these matters. Although Brasilia shares some concerns about Soviet and Cuban influence in southern Africa, it views events there with much more sympathy for African interpretations and with a political, rather than a military, criterion. U.S. support for the National Union for the Total Independence of Angola (UNITA) and the opening of a "new phase" in Washington's relationship with Pretoria did not cause open opposition but did move the Brazilian government from its previous indifference to U.S. initiatives in Africa. Washington's concrete support for opposition elements in Angola would certainly cause a significant strain in its relations with Brazil and perhaps even a public rift that would place Brazil on the side of a Marxist government.

Ill-founded rumors in 1981 about renewal of supposed U.S. interest in a South Atlantic Treaty Organization (SATO), with South African membership, also clashed with Brazil's less than comfortable position on South Africa, its regionalist idea of the South Atlantic as a conceptual link with Africa, and its view of Angola as one of the chief pillars of the African venture. The foreign ministry denies the existence of a Soviet military threat in the South Atlantic and as a semantic counterweight, some spokesmen have begun to refer to the South Atlantic as an "avenue," "basin," or "frontier" of vital national interest and a "zone of peace," pointing up their desire to prolong its status as the most demilitarized ocean in the world. This affirmation allows Brazil to take an offensive stand against persistent African accusations of Brazilian interest in a SATO and to stake a claim to a political role in South Atlantic affairs, even before it has a blue-water navy. Because this interest in keeping the South Atlantic from becoming a geopolitical chessboard is shared by Black Africa and during 1981 appeared in joint communiques with Nigeria, Senegal, and the Congo, the concept may be further developed as an indigenous strategic doctrine to promote local impact on Western policymaking on the issue.[8]

A Matter of Race and Culture

Brazil has made much of cultural similarities and its system of race relations in its approach to Africa, with low-key but persistent official statements linking Brazil's supposed racial democracy to its repudiation of apartheid. Brazilian enthusiasts of a relationship with Africa have frequently claimed that Brazil is a natural partner for African development because the African cultural roots of the country provide Brazilians with a sympathy for African customs and problems that Europeans and Americans lack. It has been argued that because of this national trait and the respect for things African that it implied, the Brazilian would not be likely to suffer culture shock in Africa, to take a paternalistic attitude, or to introduce unwanted alien ideas.

Because culture and race are major reference points in the African world view and important elements in solidarity and security matters, the accuracy of that claim of affinity was crucial to success as relations intensifed. African unfamiliarity with Brazil up to the early 1970s caused many to accept at face value official Brazil's assertions of the prestige enjoyed by the African element of Brazil's culture and of the nonexistence of a racial problem. The disparity between what they were led to expect and what they saw and experienced in actual stays in Brazil has caused numerous African officials, academicians, journalists, and business people to criticize the Gilberto Freyre—inspired white view of race and culture in Brazil.[9] At first discreetly and then more openly they have been challenging the lack of blacks in higher positions in Brazil and the scarcity of blacks in the relationship with Africa. Several initial African-Brazilian intellectual dialogues quickly raised this sensitive issue to a point of mutual uneasiness, with which even rather liberal Brazilians feel uncomfortable.[10]

Africans not only find strong racial discrimination in Brazil, but they also find that Brazil's whites give little prestige to the country's African roots. Brazil's Africanness is seen by these foreign visitors as frozen into the quaint, anthropological aspects of a museum exhibit in Bahia, rather separate from modern Brazil and more appreciated by Africans than by Brazilians themselves. Some African observers have gone so far as to contrast Brazil's racial situation unfavorably with that of the United States or of South Africa, because Brazilian blacks have not yet achieved a political consciousness of the racial dimension of their society.

Brazil is not yet a common topic in African newspapers and magazines, but the reports that do appear, often on the occasion of the visit to Brazil of a major figure, are beginning to contain references to this counter image. Despite Leopold Senghor's earlier unreserved praise of Afro-Latinite and despite Brasilia's attempts to control the exchange for public-relations purposes, the cultural-affinities assertion could become an embarrassment as the real status of Afro-Brazilians becomes more widely known in Africa. Even African leaders sympathetic to the economic advantages of a relationship with Brazil might find it difficult to justify morally the de facto exclusion of blacks from Brazil-Africa relations when Brazil claims to be second only to Nigeria in size of black population.

Brazilian authorities, of course, prefer to see Brazil-Africa relations progress on their own merits, with neither side using the relationship to push for internal political changes in the other. They are especially critical of the validity of parallels drawn between Brazil's racial system and the evolution of the racial issue in the United States, an approach commonly taken by both Africans and Americans. Some black Brazilian intellectuals, however, would very much like to see an explicit connection made between the Africa policy and Brazil's racial system, so that African criticism could be used to benefit the condition of Brazil's blacks.

Could Brazil become the target of an African "humanization" campaign on behalf of the small but vocal black civil-rights movement as relations deepen and Brazilian blacks gain political consciousness? Nigeria may prove to be the key actor on the African side, given its position as Brazil's major partner in Africa. President Shagari's expression of Nigerian concern for blacks everywhere as a principle and his use of the term *diaspora* to describe the forced scattering of blacks by the slave trade could presage a more assertive political stance, but probably only in rhetoric. At present the African governments are more attentive to racial developments in South Africa and remain pragmatically willing to facilitate ties with Brazil for economic reasons. They still see Brazil's race relations as an internal matter, although several diplomats have been involved in racial incidents. It is not beyond conjecture, however, that African governments important to Brazil may quietly make representation to the Brazilian government to address the situation of Afro-Brazilians and may require acknowledgement of the problem and visible progress toward solution before relations are allowed to grow really intimate. This supposition could become more likely if the black civil-rights movement expands but is repressed. On the other hand, in Brazil's current political climate, race is barely nascent as an issue and is far overshadowed by larger questions of social justice and political liberties for the population as a whole. This contradiction in Brazil's approach to Africa therefore highlights yet another rhetoric-versus-performance question implicit in the political consequences of the country's relatively recent official Third Worldism.

How Deep and Lasting a Relationship?

The durability of Brazil-Africa relations as a consequential link depends upon a number of political factors that are just now being tested. Internal political forces in Brazil are among these, for the future effects on foreign policy of the political opening of the government, or its occlusion, are not well defined. Brazil's political model and its international economic position are being thoroughly debated as its internal economic troubles mount and increasing attention is focused on the foreign debt. In the words of the prominent economist Celso Furtado, "How can we visualize the role which ought to belong to Brazil in the regulation of the Third World without first inquiring if this country will set a course or will continue deflecting without knowing to which port it is heading?"[11]

Within the government, the lines of African policy are now apparently well accepted, although conservative naval sectors voiced opposition to policy toward southern Africa from 1975 to 1977 and still have quiet reservations about the South Atlantic policy. The foreign ministry has had a free hand as front-runner and innovator in setting political, economic, and financial policy toward Africa, stressing the long-run view but with no clear idea where it all will lead, beyond the policy's role as a vehicle in Brazil's South-South plans. Other ministries dealing in foreign affairs (such as the treasury and planning ministries) are more prone to be wary of the uncertainties and costs. For example, cultural relations and technological assistance have been especially vulnerable to budget trimming. A serious expansion of the relationship or a contraction of its benefits would bring in new political actors and subsequent policy complications. Over time, in view of the degree of subsidization involved, the venture will need some respectable breakthrough to overcome skepticism in the bureaucracy outside the foreign ministry. The visits of Brazilian President Figueiredo to Africa and of Nigerian President Shagari to Brazil, originally planned for 1981, might have been opportune moments to gain such political coverage, but the repeated postponement of both visits provides evidence that vital national priorities lie elsewhere.

Encouraged by foreign ministry incentives to play up service in Africa for career advancement, a small cadre—albeit recent and sparse—of bureaucrats with experience in African affairs has emerged in Brazil. They are complemented by some quality opposite numbers in private-sector activities such as trade, banking, and services (Nigeria and the Ivory Coast are the countries of greatest initiative on behalf of business). The foreign ministry still has to "sell" Africa to the cautious business community, for its plans and political preparations run well ahead of private sector follow-up.

The academic world remains weak in Africa expertise, somewhat a reflection of its peripheral position in Brazilian foreign relations in general. Editorials on African questions have been more frequent in the quality press in recent years. Although certain foreign-policy stances toward Africa have occasioned controversy, the consensus on the present course of action appears to be broad. Most of the foreign-policy community and the small attentive public on the matter appear to see Africa as a natural location for projection of a Brazilian presence, even though disagreements arise concerning time frames, types of activities, and which countries to deal with.

Political instability, organizational weaknesses, and a lack of expertise on Brazil have caused the relationship with Brazil to be more problematical in Africa, although the level of acceptance for Brazil is high there. Brazilian officials are now more willing and able than previously to gauge critically the feasibility of African projects. At the same time African contact with Brazil has enabled both sides to start a direct exchange of information to overcome mutual stereotypes and false expectations induced by prior acceptance of U.S. and European images of the two areas.

The last few years have seen the establishment of institutionalized frameworks for cooperation, including numerous treaties and joint commissions. However, progress is hindered by a lack of follow-through: too many optimistic announcements have failed to bear fruit. After the intensification of relations in 1980 and 1981, the economic reverses of 1982 showed that the next several years would be trying ones for Brazil-Africa. Severe economic recession and debt crises on both sides, a decline in African ability to pay, and Brazil's search for goods to take in return for its manufactures threaten to weaken the relationship.

Only after several more years will results demonstrate whether Brazil is able to offer a new type of long-run cooperative alternative to Africa or whether essentially there will be a smaller-scale reproduction of the characteristics of postcolonial Western relations with Africa. Although it has already been demonstrated that Brazil does not have hegemonic aspirations or capabilities, so also has it been shown that it cannot become a source of foreign aid on terms the Africans require. It is not militant or participationist enough to satisfy some on security matters. Somber African economic prospects could direct Brazil's attention elsewhere, for despite South-South rhetoric it remains to be proven that developing countries are less motivated by self-interest than are developed ones. The most probable outcome is that Brazil will continue to be a useful but minor option for Africa in the 1980s. In any case, the connection merits close observation, because if the Brazil-Africa link falls short of mutual advantage, the viability of African attempts to find Third World alternatives for their development and security needs can be thrown into serious question.

Notes

1. Wayne A. Selcher, ed., *Brazil in the International System: The Rise of a Middle Power* (Boulder, Colo.: Westview Press, 1981). A Brazilian perspective from an authoritative diplomatic planner and spokesman is found in Ronaldo Sardenberg, "A política externa do Brazil nas duas últimas décadas," *Revista do Serviço Público* 109 (1981):25–40.

2. *Latin America Weekly Report* (May 30, 1980), p. 12.

3. *Latin America Weekly Report* (June 6, 1980), p. 8.

4. This diplomatic style is described in Wayne A. Selcher, "Brazil in the World: Multipolarity as Seen by a Peripheral ADC Middle Power," in Elizabeth Ferris and Jennie Lincoln, eds., *Latin American Foreign Policies: Global and Regional Dimensions* (Boulder, Colo.: Westview Press, 1981), pp. 98–101.

5. "O Brasil espera 'nova formula' para Namibia," *O Estado de São Paulo,* September 3, 1982.

6. *Veja* (October 28, 1981), p. 42; Warren Hoge, "Brazil's Arms Find Willing Buyers in the Third World," *New York Times* (August 9, 1981), p. E-3; "Armas: O Brasil invade o mercado mundial," *Senhor* (February 1981), p. 40. Reliable sales figures for Brazilian military equipment in any given year are still a matter of conjecture because of company secrecy and creative accounting.

7. "O Brasil vando alto," *Veja* (August 20, 1980), p. 122.

8. A similar view from the African side, suggesting a joint Brazil-Nigeria-Angola declaration and naval exercises, is provided in A. Bolaji Akinyemi, "The Need for an African South Atlantic Ocean Organization," *Nigerian Forum* 1 (1981):125–130. Such ideas, however, beyond their impracticality, have not been well received by the Nigerian government.

9. On this point, see Anani Dzidzienyo and Michael Turner, "African-Brazilian Relations: A Reconsideration," in Wayne A. Selcher, ed., *Brazil in the International System: The Rise of a Middle Power,* pp. 207–214.

10. African views of Brazil's racial system are still scarce in print, but a typical firsthand account is given by journalist Clem Baiye of the *New Nigerian* in "Nigerian View of Brazil," *West Africa* (September 1, 1980), pp. 1655–1657.

11. Celso Furtado, "El orden económico internacional y el Brasil," *El Trimestre Económico* 48 (1981):533.

5. A Giant Staggers: Nigeria as an Emerging Regional Power

Pauline H. Baker

Shifting Fortunes

Although Nigeria has followed a moderate and pragmatic foreign policy since independence in 1960, a new trend toward greater autonomy and unpredictability has emerged over the last decade. The origins of this trend can be dated from the time of the Nigerian civil war (1967–1970) when, after being rebuffed by the United States and Great Britain, Lagos unexpectedly turned to the Soviet Union for arms to suppress the Biafran rebellion. In 1967, Nigeria purchased twelve reconditioned MIG-17 fighters and several trainers, its first major weapons procurement from Moscow.

Nigeria's opening to the East stunned Western observers. However, what was significant was not that Nigeria went to the Soviet Union for military assistance, but that it maintained its steadfast resistance to Soviet penetration in the midst of disintegration. Several African states have experienced sharp reversals in international alignment and ideological orientation when they sought external military aid to meet urgent internal political crises. Nigeria, by contrast, sustained the basic tenets and integrity of its nonaligned foreign policy. Remarkably, the country managed both to hold itself together and remain free of foreign domination during the most difficult stage of its postindependence history.

Nevertheless, although there were no radical ideological transformations consequent to the civil war, there were fundamental policy reappraisals resulting from the ordeal and its aftermath, the results of which can be seen today. National interest has taken priority over emotional, cultural, and historic ties that had previously favored the West; diversification of relationships has been actively sought, if only to ensure that the country will never again be placed in a position of depending primarily upon one country or political bloc for critical defense needs; a more sophisticated understanding of world politics and a greater appreciation of the flexibility necessary to achieve international objectives has emerged; and Lagos has exhibited a willingness to speak out against transgressions by other African states and use its resources in support of its policy. In global politics, nonalignment has become a far more meaningful political doctrine, implemented through a balanced series of steps that has distanced Nigeria from both power blocs. The net result is that over the last several years Nigeria's public positions have carried more weight, its policy has been backed by more clout, and its role as a Third World power has been more credible.

In a pithy statement heralding the arrival of Pres. Shehu Shagari to London in 1981, the *Times* of London summarized the extent to which Nigeria's regional influence had grown:

> Nigerians, justifiably, see themselves as the giants of Africa. It is the one element they are agreed upon. And they are now seeking to use their oil and emerging industrial muscle to influence opinion and guide events. The December [1980] Lagos summit to determine the future of Chad, showed how once the Nigerian elephant had taken a position, the rest of Africa had to acquiesce and swallow its bile. To that extent Lagos is already a point of political pilgrimage for the smaller, weaker, more dependent African heads of state. In a good week, African ministers flock to this capital like compliant sheep seeking their shepherd, Shagari's blessing, and return home strengthened by promises of Nigerian support and more importantly, large gifts of money. . . . It is Nigeria's foreign policy, more than that of any other black African country, that most determines Africa's collective future. . . . The threshold upon which Nigeria is today poised is then not just a watershed in its pursuit of democracy, but also a potential turning point in its international outlook and position. . . . Nigeria is determined not just to play its natural leadership role in Africa, but to also build upon it.[1]

Foremost among the emergent themes in the country's more assertive foreign policy over the last decade has been the increased emphasis placed on national security. During the early days of the First Republic, this concept was far from the minds of the Nigerian foreign-policy elite. Anxieties about external threats existed, but they were largely attributed to scheming opposition politicians and jealous international rivals and dismissed as nuisance issues of a personal or transitory nature. Deep concerns lingered, as they still do in much of Africa, about the general dangers of "neocolonial" intervention and hostilities connected with white-minority rule in southern Africa, but neither were deemed to be urgent threats against which the state needed to defend itself militarily. Formidable natural resources, a fortuitous geographical location far from the continent's shooting wars, and the absence of credible adversaries on its doorstep have kept the country relatively secure.

By the 1980s, however, the international climate had changed dramatically. Challenges to the regional balance of power were occurring across the broad belt of Africa from Morocco in the west to the Horn in the east. Libyan activities, once ignored, presented new threats to Nigeria's interests, including a violent Islamic uprising with an anti-Western bias in the northern heartland of the country. Political transformations in neighboring Ghana, Liberia, and Chad created other flashpoints of instability in territories close by. Great-power conflict also has become more overt in Africa, affecting key conflicts in which Nigeria has staked out strong positions.

Internal events have clouded the picture further. Continuing ethnic rivalry, religious unrest, border disputes, the mass expulsion of illegal African immigrants, electoral tensions, and a spate of fires believed to be set by arsonists to impede investigations into government corruption have underscored the extent to which the country's domestic stability has been shaken. Inflation, unemployment, import dependency, and rapidly falling oil prices—perhaps the greatest shock of all—have added to Nigeria's hard times, shattering the popular presumption that the country has unlimited resources.

At a time when most observers expected the country to forge ahead strengthened by a renewed self-confidence, precisely the reverse has happened. The "giant of Africa" is staggering from the combined weight of a collapse of the market for oil, its most critical export; a test of its American-styled democracy at the polls during a period of economic hardship; internal political pressures deriving from a mismanaged economy, religious upheaval, and pressure for more states; and deteriorating external conflicts, ranging from the Organization of African Unity (OAU) stalemate to heightening tensions in southern Africa, conflicts that Nigeria has always considered its natural destiny to shape. Thus, the trend toward unpredictability fostered initially by a thrust for greater independence may be even more pronounced in the years ahead, promoted by the stresses and strains of suddenly shifting fortunes.

An African "Manifest Destiny"

Self-image plays an important part in shaping a country's international role. Despite several changes of government and widespread political upheaval, there has never been any doubt in the minds of most Nigerians that as long as their country remained united it was a born leader of Africa. A 1966 Ministry of External Affairs working paper stated bluntly that "Africa is Nigeria's natural sphere of influence. To shirk this manifest destiny is not to heed the logic of history."[2]

This theme has been repeated by the country's top political leaders and emphasized by outside observers time and again, albeit for somewhat different reasons. In a variation on a theme of nineteenth-century colonialism, Lagos has often interpreted its "manifest destiny" in racial terms—conceiving of itself as a nation bearing the "black man's burden." Pres. Shehu Shagari stated in a speech before the United Nation's (UN) General Assembly on October 7, 1979, that "the problems of no other continent define the international agenda better than those of Africa. . . . The destiny of Nigeria is inextricably linked with the fortunes of all the countries of Africa and all the peoples of African descent abroad. As a result, we have, and will continue to strive vigorously for the restoration of the rights and dignity of the black man everywhere; for too long he has suffered humiliation and discrimination."[3]

Nigeria's self-image notwithstanding, racial leadership has not been the most important factor accounting for Nigeria's influence in the eyes of the outside world—at least, not yet. To the West, Nigeria's importance lies in its huge population, estimated to be close to 100 million people, and in its rich reserves of high-quality oil near major European and North American markets. Until recently, Nigeria was the second-largest overseas supplier of oil to the United States and a "price hawk" among OPEC members.

But petroleum has been one of Nigeria's weaknesses as well as one of its greatest strengths. Its oil wealth has led to nearly a total collapse of agriculture, the economy's backbone until commercial petroleum production took off. Instead of taking steps to assure food self-sufficiency to keep pace with an exploding population, the government permitted agricultural production to drop 13 percent in the last decade, and major food items, including rice, have had to be imported. Moreover, the distribution of national income is highly imbalanced, with rural poverty contrasting sharply with ostentatious wealth in the cities. Nevertheless, as long as the oil spigot flowed, Nigeria was able to sustain growth in the midst of these development distortions. Eighty percent of Nigeria's income and 90 percent of its export earnings come from oil.

Price and production fluctuations recently began to play havoc with Nigeria's finances, however. The country lost an estimated $3.5 billion, or 14 percent of its budget, in 1981. Further competitive pricing by non-OPEC (Organization of Petroleum Exporting Countries) producers encouraged buyers to go elsewhere. By February 1983, Nigeria's production sagged to 550,000 barrels per day, as compared to 1.2 million barrels per day in December 1982 and a 2.1 million-barrels-a-day average production in 1980. Annual revenues dropped from a high of $26 billion in 1980 to an expected low of $8.6 billion in 1983. At a time when Nigeria held the presidency of OPEC, it split with the organization by unilaterally slashing prices by $5.50 a barrel and committing itself to match any further cuts by competitors. As Shagari predicted earlier, Nigeria proved to be the weakest link in the OPEC chain. The break was inevitable, commented a Western analyst, because Nigeria was "slowly going bankrupt."[4]

Under these conditions, barely anyone now raises the question of Nigeria's use of oil as a political weapon, a subject of considerable speculation two years earlier. Nigeria has become far more dependent on its trading partners for assured markets than they are dependent upon it for supplies. However, as a local Nigerian saying goes, no condition is permanent. With a recovery in the world economy and stabilized oil prices, the old question may well assume new importance. "People tend to think that as a result of a temporary glut in the world oil market, Nigeria will have to jettison its foreign policy," Dr. Chuka Okadigbu, a senior political advisor to President Shagari, stated. "That is naive. A temporary situation should not be considered a permanent situation."[5]

From time to time, producing companies have stressed Nigeria's willingness to consider oil as an instrument of foreign policy. Melvin J. Hill, president of Gulf Oil Exploration and Production Co., confirmed that President Shagari had given "a frank warning that Nigeria would be prepared to use a variety of economic sanctions as a political weapon, including oil."[6]

Certainly, there is ample precedent. Lagos nationalized British Petroleum in 1979, on the eve of the Commonwealth-sponsored talks on Rhodesia, to underscore the commitment to majority rule and the desire to make the negotiations work. Oil shipments to Ghana were withheld to protest the summary executions of former leaders by the first regime of Flight Lt. Jerry Rawlings; they were suspended again after Rawlings's second coup, ostensibly because Ghana had not paid a $150 million oil debt. Nigeria also stopped oil supplies to Chad to protest the collapse of the peacekeeping operation prior to the Libyan intervention. As these examples show, whatever government is in power, Nigeria may use its economic resources for political reasons, if sufficiently provoked. Though the impact of the oil glut is certain to divert international concerns to domestic issues for the foreseeable future, it is not likely to alter the basic trend toward a more assertive foreign policy in the long term. As the largest market in Africa with substantial Western investments, Nigeria retains the capacity to send sharp messages through means other than oil, if that weapon continues to dwindle in strength.

In better times, Nigeria's perception of its full range of capabilities in international affairs has gone beyond the conventional view of the country as an oil power. Nigeria prides itself on an accumulated influence and range of diplomatic achievements based on size, military strength, and stature. A comment by the Nigerian Ministry of Information boasted, for example, that

> Nigeria now enjoys more international influence than ever before. This is based partly on her position as the most populous country in Black Africa, and the one whose military forces, although in numbers they have been considerably reduced since the Civil War, are still Black Africa's biggest, with their equipment constantly being improved. It is based, too, on her recognition of her responsibilities to her neighbors and her ability, at least until recently, to afford to other African countries considerable financial help, and to invest in their enterprises. . . . Above all Nigeria has been, and is, the moving spirit behind the Economic Community of West African States (ECOWAS) whose object is to create a great area of free trade and free movement in an area of 16 countries stretching 2,000 miles from Mauritania to Nigeria, with a population expected to exceed 200 million by the century's end. . . . Nigeria also belongs to a wide range of regional bodies in West Africa. . . . She is always anxious to be a good neighbor and never to use her strength to claim hegemony. . . . In wider continental problems, African countries always look to Nigeria.[7]

The claim to be a "moving spirit" behind West African unity has been placed in serious question following the expulsion in January 1983 of an estimated 1 to 2 million illegal aliens who originated from neighboring

ECOWAS states. (Former Internal Affairs Minister Alhaji Ali Baba reported that 1.15 million Africans left Nigeria at that time—700,000 from Ghana, 180,000 from Niger, 150,000 from Chad, and 120,000 from Cameroon.) On the heels of international criticism over this action, Shagari tried to defend his nation's image and reputation on this score. "We have vigorously contributed to the sustenance of the unity of Africa, to reinvigorate regional organizations within Africa, and we have positively projected the image of Nigeria as a stable and virile democracy," asserted Shagari as he kicked off his party's election campaign less than a week after the expulsion directive was issued.[8] Former president Nnamdi Azikiwe, himself a candidate for president in the last election, took exception, maintaining that the order had dealt a "mortal blow" to the foundations of African unity.[9]

Much as the move was resented, particularly within ECOWAS (which promotes free movement among member states as one of its principal goals), there has not been much open criticism of the action by African states. This is partly because some had taken similar action on a lesser scale against illegal aliens in their own countries, partly because they do not want to stir up ill feelings against Nigerians still living among them, and partly because they do not want to alienate what is still the most powerful country in the region.

For all the proverbial fears of domination harbored by smaller states in the region, however, Nigeria's size and resources have not been used to threaten weaker neighbors, overwhelm less powerful states, or impose its views unilaterally. Rather, Nigeria has a record of stressing diplomatic negotiations to solve regional conflicts.

It was Nigeria, for example, that swung the majority of African states in the OAU toward formal recognition of the ruling Popular Movement for the Liberation of Angola (MPLA) government in Angola in 1975, after it was disclosed that the United States was providing covert support to rival groups and South Africa had invaded the territory. Nigeria rebuffed Secretary of State Henry Kissinger three times in his efforts to achieve a settlement in Rhodesia (now Zimbabwe) in 1976, crippling that initiative from the start. Lagos played a key role as a broker among the Front-Line States in Anglo-American negotiations on Rhodesia during the Carter administration. Its military role under OAU auspices was critical in pushing the Libyans out of Chad, and it has been a key player trying to patch up the differences and work out a compromise to overcome the divisions within that organization.

Over the years, then, Nigeria has come to see itself as a regional power with the duty and obligation to intercede in African issues, particularly those involving racial domination, extracontinental intervention, and, more recently, territorial aggression. What this means in terms of material support, military involvement, and great-power relations is not completely clear, especially during times of financial hardship and domestic political uncertainty. However, a measure of the degree to which Nigeria's self-image as a major regional power has been accepted internationally may be found in an ironic footnote to the early politics of the Reagan administration. After months of delay in the Senate confirmation of Chester A. Crocker as assistant secretary of state for African affairs, aides to Senator Jesse Helms—who held up the nomination—explained that the senator felt that Crocker might look at Africa "through Nigerian eyes," putting regional concerns above strategic considerations.[10] Paradoxically, Helms's staff were enhancing Nigeria's image, implying that Lagos exercised enough clout to shape U.S. policy even with the Reagan administration, the views of which were not nearly as close to Nigeria's as were its predecessor's.

Threat Perceptions

While Nigeria has consistently argued for African unity and regional political cooperation to resolve continental conflicts, it has become more outspoken in African issues, having overcome its previous reluctance to publicly condemn sister African states and identify specific actions or regimes as threats to its own national security.

Ghana was the first state to be openly identified as a potential threat. The height of hostility between the two former British colonies occurred under the regime of Ghanian Pres. Kwame Nkrumah, a leading proponent of Pan-Africanism, an African High Command, and continental government. Despite nodding support of Pan-Africanism during the 1960s, Nigerian leaders saw real dangers behind Nkrumah's policies and attributed sinister motives to his idealistic goals. After Nkrumah's overthrow, the Nigerian Ministry of External Affairs spelled out its views of the prominent leader who, in the Third World as a whole, had been widely hailed as an African hero:

> On attainment of independence . . . [Nkrumah] was quick to sever all the common links which existed between British West Africa and so the very foundation on which West African Unity could have been built was shattered. . . . [Ghanaians] not only discriminated against Nigerians [living in Ghana] in the matter of employment but even engaged in subversive activities against Nigeria and heaped unbearable insults on our leaders. Jealous of Nigeria's resources and her size which marked her out for leadership in Africa, they did everything possible to discredit us the world over.[11]

Nigerian-Ghanaian rivalry has deep roots reaching back to precolonial times. Ghana claimed a cherished role in African history, not only as the pioneer of anticolonialism and the first to gain independence, but as a state with a sound economic base, skilled manpower, and a commitment to development at the time of independence that gave it a favored status in Western eyes in the early 1960s. Nigerian attitudes toward Ghana, on the other hand, were mildly contemptuous, with the local press viewing its neighbor as an inconsequential rival.

Evidence of Ghana's interference in Nigeria's internal affairs was presented during the 1962 treason trial of Chief Obafemi Awolowo, then (as now) the major opposition leader. In addition, Nkrumah was believed to have been behind the assassination of Pres. Sylvanus Olympio of Togo. Lagos launched a concerted effort to isolate Nkrumah throughout the continent. Its success in this endeavor was demonstrated by Ghana's exclusion from the preliminary meeting of African foreign ministers in Lagos before the formation of the OAU and from subsequent efforts to shape the organization as a device to combat subversion throughout the region. Following Nkrumah's downfall, tensions between the two countries eased. Ghana's subsequent economic misfortunes and political instability further lessened the threat. However, the perception of Ghana as a potential danger to Nigerian interests has been revived with the seizure of power by Flight Lt. Jerry Rawlings, a reputed admirer of Nkrumah and Col. Muammar Qaddafi. Relations have been further strained by the January deportation of illegal residents, more than half of whom were Ghanaian. (Four years earlier, Ghana had similarly expelled Nigerians.)

Lagos has had a range of difficulties with other neighboring countries over a host of issues. These include boundary disputes, allegations of mistreatment of nationals, smuggling, escape of fugitives, and foreign support of dissidents. Usually these have amounted to no more than passing skirmishes or minor diplomatic confrontations that were quickly resolved—typically conflicts complicated by ethnic, tribal, or regional linkages. Nevertheless, they are indicative of two important aspects of Nigeria's foreign policy: the inclination toward peaceful resolution of international conflicts and the lack of experience in distinguishing between these more moderate disturbances, on the one hand, and the more serious and formidable threats emanating from beyond her borders on the other.

Benin (formerly Dahomey) offers a useful example. Thousands of Yorubas, whose homeland is in Nigeria's western region, inhabit this small Francophone state to the west, which had provoked Nigeria in the past by permitting its territory to be used as a staging area for Red Cross relief supplies to Biafra during the civil war. Economic sanctions quickly put an end to the airlift operation, and Nigeria mended relations shortly after the war ended, offering Benin the first interest-free loan that Nigeria had granted to another country. Nigeria remains only moderately concerned about its tiny western neighbor that has ethnic ties to one of the country's three largest tribes, a record of having had the greatest number of coups d'etat in Africa, a terrain that functions as a convenient outlet for contraband, and a Marxist-Leninist ideology that contradicts Nigeria's vibrant capitalism.

To the east, Nigeria has also had long-standing border disputes with Cameroon. The latest clash came in May 1981 between Nigerian and Cameroonian troops in an episode that former Nigerian Minister of External Affairs, Prof. Ishaya Audu, described as "very serious."[12] Five Nigerian soldiers were killed in the incident, sparking extensive controversy as the local press, army officers, and opposition politicians uniformly called for swift retaliation. Instead, President Shagari acted with characteristic moderation, issuing a note of protest to the Cameroonian government and demanding an apology, punishment of the Cameroonian soldiers, and payment of compensation to the families of the deceased. Concerned that the flare-up might generate discontent within the army, Shagari personally warned the soldiers at the annual passing-out parade of the staff college that this was a matter for civilians to handle. Though praised internationally for his restraint, Shagari's actions fell short of the expectations of many internal critics. The Nigerian Senate Foreign Relations Committee, among others, registered unhappiness over the Cameroonian response, calling the killing of Nigerian soldiers "an act of aggression and provocation."[13]

By far the most recent source of concern for Nigeria's national security is one that the country never had to confront before: military aggression and subversion from a rival regional power. Before the Libyan intervention in Chad, warnings of Libyan aggression were not taken seriously in Lagos. Just as they had once regarded Ghana as too puny to constitute a serious threat, Nigerians tended to shrug off the suggestion of danger from a small country hundreds of miles across the Sahara Desert with a population of merely two million. Moreover, an underlying suspicion existed that much of the international alarm about Libya was manipulated by the West for ideological reasons, especially by the French, who have been resented in Nigeria for their continuing "neocolonial" role in several Francophone states, their trade with South Africa, and their former support of Biafra. Throughout the protracted fifteen-year conflict in Chad, therefore, Nigeria was as determined to minimize French influence in the territory as to contain the reputed Libyan advance.

This did not mean that Nigeria supported Libya's wider objectives. Col. Muammar Qaddafi's Pan-Islamic ideology, vaguely reminiscent of Nkrumah's Pan-Africanism, disturbed more conservative minded Nigerian leaders who saw Qaddafi's campaign as a potential threat to political stability throughout the Sahelian states. Nigerians were also embarrassed by Libya's support of the regime of Uganda's Pres. Idi Amin. They watched silently, but disapprovingly, as Qaddafi futilely tried to save the unpopular dictator. However, it was not until Libya militarily intervened in Chad after the collapse of the transitional government and the failure of the Nigerian-led peacekeeping mission that Lagos saw Tripoli, without qualification, as a direct threat to Nigerian security and to the political resolution of the Chadian civil war.

Adding to fears of Libyan external aggression, and underscoring the connection between national security and internal stability, was a fundamentalist Islamic insurgency that originally erupted in Nigeria's northern city of Kano. Attributed to the Maitatsine sect, a newly formed secret society that challenges traditional Islamic theology, the original outbreak of violence in December 1980 took the government by total surprise. It was suppressed only after the army was called in and after a thousand people were reportedly killed, the largest disturbance to have occurred in Nigeria since the end of the civil war. While lacking concrete proof of a Libyan hand in the unrest, many Nigerians concluded that Qaddafi was behind the riots. Later disturbances that provoked additional bloodshed in October 1982 in Kano, Maiduguri, and Kaduna were attributed to displaced persons who had earlier fled from Libya's invasion of Chad, together with refugees seeking asylum from the defeat of the Libyan-backed faction led by Goukouni Oueddei. The fierce nature of these religious riots enflamed Nigerian xenophobia, alerted the country to the Libyan threat, and sparked calls for the renunciation of the ECOWAS treaty.

At the initial outbreak of violence, Lagos reinforced its northern border with federal troops in response to clashes between Nigerian soldiers and people described as "armed Chadians" crossing the frontier. Nigeria significantly increased its military budget to fill the gaps in its defense against Libya's modernized arsenal. Libyan diplomats were expelled from Lagos in February 1981, after Tripoli announced it was converting its embassy into a "people's bureau." The forty-eight-hour expulsion order was issued just a day before Libya announced its abortive plan to merge with Chad. A meeting was called between Shagari, Qaddafi, and Goukouni for the following month, but Libya refused to attend because Nigeria insisted that only a timetable for withdrawal of Libyan troops be discussed.[14] Shagari again put his prestige on the line over this issue when he later flew to N'Djamena, the capital of Chad, to meet Qaddafi in person. Qaddafi attended this session, but defied Nigeria by flatly refusing to withdraw his troops from Chad.[15]

That laid the foundation for wider action. Nigeria's deep concerns and frustrations with Libya led it to cooperate with the West in pushing for Tripoli's ouster. This was a turnaround from established policy of discouraging Western intervention in African conflicts, particularly by the French. Essentially, the French-inspired strategy was to persuade Goukouni to request the Libyan troops to leave Chad by promising him direct military aid and an inter-African peacekeeping force. It was truly a historic step when Nigeria accepted the plan, the centerpiece of which was an OAU-sponsored force, with Nigerian troops constituting the strongest component and France and the United States jointly footing the bill. Paris and Lagos worked toward the common objective of mobilizing African opinion in the OAU, in which Qaddafi was due to become the next chairman.

The decision to participate in the Chadian peacekeeping plan involved grave political risks for Nigeria and the impact of its eventual outcome is still not fully known. The humiliation of a second defeat of its military mission in Chad or controversial involvement in a neighboring civil war could have caused unrest in the Nigerian army, discontent among civilians already critical of Shagari's peaceful handling of the Cameroonian incident, and alienation among the masses resentful of the economic costs of involvement. That Lagos went ahead in the face of these considerable political constraints is indicative of the gravity with which Nigeria assessed the threat from a country once thought to be harmless.

Although none of the worst fears materialized, Nigeria's plans did not work out as hoped. Despite the OAU peacekeeping presence, there was a military solution in Chad following the departure of Libyan troops. The faction led by Hissène Habré marched to N'Djamena with the OAU forces standing by, unable to stop the assault—because, the Nigerian commander explained, it was not part of their mandate to intercede. The question of which of the rival factions—that of Habré, who established physical control, or that of Goukouni, who took refuge in Libya—should be recognized by the OAU has become a contentious issue that prevented the convening of the OAU 1982 summit. Chad thus remains a troublesome issue, not only because it is one of the issues depriving Nigeria of an OAU forum but also because of the lingering possibility of a resumption of hostilities, a reinvolvement of Libya, or even worse, an interminable African conflict on Nigeria's borders in which Lagos would inevitably be sucked in. Shagari met with Habré, the de facto Chadian ruler, late in 1982, but relations remain distant due to continuing religious troubles, the refugee situation, the expulsion order, and a dispute over oil claims in Lake Chad.

Southern Africa Policy

No matter how significant is the continuing threat from Libya, how extraordinary is Nigeria's cooperation with the West over Chad, and how hard pressed is the economy during the oil glut, none of these developments is likely to divert Nigeria's stated posture with regard to southern Africa, the one foreign-policy issue around which all Nigerians unite. On the occasion of the independence of Zimbabwe in April 1980, President Shagari reiterated the nation's long-standing commitment to combat racism in Namibia and South Africa: "I think that it is important for me to underline the fact that as far as we in Nigeria are concerned, we will continue to give our total support to the uncompleted struggle for the total liberation of the continent from the clutches of minority regimes and all the vestiges of colonialism. This is a basic principle of our foreign policy from which no Nigerian government can deviate and it is a position which is in accord with popular sentiment in our country."[16] In an address to the Foreign Policy Association in New York later that year, Shagari defined the role he expected the United States to play in this context:

> We, in Nigeria feel that the history of [the United States] . . . places on the government and people of [your country] a great responsibility to use your powerful international economic and financial position to discourage and, eventually, destroy apartheid in South Africa. . . . Your policy towards South Africa has been largely dominated by a single-minded pursuit of economic and strategic considerations. This in my view can at best offer only a temporary advantage, for in the final analysis, only a South Africa which accepts majority rule can truly offer a lasting guarantee to the security of your economic and strategic interests.[17]

Nigeria would regard it as a great setback if the United States tilted irrevocably in favor of South Africa, either on the question of apartheid or on regional issues, in such ways as supplying arms to anti-MPLA forces in Angola or backpedaling from United Nations (UN) Resolution 435, which contains the guidelines for an internationally recognized settlement in Namibia. Apartheid, Namibia, and Angola are the three keystones of U.S. southern Africa policy that Nigeria watches like a hawk.

In fact, with an eye on the 1983 elections, the Nigerian government sent top officials to an anti-apartheid seminar held at Jos, northern Nigeria, in December 1982 and announced an official investigation of multinational companies (Siemens, Hoëchst, and Union Carbide) and other organizations involved in South Africa. A campaign was also launched to involve European Economic Community (EEC) countries in anti-South African policies. The Nigerian ambassador to Brussels confirmed that his country will raise the issue when Lomé III negotiations commence.[18] Southern Africa is the one sure issue in which a militant position can be counted upon to be domestically popular.

Nevertheless, Shagari has been patient with the Reagan administration, indicating that while he was skeptical of constructive engagement, the term used by the United States to describe its policy of getting South Africa's cooperation, he would give the West time to push Pretoria into an agreement on Namibia. But he has warned that Nigeria "will use every means at our disposal" to fight "the evil system of apartheid" and any "collusion and encouragement of Western powers."[19] Referring to Angola, he has noted that "if the United States is willing to support rebels in a sovereign African nation, it would be extremely serious. I don't believe [Washington] will do it because it would be very unwise." Until minority rule is abolished, there is little question that Nigeria, in Shagari's words, will continue, at least in spirit, to give "all necessary aid to freedom fighters in Namibia and South Africa."[20]

The Nigerian president has taken pains to point out that his government's opposition to apartheid is not a passing phase or a personal priority. It is a matter of national honor and racial pride "based on the deep-seated conviction that the whole philosophy of racism and apartheid is not only reprehensible, but is one which is deeply offensive to every civilized man or woman throughout the world."[21] To retreat from this position would be tantamount to repudiating the principles which every Nigerian leader since independence has espoused and forfeiting the one foreign-policy issue that is sure to arouse mass public support.

Given this degree of commitment, it is not surprising that Lagos was disturbed by Washington's decision to veto the UN resolution condemning South Africa for its attack on Angola in September 1981. In reaction, Prof. Ishaya Audu, former Minister of External Affairs, obliquely hinted of Nigerian military assistance to Angola to resist future incursions: "There is definitely a feeling Africa should participate in the defense of Angola. There is a feeling that if Cuba is in the position to help then Africa should be even more in a position to help. . . . As far as Nigeria is concerned, if asked, Nigeria would look at it objectively."[22]

It is highly unlikely, despite the rhetoric, that material assistance would be forthcoming in the near future. But Audu's reference to Cuba raises the fundamental question of Nigeria's perceptions of the Soviet and Cuban presence in Africa. While the United States would place the Cuban troop presence in Angola high on the agenda of national-security threats to Africa, Nigeria regards the major threats to African political stability as arising principally from indigenous problems. Indeed, Shagari has been critical of those who treat "the struggle of African peoples and governments . . . in terms of ideological differences between East and West."[23] Even the recent concerns over Libya are not laid at the doorstep of Moscow. Rather, Lagos sees Libya much the same way as it saw Nkrumah's Ghana— as a nation led, not by a puppet of a foreign power, but by an irresponsible leader with dreams of power and dominance.

This is not to say that the presence of Cuban troops in Africa has not caused mixed feelings in Lagos, especially as regards Angola. On the one hand, Nigeria resolutely defends the right of the MPLA government to ask for external assistance to defend itself against South African aggression. The Cuban presence is justified, from this perspective, as long as South Africa continues to threaten Luanda. On the other hand, Nigeria is adamantly opposed to foreign intervention in Africa and would welcome a settlement of the Namibia dispute, both to bring majority rule to the territory and to create the conditions under which South African forces would be withdrawn and the Cuban troops sent home. In an address to heads of state at the 1978 OAU summit meeting in Khartoum, Nigeria's then head of state, Lt. Gen. Olusegun Obasanjo, conveyed this sentiment in a widely celebrated comment: "To the Soviets and their friends, I should like to say that having been invited to Africa in order to assist in the liberation struggle and the consolidation of national independence, they should not overstay their welcome. Africa is not about to throw off one colonial yoke for another. Rather, they should hasten the political, economic, and military capabilities of their African friends to stand on their own."[24]

Lest he appear one-sided, however, Obasanjo also sent a parallel, and less publicized, warning to the West: "To the Western powers, I say that they should act in such a way that we are not led to believe they have different concepts of independence and sovereignty for Africa and Europe. A new Berlin-type conference is not the appropriate response to the kind of issues thrown up by the recent episode (in Shaba). Paratroop drops in the twentieth century are no more acceptable to us than the gunboats of the last century were to our ancestors."[25]

Nigeria is thus of two minds—more so now than ever—with regard to its relationships with external powers. The country recognizes the need to cooperate with extracontinental states on some security issues, as it has done to contain Libyan expansionism. At the same time, it maintains a keen awareness of the dangers inherent in allowing Africa to become a victim of foreign domination. This ambivalence is likely to be an enduring feature of Nigeria's foreign policy as long as the majority of African states lacks the means to respond to legitimate defensive needs on their own and Nigeria sees itself as one of the few regional powers able to fill the vacuum.

Economic Strains

Judging by objective indexes of power, Nigeria should be invincible to threats arising from anywhere in Black Africa. With a land area of over 350,000 square miles, Nigeria's size is greater than that of France, Netherlands, Belgium, and Britain put together. It also outnumbers all other states in the continent. There has not been a reliable census in over thirty years, but most estimates place Nigeria's population between 80 to 100 million. Informed observers speculate that the actual figure is probably higher. At the current rate of population growth, the United Nations projects Nigeria's population in the year 2000 at 161 million, and 450 million in the year 2105, when it is predicted that Nigeria will be the third most populous country in the world, lagging only behind China and India. Today, as Africa watchers are prone to point out, one out of every four Africans is a Nigerian.

By African standards, Nigeria's economy for the past several years had been judged to be relatively strong, thanks to oil—which until recently had brought in approximately $30 billion in average annual income. The drop in oil revenue has suddenly plunged the economy into deep trouble, making all prior economic forecasts wrong. By February 1983, the nation's foreign reserves had dwindled to $1 billion, approximately equal to one month's imports. But oil is not the only villain undermining Nigeria's economic health. A history of ignoring the pressures of an exploding and rapidly urbanizing population, ambitious spending, widespread corruption, smuggling, mismanagement, and misplaced economic priorities has deprived Nigeria of the safety net now desperately needed as the oil market collapses.

Nevertheless, considering the shape of other Third World countries strapped for funds, Nigeria still has reasonable options. With oil reserves of about 25 billion barrels, a large market potential, and a reputation as an underborrowed country whose political importance cannot be ignored, Nigeria has the capacity to pull through this crisis just as it pulled through the civil war. What is less certain is the political impact that these conditions will have internally and the willingness of the general population to pay the price of recovery.

Political Uncertainties

The political corollaries of the economic crunch are the most difficult variables to assess, especially as regards the role of the armed forces, still the mightiest in Black Africa. As N. J. Miner noted, Nigeria's military organization began with "miniscule armed forces that had been left behind by the colonial regime—small in numbers, defective in equipment, with few experienced African officers and generally despised among the politically conscious citizens of the new states."[26] By 1966, the army numbered 10,500. During the civil war, the forces ballooned to over 250,000. Through gradual postwar demobilization the armed strength of the country was trimmed down to its present estimated 120,000 to 140,000—still the largest in Black Africa. Nigeria's 8,000-man navy is considered to be the most highly developed on the continent, except for South Africa, and the country's air force has been undergoing extensive modernization. The professionalism and prestige of the army reached a high during its performance as part of a UN peacekeeping operation in Zaire in the early 1960s; it suffered severely during the internal upheavals, but was given a big boost when the soldiers turned power over to an elected civilian government in 1979, launching Nigeria on its present democratic experiment.

The new presidential system modeled after the U.S. system of checks and balances has further enhanced Nigeria's international prestige. It faced a critical test when the first civilian-run elections of the Second Republic were held over a five-week period beginning in August 1983. If Nigeria progresses peacefully through the second term of civilian rule, its standing in the world community will be elevated considerably, especially in light of the economic difficulties being faced.

Many observers, looking at the social and political fabric of the country, are pessimistic about Nigeria's long-range prospects. Certainly, on the basis of the nation's internal weaknesses alone, one could make a persuasive case that Nigeria is far from reaching the heights of regional influence often expected of it. Throughout Nigeria's history, the gravest threats to national survival have come not from external aggressors, resource competition, ideological struggle, or territorial aggrandisement—conflicts for which conventional indexes of international power are relevant. Rather the real threats to survival have originated from the cultural pluralism, economic disparities, and ethnic hostilities emanating from uneven and rapid modernization. These are internal vulnerabilities for which conventional power formulations have little application.

More than 250 tribal groups live in Nigeria, with three large communities—the Hausa-Fulani, the Ibo, and the Yoruba—representing about 60 percent of the total population. Roughly half the country is Muslim, 35 percent is Christian, and 15 percent animist. English is the official language, but numerous other tongues are spoken. Literacy is estimated to be 25 percent. Universal primary education is accelerating the education of youths fifteen years of age and under, thought to account for more than half the population. With great class disparities, the creation of states (which may go as high as forty), and the widening urban-rural gap, Nigeria is more culturally and socially diverse than any other country in Africa.

The new American-style constitution was designed to diffuse authority and moderate the opposing views of this highly pluralistic and politicized society, in an attempt to avert the violence that characterized Nigeria's earlier political contests. However, despite this achievement, many observers feel that Nigeria still lacks a broad-based political consensus that will ensure smooth governmental operation. The *Times* of London opined that: "With the absence of a majority view as to limits and goals, the methods and character of Nigerian democracy will corrode, and indeed, already is corroding the delicate framework, as yet still precariously constructed, to lay bare the simmering squabbles and jealousies that have always been there. Without that general agreement, Nigerian democracy is at best only technically proficient."[27]

Moreover, while the idea of secession seems to have been buried for good, the civilian government continues to live under the shadow of the army that gave it birth. The Shagari government has never lost sight of the possibility of unrest from disgruntled army officers smarting from their diminished roles or dissatisfied with the performance of civilians. While senior officers have a stake in the survival of democracy, the chance of another military coup d'etat, initiated from junior ranks, cannot be discounted.

Other economic and political problems are also sorely testing the system. Federal revenue sharing among the nineteen states and agitation for new states are nettlesome issues that have caused continuing strife. Rapidly growing class differences point up Nigeria's oceans of poverty amid islands of staggering wealth, leading opposition politicians to attack government measures that produce "mandarin millionaires at the expense of the poor." In spite of much talk of a "green revolution," the overtaxed and underpaid peasant population never really reaped the benefits of the country's wealth, even in better times. Divisive party politics, intimidation of the press, and a restive labor movement add to the fissures in the country.

Grounds for optimism about Nigeria's political future can in no measure be based on an assumption of a diminution of serious problems. Nigeria is likely to continue to face formidable difficulties for years to come, and these problems will have an inevitable impact on Nigeria's ability to act as a regional power. Nigeria exercised considerable influence on all the major OAU committees, provided aid to neighboring states, financed the development fund of ECOWAS, and was the sole supporter of a separate trust fund for the African Development Bank. Such subsidies and leadership will have to be cut back, at least temporarily, during the oil crunch, as may other external bilateral loans and obligations, including those to the Southwest Africa People's Organization and the African National Congress, which are fighting white-minority rule in southern Africa. Given the ramifications of Nigeria's diminished economic position, one commentary described the domestic constraints on Nigeria's regional activities as possibly "the most significant development in Black Africa in the decade."[28]

Defense Programs

The Nigerian armed forces have had more international experience than those from any other Black African country. With the decision to contribute to the inter-African force in Chad, Nigeria launched its sixth military mission beyond its own borders (four of them since independence). Nigerians fought during World War I in German Tanganyika and Cameroon, and in World War II Nigerian forces were sent to Burma and to Ethiopia to restore Emperor Haile Selassie to the throne. Although these wars were fought under a colonial flag, the armed forces are proud of their role in the Asian and North African campaigns.

Following independence, two Nigerian infantry divisions served with distinction under UN command in Zaire, where they became the backbone of the international force from 1960 to 1964. Shortly thereafter, Lagos sent a battalion of soldiers to Tanzania to help Pres. Julius Nyerere resist a mutiny. (Nyerere's decision to recognize the Republic of Biafra four years later was therefore particularly galling to Lagos.) Nigeria sent a peacekeeping force to Chad in 1979, but was forced to pull out when the transitional government collapsed and Chadian armies began fighting again. One battalion of Nigerian soldiers served in the UN peacekeeping force in Lebanon, but it was withdrawn with the Israeli invasion of Lebanon.

In line with the postwar demobilization program, the government of President Shagari had decided to reduce its defense budget for the 1980–1981 financial year by more than $500 million. Following the Muslim riots and the Libyan takeover of Chad, however, Shagari reversed his decision to cut back on defense expenditures. In January 1981, Lagos announced a five-year national development plan that provided for $6.4 billion in defense spending. Significantly, the 1982 defense budget, providing for $1.85 billion, met no serious internal opposition. In fact, military expenditures are likely to be among the last items touched in cutbacks necessitated by declining oil revenue.

Nigeria is only just beginning to put together its programs and strategies to meet its modern defense needs. Nigerian forces are relatively well equipped for internal security as a result of the nation's preoccupation with internal crises, but there are deficiencies in external defense, particularly in strike aircraft and heavily mechanized armored equipment. Most of the country's current stock consists of outdated British and Soviet matériel, considered ineffective against Libya's modern arsenal. Nigeria thus has been shopping for tanks, fighter planes, antitank weapons, and antiaircraft guns. It negotiated a $1.3 billion arms package with Britain that included Jaguar attack jets and Corvette vessels, acquired twelve Franco-German Alpha jet attack aircraft, and negotiated with the British for forty new Vickers battle tanks. Other recent acquisitions include frigates, helicopters, patrol boats, gunboats, missiles, cannons, electronic communications equipment, and air defense systems. Nigeria's air force has been upgraded with the addition of MIG-21 fighters equipped with air-to-air missiles.

Still dependent on foreign sources for all its military requirements, Nigeria has been exploring the technology to produce its own arms. The government has offered an Austrian firm a contract to assemble armored personnel carriers and jeeps. There have been further reports of talks with

Brazil for the technology to construct an automatic-rifle factory. These efforts represent the beginning of the first domestic arms industry in Black Africa.

Thus far, Nigeria's arms purchases have been based on cash transactions. Its suppliers have included the Soviet Union, the United Kingdom, France, United States, the Federal Republic of Germany, and Italy. From 1974 to 1978, arms supplies worth $210 million were obtained, roughly a third from the Soviet Union and two-thirds from the West, though little originated from the United States. Through the International Military Education and Training Program (IMET), Nigeria received only $1.5 million for military training from the United States from 1950 to 1980. In 1978, Nigeria's request for TOW-equipped Bell helicopters[29] was turned down by the Carter administration, although Lagos spent $2.8 million on U.S. arms supplies the following year, chiefly communications equipment, riot-control gear, small arms, and spare parts.

In justifying the increase in military expenditures, Nigeria has focused on obtaining sufficient equipment to counterbalance Libyan ambitions in the region. President Shagari told the National Assembly that Nigeria "is being forced by recent and unanticipated world events to reassess its security and defense preparedness," a not so thinly veiled reference to Libya, which the *Daily Times*, a semiofficial newspaper, openly labeled "a threat to our national security."[30]

However, the recent surge in military spending is only one line of defense that Nigeria is relying upon. The more conventional approach has been and—unless it proves hopelessly unequal to the task—will continue to be a strategy of collective defense through regional coordination and cooperation.

The principal regional organization, the OAU, reached one of its lowest points ever in 1982 when the nineteenth summit in Tripoli, Libya, failed to take place as a result of a dispute over recognition of the POLISARIO (Popular Front for the Liberation of Saguia el Hamra and Rio de Oro), which claims to be the legitimate government of the western Sahara, and a second dispute over recognition of rival factions in Chad. The meeting was boycotted by a substantial number of states taking sides in these disputes until a settlement was reached months later. The OAU's effectiveness in responding to regional crises therefore will be severely limited until it puts its own house in order. In addition to these political logjams, the OAU suffers from lack of adequate funding, as might be expected in a continental body whose members can barely meet their own national debts. Only two (Libya and Zimbabwe) out of the fifty members are completely paid up in their subscriptions, according to OAU documents.[31]

As one of the moving forces behind formation of the OAU, Nigeria has traditionally viewed the OAU as an organization that has served its national interests. Lagos has used the organization to extend its own influence in the continent, to keep external powers at bay, and to block moves toward support of Biafra, the former secessionist region. In response to a suggestion that Lagos withdraw from the OAU at an earlier time when it was likewise encountering enormous difficulties, an internal policy paper predicted that without the organization "many more states would fall upon each other's throats and that Africa would become a battleground without an umpire for the big world powers. Reduced to a lone wolf," the memorandum noted candidly, "Nigeria cannot hope to effectively shield herself from international intrigues either by her size or natural resources."[32]

Frustration with the organization's problems has stimulated some negative reactions in Lagos. But the leadership role to which Nigeria is accustomed in African matters and the time and effort invested in keeping the OAU together in the past suggest that Lagos will employ every means at its disposal to revive the organization and use it to Nigeria's own advantage, especially on issues concerning southern Africa.

Inroads have likewise been made by Nigeria in Francophone Africa through economic associations such as the Chad Basin Fund, the Niger Basin Authority, and, as noted earlier, ECOWAS, now reeling from Nigeria's deportation order, allegedly promulgated without prior consultation with the affected states. Actions such as this are precisely what fosters fear of Nigeria by other states. Be that as it may, Lagos has managed to keep up the momentum of its inroads. In response to Libya, for example, ECOWAS concluded a mutual-defense pact, a gesture demonstrating a common-threat perception, albeit with little actual military collaboration.

Despite its efforts to stem Libyan influence through regional cooperation and diplomatic negotiations, Nigeria recognizes the limitations of this approach. Nigerian frustration with unsuccessful peace efforts in Chad, for example, was evident at the 1980 OAU summit meeting in Freetown, Sierra Leone. Shagari provided a rare glimpse into Nigeria's evaluation of its own failure in employing traditional diplomatic pressure when he said:

> We, in Nigeria, are much concerned and unhappy about the war now raging in Chad. When war first broke out there, Nigeria, in concert with ten other neighboring countries, offered its good offices by mediating between various Chadian factions involved. A series of peace meetings were held culminating in the Lagos Peace Accord signed by all the parties to the dispute on August 21, 1979. . . . But for some inexplicable reasons, the terms of the Lagos Accord still have not been fully implemented by the various Chadian factions. The peacekeeping operations, which were intended to demilitarize N'Djamena and keep foreign military adventurers at bay, have been a total failure. All bilateral and OAU peace efforts have failed to resolve the Chadian dispute and to bring the country back to normalcy. Today, the situation in Chad is worse than ever, and has assumed dangerous dimensions with the possibility of international military intervention and ominous consequences for Africa.[33]

Nigeria's call for extracontinental help to resolve the Chadian conflict introduced a significant new dimension to Nigeria's evolving defense strategy, for it was the first time that Nigeria ever requested external assistance for a military operation in which it was a prime player acting to resolve an African dispute. While fundamental foreign-policy goals have not changed, the decision suggests the primacy of national security, the rethinking of strategic policy, and the importance of flexibility and pragmatism in the country's foreign policy. Whether Nigeria can continue to plead the cause of inter-African cooperation credibly and successfully while coping with intense internal pressures is open to debate. The expulsion of non-Nigerian aliens has deepened Nigeria's unpopularity among West Africans, diminishing her authority to speak on behalf of African unity in regional councils. The break with OPEC, lingering embarrassment over the outcome of the peacekeeping mission in Chad, continuing allegations of Libyan subversion in the continent, mounting conflict in southern Africa, and the prospect of a disintegration of the Namibia initiative add complicating external pressures to a nation whose ruling elite is understandably jittery about the circumstances in which it finds itself.

Prospects

What are the implications of these developments for the future? There is little doubt that Nigeria desires to play an even more activist role in the continent than it has to date, utilizing not only its diplomatic skills but also military force (preferably in concert with inter-African support) and economic weight to achieve its political objectives. However, while Lagos is capable of taking decisive action when aroused, it is neither psychologically disposed nor, at this time, materially equipped to engage in a significantly more activist role. Indeed, for the immediate future, Nigeria might be expected to retreat considerably from international concerns as it devotes its considerable energies to domestic issues.

Looking ahead somewhat, it is not easy to speculate about how Lagos will react to a range of issues. Domestic political consensus exists among the electorate about most foreign-policy issues, but the situation could change overnight if, for example, Nigeria got bogged down in the Chadian civil war or the drop in oil revenue became so severe that Nigeria was forced to cut back on basic commitments, including defense and security. A number of other questions also remain unanswered. At what point will Lagos conclude that diplomatic options have been exhausted in pressuring the United States to reach an internationally recognized settlement in Namibia or to bring down apartheid in South Africa? Under what conditions will Lagos feel that Libyan threats require more substantial action and that it can no longer tolerate a hostile regional rival? More to the point, what would Nigeria be capable of or willing to do about these issues, once action was called for?

Western analysts have traditionally misinterpreted Nigerian political behavior. From the time of independence, when Westerners thought Nigeria was a "showcase of democracy," to the aftermath of the civil war, when international public opinion was convinced there would be genocidal retribution or a precipitous shift to the Soviet camp in gratitude for its assistance during the civil war, Nigeria has confounded the West. Prior misjudgments should discourage snap conclusions about Nigeria's foreign policy as the country assesses its capabilities as a regional power and adjusts to severe internal pressures.

The truth is that in global politics, neither East nor West can currently take Nigeria for granted. Foreign-policy issues will be treated on a case-by-case basis, without the favoritism, sentimentality, or reciprocity that had been customarily reserved for countries with whom Lagos had traditional relationships, historic ties, or economic or military connections. This pattern is evident in a number of recent examples. Even though it condemned the Soviet Union at the United Nations for the invasion of Afghanistan, Lagos attended the Moscow Olympics in defiance of Washington's campaign for an international boycott. Nigeria supported the Commonwealth-sponsored talks on Rhodesia in 1979, but nationalized British Petroleum on the eve of negotiations, a sharp warning to London not to lean too far in favor of the white-minority regime.

The great imponderable regarding Nigeria's international status relates to the country's ability to sustain leadership in Africa. There is little doubt that whatever government is in power, the country will continue to regard itself as a leader, promoting the self-image that is now part of the nation's political fabric. What is less certain is whether Lagos will be able to fulfill the role as expected. Will it maintain its reputation as a conciliator, shaping African positions through compromise and consensus, or be inclined toward a more forceful role, strong-arming sister states into supporting its positions on regional issues. Other African states will shed crocodile tears over Nigeria's current economic misfortunes, privately pleased that Nigeria has finally joined the ranks of most other African states in facing severe economic hardships. As time passes, however, the gloating will fade as Nigeria's neighbors find they can no longer turn to their traditional patron for financial bailouts, a strong political voice in world councils, or arbitration in regional disputes. It will be interesting to observe inter-African dynamics as Nigeria tries to regain its balance, for the results will have a profound impact from Addis Ababa to Pretoria.

Notes

1. *Times* (London), March 16, 1981.
2. RCHM-A, Working Paper no. 2, "Nigeria's Role in the OAU," Lagos, June 1966, quoted in John J. Stremlau, *The International Politics of the Nigerian Civil War* (Princeton, N.J.: Princeton University Press, 1977), pp. 79–80.
3. Shehu Shagari, *My Vision of Nigeria*, Aminu Tijjani and David Williams, eds. (London: Frank Cass, 1981), p. 91.
4. *Washington Post*, February 21, 1983.
5. *New York Times*, July 27, 1981.
6. "West African Oil," *Business Week*, August 10, 1981, p. 58.
7. *West Africa*, October 5, 1981, p. 2318.
8. *Africa Confidential* 24, no. 3 (February 2, 1983), p. 1.
9. Ibid.
10. *Washington Post*, March 6, 1981.

11. RCHM-A, Working Paper no. 2, "Nigeria's Role in the OAU," quoted in Stremlau, *The International Politics of the Nigerian Civil War*, p. 15, n. 38.

12. Federal Broadcasting Information Service (*FBIS*), May 19, 1981.

13. Ibid., August 19, 1981.

14. *Washington Post*, March 30, 1981.

15. *Africa Confidential* 22, no. 17 (August 19, 1981).

16. Shagari, *My Vision of Nigeria*, p. 68.

17. Ibid., p. 78.

18. *Africa Confidential* 24, no. 3 (February 2, 1983), p. 2.

19. *Washington Post*, March 21, 1981.

20. Ibid.

21. Shagari, *My Vision of Nigeria*, p. 68.

22. *West Africa*, October 5, 1981, p. 2292.

23. Shagari, *My Vision of Nigeria*, p. 77.

24. William H. Lewis, ed., *The United States, the Soviet Union and Africa* (Washington, D.C.: The Institute for Sino-Soviet Studies, George Washington University, March 1979), p. 4.

25. Ibid.

26. N. J. Miner, *The Nigerian Army, 1956–66* (London: Methuen and Co., 1971), p. 2.

27. *Times* (London), March 16, 1981.

28. *Business Week*, May 10, 1982, p. 54.

29. TOW stands for Tube-launched, Optically-tracked, Wire-guided antitank guided missile.

30. President Shagari's speech and *Daily Times* comments as reported in *New York Times*, January 15, 1981.

31. *Africa Confidential* 24, no. 3 (February 2, 1983), p. 8.

32. Quoted in Stremlau, *The International Politics of the Nigerian Civil War*, p. 17.

33. Shagari, *My Vision of Nigeria*, pp. 52–53.

6. Social Incoherence and the Mediatory Role of the State

Donald Rothchild

with the state there comes security . . .
Harold J. Laski[1]

In any society, security is inextricably linked to the coherency of domestic social relations. To the extent that the patterns of interaction among group interests are regular, the state's political capabilities will be enhanced and threats to the political order are likely to be momentary and contained within the system. What choices are open to political actors as they seek to channel ethnoregional and related class conflict along constructive lines? This question is obviously too broad to discuss comprehensively in a short essay, but it is possible to treat one aspect—namely, the role of the state as a facilitator of political exchange under conditions of economic scarcity and the ineffectuality of institutions.

In the some twenty or more years since independence, Africa has had broad experience with both coherent and incoherent domestic social relationships. These range currently from the relatively regularized societal relationships in Nigeria, Tanzania, the Ivory Coast, and Cameroun to the relatively incoherent factional encounters occurring in Chad and Uganda. In the latter cases, the state is fragile not only because the organizing rules governing state-societal relationships are not accepted but also because state institutions are unable to accomplish critical tasks such as coping with reasonable public demands, establishing priorities, implementing policies, and monitoring results. As critical as these organizing rules are to the regulation of social relations and the achievement of societal goals,[2] it is important to keep in mind that they need not be explicitly written down to be meaningful. Such basic principles can also rest upon conventions, customs, judicial interpretations, and even unspoken rules and understandings regarding decisions. The Lebanese practice of appointing a Maronite Christian as president and a Sunni Moslem as prime minister was rigidly adhered to in 1982 appointments, even though it is essentially an unwritten tradition. Provided these rules are understood and, to some extent at least,

The author wishes to express his appreciation to Ruth Collier and Zaki Ergas for comments on the first draft of this chapter.

accepted as legitimate by the decision-making elite and its attentive public, they may prove a sufficient basis for coherent group encounters.

To probe issues of African security, then, it is necessary to examine the link between the state and the political processes normally taking place under its aegis. As Harold D. Lasswell and Abraham Kaplan contend, the state "maintains a framework of interpersonal relations with which particular interests can be expeditiously satisfied."[3] Class, ethnic, and regional conflicts are certainly to be anticipated wherever groups seek contradictory outcomes. What is critical to the well-being and even the survival of societies is not an absence of such conflicts but a set of predictable norms and rules for channeling these divergent interests into mutually beneficial outcomes. Hence the state and its institutions, by providing organizing principles and agencies of action and control, emerge as indispensable instruments for managing conflict in a given society. Provided that groups adhere to these basic rules of relationship, the state, though in some African cases buttressed by institutions that are all too fragile, offers a means of finding convergent objectives and avoiding mutual damage. It allows conflict to occur and yet possibly to be constructive.

An effective and responsive state clearly facilitates the process of regulating intergroup exchange, thereby allowing manageable conflict to take place. To better understand the state's role in regulating these exchanges, it will be necessary first to describe the characteristics of the state and to relate the concept of the state as a set of organizing principles to the concept of the state as a relatively autonomous actor. It is as the active state closes the gap between these two aspects that it emerges as a critically important mediator of interclass and interethnic conflicts. It will then be possible to analyze the modalities of political exchange and the constraints upon the exchange process under African conditions. Finally, I will conclude with a brief discussion of the policy implications of the state's mediatory role in middle Africa.

The State as a Set of Organizing Principles

Policy analysis, with its primary focus on choice, can effectively utilize the state as an important unit. In this view, the state is both a set of organizing principles used as a general guide to public action (the wide perspective) and a group of public institutions that allocate values authoritatively and strive to achieve systemic goals (the narrow perspective). Many writers, both Marxist and non-Marxist, play down and even dismiss the state's normative role, its capacity for autonomous action, or, in some cases, both of these. Such a reductionist orientation has grave consequences, not least with respect to analyzing and prescribing on matters pertaining to societal coherency. Social relations are expressed in institutions that may in turn structure the nature of the interactional process. A comprehensive view of reality requires attention to the broader norms and values legitimizing the state as well as to the manner in which state agencies convert specific policy preferences into authoritative allocations of value. To stress only one perspective, the narrow or the wide, is to fail to explain persistent societal incoherency and the possible means for coping with "shortfalls" in group relationships.[4]

An understanding of the wide perspective—the state as a set of organizing principles—is critically important to facilitating behavioral regularities. That these organizing principles exist and legitimize the actions of state agencies, that they define the terms on which class and ethnoregional conflict take place, and that they are distinct from the institutions of government— even under "soft" state conditions (i.e., where state control over society is relatively ineffective)[5]—is evident to a variety of observers. Thus J. Isawa Elaigwu and Victor A. Olorunsola describe Nigeria's 1979 constitution and subsequent basic laws such as the Revenue Allocation Act (which applied a 55-35-10 formula to federal-state-local distributions) as going a long way toward restructuring the imbalance in subunit-central relations so evident at the time of independence. Not only did the nineteen-state federal system establish many centers with limited autonomy, but the new norms on the formation of political parties and government recruitment to reflect the "federal character" of Nigeria and on the distribution of revenues between the center and the state and local governments according to the principles of need and equity provided "a new platform" on which to build a more stable and equitable relationship.[6] In Uganda, the republican constitution of 1967 affected subnational conflicts in Ankole and Toro by increasing central control over the district administrations and abolishing the institution of kingship in Toro. Such changes affected inter-ethnic relations in the subunits by altering the processes of political recruitment, decreasing subunit control over minority-group affairs, and increasing the center's capacity to regulate political matters throughout the country. As Martin Doornbos concludes with respect to the state's role as a manager of these intergroup relationships:

> the center's ability to act as arbitrator is closely linked to, and circumscribed by, the fact that it is also the body which defines the rules of the game: it determines what rights can be maintained and what actions are permissible. But in doing so it also sets the terms for conflict in a wider sense because it simultaneously to a large extent predetermines what issues will be contended next, legally or illegally. Seen in this light, the rules are more than just "legal" prescriptions; they also fix the boundaries for actions to change or uphold the status quo. The major turning points in the development of protest in both Ankole and Toro, for instance, were brought about by central government rulings which defined, redefined, or reaffirmed the issues and, by implication, the targets. In other words, the center establishes the objects of competition by the opposing groups in a subsystem.[7]

Yet organizing principles can be a reality without being as formally articulated as they are in the foregoing constitutional examples. Thus David Laitin noted that both before and after the 1969 Somali coup that brought

President Siad Barre to power, the military "has respected lines of authority, and its members have adhered closely to their rôles."[8] Moreover, Ronald Libby, characterizing the state as both a permanent institution and a "repository of authority for the political system," cautiously argues the existence of such organizing principles in patrimonial Zaire. "I would suspect that in the case of Zaire," he writes, "subcentral government *vis-à-vis* central administration is the crucial relationship of power in the state system. Scholarly preoccupation with the ineffectiveness of Zaire's political system has tended to deflect attention away from the relatively unchanging character of the local-center relationship of the Zairean state."[9] For these analysts, and others as well, the state represents more than the sum of public institutions. It is a framing fact of the profoundest importance to society, acting as an authority and a legitimizing apparatus and determining the rules under which—and arenas in which—class and ethnoregional conflicts are played out.

To contend that an important dimension of the state is that of an organizing set of rules is by no means to argue its neutrality as regards class or ethnic interests. As Ralph Miliband asserts, "the intervention of the state is always and necessarily partisan."[10] This principle applies whether the state is polyarchical or hegemonic, capitalist or socialist. It may be expected that state rules will reflect class or ethnic biases in their conception and that these preferences are likely to become more clearly visible as the rules are put into effect by state institutions controlled in practice by class and ethnic interests. Certainly the dominant political class, by dint of its control over the various state agencies, is in a position to alter the rules of relationship as new circumstances prevail. Nigerian leaders have changed the number of states periodically—from three to four, then to twelve, and then to the current nineteen; the effect of these actions has been to change the arena of conflict in society. President Jaafar el Nimeiry's attempt in the early 1980s to decentralize administrative authority in the Sudan and to redivide the Southern Region (which had been treated as a single entity under the Addis Ababa Agreement and Self-Government Act of 1972) represented an effort on his part to strengthen his own position and to alter the context of societal class-ethnic relations. As the ensuing class-based and ethnic-based (Dinka versus non-Dinka) conflicts in the South made clear, the proposed change of rules on the nature and composition of the Southern Region(s) would have worked to the benefit of certain political interests, at the expense of others. Interestingly enough for our purposes, the basic constitutional rules of relationship proved to be critical in mediating the dispute, for anti-redivision politicians successfully appealed to Nimeiry's legal advisors in mid-1980 against the hasty violations of the rigid guarantees of the South's status as a single entity that were being proposed under an amendment to the 1972 Self-Government Act.[11] The attempt to restructure the rules to Nimeiry's (and, in the context of Southern politics, Joseph Lagu's) advantage has failed—at least temporarily.[12]

Clearly, regularized rules of relationship are a reality in numerous middle-African contexts, existing at various levels of political life. As already noted with regard to the conflicts in Nigeria, Sudan, and Uganda (1967), these rules may operate in the constitutional life of a country, setting out the parameters of choice and the general terms under which intergroup conflict occurs. In a related way, both explicit and implicit rules of relationship also outline the manner in which the state's machinery is to be employed to formulate and implement policy: by stipulating political recruitment and training practices, determining the perquisites of public office, organizing election procedures, governing revenue allocation practices, setting out the basis upon which national coalitions are formed, and defining local-central relations.[13] In fact, in the soft state conditions of contemporary Africa, these norms may well be accepted practice in advance of any formal legal recognition. Even in the extreme case (from the standpoint of incoherency) of military coups, it is possible to detect "repetitive practices . . . gradually acquir[ing] a tacit and resigned acceptance."[14]

Contrary to the opinions of some, a recognition of the existence of the state as an embodiment of a set of organizing principles or rules in the African context is not necessarily incompatible with a view of the state as a reflection of class or ethnic dominance—as a nonneutral arena.[15] These two realities can be coextensive. Although a state may indeed be dominated by a particular socioeconomic class or ethnic people, this does not in itself preclude the establishment of rules constraining the particular actors involved in the decisional process. The state, whether a capitalist or socialist framework, can represent organizing principles to which the dominant class adheres for the sake of the collective benefits it perceives as resulting from the achievement of community purposes. Such adherence may place some constraint on choice, narrowing the scope for state action to defined areas. This possible coextensiveness of class hegemony and limitations on choice is recognized by the Italian neo-Marxist Antonio Gramsci, who observes on the state's role as a leader of society as follows:

> It is true that the State is seen as the organ of one particular group, destined to create favourable conditions for the latter's maximum expansion. But the development and expansion of the particular group are conceived of, and presented, as being the motor force of a universal expansion, of a development of all the "national" energies. In other words, the dominant group is coordinated concretely with the general interests of the subordinate groups, and the life of the State is conceived of as a continuous process of formation and superseding of unstable equilibria (on the juridical plane) between the interests of the fundamental group and those of the subordinate groups—equilibria in which the interests of the dominant group prevail, but only up to a certain point, i.e. stopping short of narrowly corporate economic interest.[16]

If the rules of state are less than neutral, they are also incompletely accepted by African societies, especially those peoples in the rural areas beyond the reach of central competency and power. The modern African state, paradoxically, is overcentralized, consuming extensive resources, yet soft and lacking in the ability to carry out its extensive program. It can make no claim to "binding authority" over all activities in the domain under its jurisdiction.[17] Some of the factors explaining this paradox are incoherent social relations, lack of resources, overdeveloped state structures, insufficient state legitimacy, and inadequate state coercive power.[18] J. P. Nettl pessimistically concluded that

> The very instability of governments in developing countries suggests that the competition for norms is very strong. A state could therefore develop only if a politically supported regime remains in power for a considerable time and is able to transpose its own norms across the high threshold of time and internalization of legitimacy into a situation of stateness, within which interests can eventually be articulated and institutionalized by cleavage structures. All the current evidence from the third world is to the contrary. . . .[19]

The abortive coup in 1982 in seemingly stable Kenya would seem to support Nettl's argument on the fragility of state norms in the African setting. In many African countries regularized rules of interaction have achieved a fragile and partial existence and still must go a substantial way to gain legitimacy throughout the realm of the state. To the degree that its parameters remain in doubt and its rules unaccepted, the state remains weak, and the ability of its institutions to regulate societal conflict depends upon coercion and chance. In such context, therefore, it seems more appropriate to refer to "stateness" and thereby to leave open a sizable space for the development over time of fully understood and accepted organizing principles.

The State as Autonomous Actor

We turn now to the narrow perspective of the state: the state as the institutionalization of public power. Here there can be considerable agreement between many of those with Marxist or non-Marxist perspectives on a concept of the state as a bounded core of hierarchically organized public officials who wield administrative and coercive power, engaged in an ongoing process of competition "with other political economic and social organizations both internally and externally."[20] In policy terms, the significance of the state can be seen in its ability (or inability) to establish priorities, make decisions, and implement public policies. Rather than being a disinterested actor, the state as decision maker is more likely than not to reflect dominant class and/or ethnic interests. As discussed above, class or ethnic dominance need not connote a complete lack of a normative order; nevertheless, it does imply the utilization of state power in such a way as to affect internal regulations as well as relations to the international economy.

In the soft state conditions of Africa, where system rules often lack acceptance and reach, the state's role as administrator and regulator is likely to prove critical to the achievement of collective goals and, with reference to the topic at hand, to the maintenance of coherent social relations. However, given the fragility of the state as an authority and legitimizing apparatus in contemporary Africa, a lack of fit may be apparent between the state as a set of organizing principles and the state as autonomous actor. Particularly in patrimonial societies, where the personality of the leader is a critical factor, the norms regulating relations may be partial and ineffective, and administrative agencies may find themselves relatively unrestrained. In such circumstances, *coherency requires greater convergence between the two aspects of state—as a set of organizing principles and as autonomous actor.* After analyzing the characteristics of the state as actor, I will turn to the question of the state's role in facilitating coherent relationships.

In contemporary Africa, the state as autonomous actor implies an interrelated set of characteristics: the capacity for action, an ability to accumulate power, and a perception of its interests as separate from the rest of society. Partial autonomy is critical to the others.

Recognition of the state's autonomy, whether partial or full, is important to a policy approach, since such an approach involves assumptions about the power of central decisional authorities to make and implement choices. Certainly some writers, primarily those in a more orthodox Marxist tradition, tend to reduce the state to little more than an instrument of dominant class interests; others, however, including a number of contemporary neo-Marxist analysts, describe public institutions as uniquely unfettered by domestic African interest groups in their formulation and execution of public policy. If the neo-Marxists and others vary considerably in their views of the constraints of international forces on the African state, they tend to find common ground with respect to the state's extensive maneuverability vis-à-vis internal classes within society. No current author better represents this orientation than Ralph Miliband. In a recent analysis of Marxist thought, Miliband argued that "the first and most obvious feature of the state in both 'Third World' and Communist societies is a very pronounced inflation of state and executive power . . . with which is usually associated a very high degree of autonomy, at least from the civil society over which the state holds sway."[21] By comparison with the diversity of modern-sector economic interests in the relatively developed countries, the indigenous-African private sector operates from a weak resource base, and the economy is heavily influenced by a variety of foreign interests as well as by active state interventions. Politically exposed ethnic elements— the Asians in East Africa and their Syrian-Lebanese counterparts in West Africa—represent anything but an effective countervailing force. Rather than curbing the power of the state-party elite, the survival of these economically important groups depends largely upon their conciliating the dominant political class by a marginal process of tacit exchanges.[22] The consequence of this interest-group weakness on the domestic political scene is to insulate the state from society to a greater extent than in the industrialized countries.

If this interest-group frailty leaves the African state, mainly by default, in a potentially powerful position, such strength at the center often remains more potential than real. This is due to the heterogeneity of the state actor itself. The state, as an arena in which interests collide, is anything but uniform in its composition. Even after assuming public office, various members of the executive or bureaucracy continue to maintain connections of interest, kinship, and loyalty to class and ethnic groups in society, thereby intensifying conflict within the state's decisional and administrative agencies as well as complicating the state's task of mediating class- or ethnic-based conflicts.[23]

Continuing ties on the part of government or civil-service leaders to societal interests place some limits on state independence; however, the state as a whole still retains a very considerable autonomy to determine on its own what it regards as being in the general interest of society. The extent of this autonomy no doubt differs from society to society depending on the configurations of class- and ethnic-based power, but all states can be said to exhibit some independence from the various groups that make up the society. The state, which is supposed to represent no single class or ethnic group and to be guided in its formulation of policies by society's organizing principles, can be expected in its day-to-day policy decisions to give heed to transclass and transethnic principles. Mobutu Sese Seko's efforts to apply the principle of "ethnic scrambling" when recruiting candidates for provincial posts in Zaire—creating an administrative cadre with no local ethnic ties and dependent for political survival upon projecting a statist viewpoint—is an example of this behavior.[24] Moreover, some socialist-oriented regimes (Mozambique, Tanzania) have nationalized industries and increased the role of the state in economic management and distribution with the effect, if not the intent, of insulating themselves from the pressures of "capitalist" interests in their societies. Although others have been more accessible to these interests, it seems a mistake to conclude that state authorities maintain no distance from class influences. As Nicos Poulantzas observed: "Although the State is not created *ex nihilo* by the ruling classes, nor is it simply taken over by them: state power (that of the bourgeoisie, in the case of the capitalist State) is written into this materiality."[25]

State autonomy is critical to the African policy process, being the basis upon which independent policy choice rests. But one must be careful here not to overestimate the state's capacity for effective decision making under the soft state conditions of contemporary Africa. Such factors as an inadequate resource base, an overextended state bureaucracy in relation to resource capacity, an insufficient regulatory capacity at the periphery, and an inability to gain a public consensus as to the valid exercise of state power may give rise at times to something of a governability problem. Yet despite such constraints, we can nonetheless recognize that the African state is not without some capacity for autonomous policy formulation and implementation. Put another way, *the state as autonomous actor can make demands in its own right as well as process and resist demands put forward by class or ethnic interests in society.* As a maker of demands, the state appears as an important autonomous actor in the policy process, able to initiate and implement actions that define the terms of relationships and mediate conflicts in society. It designs policies to cope with competing domestic or foreign demands and alters structures affecting social relationships at home or economic relationships abroad. Ghana's decisions at different stages on unitary government or limited subregional autonomy or on single-party, multi-party, or no-party electoral systems have greatly affected the way in which class and ethnic interests have articulated their political demands upon the state. In setting out the terms under which such encounters take place, the state displays a capacity to affect, in a positive or negative manner, intergroup conflicts.

A certain amount of state autonomy also facilitates the accumulation of power by public officialdom, giving officials room to make their own decisions on extending their administrative functions and powers as well as on overpowering, coopting, or remaining inattentive to the claims of ethnoregional groups in hinterland areas. Because of past institutional investments and the coercive resources at their disposal, administrative organs of state have an advantage in their competition with other organizations in society. And given the need for political and economic leadership in the postcolonial period, it is not surprising that the autonomous state actor moves rapidly to attempt to consolidate and strengthen the institutions inherited from colonialism. Such statist inclinations result in determined bureaucratic efforts to prevent a weakening of central powers (e.g., the Nigeria civil service's opposition to regionalization of authority just prior to the war with Biafra); they can also lead to an "aggressive expansionism of the state" into new activities and previously uncontrolled parts of its territory.[26]

This trend toward consolidating central state power has not proceeded smoothly, reflecting the soft state environment in which the various leaders have operated. In nineteenth- and twentieth-century Ethiopia, Emperors Menelik and Haile Selassie encountered stubborn resistance to the ethnic and class dominance of the Amhara core. "Cries for self-determination of several of the peripheral groups in the Ethiopian Empire had been an everpresent fact of history," notes Edmond Keller. He continues: "The Somalis, Eritreans, and Oromos (to a lesser extent the Afars) had never accepted the idea of Ethiopian hegemony. No doubt this was in part due to the fact that they were never considered full citizens as groups."[27] Similarly, the current leader, Lt. Col. Mengistu Haile Mariam, has met determined opposition from the Oromo, Somali, and Eritrean peoples, who resist efforts made by the Amhara-led state to consolidate power and to set the terms on which ethnoregional units at the periphery are to be integrated into the Ethiopian community. Mengistu's unwillingness to engage in a serious process of exchange has led to social incoherence, including bitter and protracted warfare with the Somalis, Eritreans, and other nationalities.

Similarly, in Chad, Uganda, Zaire, Mozambique, and elsewhere, the partially autonomous state, lacking the necessary resources to accomplish a full consolidation of power, is not in a position to impose an effective administrative unity on fragmented and fluid social structures. The Zairean state, reconstituted along highly centralized lines by the regime of Mobutu Sese Seko, by the 1980s proved less and less able to impose its will on provincial affairs.[28] And while the Uganda army did manage, after heavy fighting, to secure the West Nile district in fall 1980, the government of A. Milton Obote nonetheless continued to list Kampala, Arua, Mukono, Luwero, and Mpigi districts as insecure. Conditions in Karamoja, where remnants of Amin's force reportedly led large units of Karamojong warriors on raiding expeditions, also remained unaffected by central sanctions.[29] In brief, the unification envisaged on paper may not be matched by the bureaucracy's capacity to extend its jurisdiction throughout the realm. The resulting gap between the center's urge to accumulate power and the evidence of persistent local autonomy can give rise to state incoherency, especially where the state refuses to respond constructively to local demands for the right to make authoritative decisions.

Finally, state autonomy encourages a sense of separate interests on the part of public officials. "The very notion of the state as an entity separate from civil society implies a certain distance between the two, a *relation* which implies a disjunction."[30] The state's relative insulation from the pressures of other classes in society may strengthen its ability to compete with other organizations for the scarce benefits of modernity. Public officials use the expansion of state responsibilities that has occurred since independence to justify increased budgetary allocations, the recruitment of additional personnel, and improvements in administrative and infrastructural support. A degree of autonomy, then, buttresses the state as a competitor for scarce societal resources; it also opens the door to misuses of public office for private purposes. State responsibilities for engaging in and regulating commercial and business activities give public officials great scope for individual self-maximization. The temptations here are enormous, and many officials have succumbed, gaining great wealth in the process. In some of the worst situations, where corruption comes to be seen as a system in itself (*kalabule* in Ghana and *magendo* in Uganda), the unwritten norms of state exploitation may be viewed as replacing the supposedly disinterested norms regulating intergroup conflict. This change epitomizes a process of political decay. Where the norms are seen to be manipulated in the interest of a particular class (Zaire) or ethnonational interest (Sudan, 1960s), such decay has the gravest of implications for incoherence and state instability.

To summarize, then, the state is both an organizing set of principles and a partially autonomous actor. A degree of autonomy from other class and ethnic groups in society strengthens its ability to compete with other organizations in society. In engaging in such competition, the state displays a capacity for action on its own and a tendency to accumulate power over competitors and comes to define its interests as separate from those of society at large. To the extent that state actors replace disinterested norms of relationship with biased and exploitative behavior, political decay and incoherency can be anticipated. On the other hand, a possible route to successful conflict management would seem to lie in movement toward a convergence between the normative state and the autonomous actor state. *As the active state, the maker of demands, leads society toward this convergence of the wide and narrow perspectives, it may emerge as a key facilitator of conflict mediation in the society.* In such circumstances, the state is responding constructively to society's most basic imperatives. How have states performed in these roles? In the next section, I will discuss state behavior under soft state conditions in Africa. This will set the stage for an examination of the ways of increasing state responsiveness, and with it the coherency of social relationships, in contemporary Africa.

The State as a Mediatory Institution

The state clearly is part of an interlinked and self-reinforcing policy process. The relationship between claims, policies, and impacts is close and complex; state authorities inevitably play an important role in promoting policies that they regard as best suited for managing demands, attaining goals, and regulating societal relationships. Under conditions of mounting economic scarcity, the imbalance between societal claims and state capabilities seems likely to grow, creating problems of malperformance of the state and ungovernability of the society. Such situations of demand overload, accompanied by a growing gap between expectations and achievements,[31] weaken government institutions at the very time they need to expand their activities. To the extent this expectation-achievement gap continues to widen, the environment tends to overwhelm public institutions, exposing their fragility and lack of capacity to full view. As the December 1981 Rawlings intervention in Ghana showed so dramatically, government immobility, even under a constitutionally elected government, is not likely to be tolerated for long by an elite that has lost confidence in the state's capabilities and probity.

In this context of demand overload, constraints on state responsiveness are readily evident. States that can successfully respond to both immediate public demands and the broader needs of society are somewhat unusual the world over; in middle Africa's soft state circumstances they are inevitably a rarity. Not only are domestic African expectations frequently in excess of the capacity of the state to achieve desired outputs,[32] but external demands upon these dependent African states add to the heavy burdens already existing. Pres. Hilla Limann, nine months prior to the Rawlings takeover, fully recognized the extent of the domestic and international demands upon Ghana's overburdened polity:

> Our mature and candid appreciation of the facts of our present situation reveals the depressing enormity of our national problems and the ever-

decreasing resources at our disposal to solve them. The most telling example of this bleak picture of our present economy is that while our demands for local and foreign goods have continued to grow with the rapid growth of our population, our domestic production and foreign earnings have been dwindling sharply for more than a decade now. Thus our main foreign exchange earner, cocoa, which fetched over £3,205 per ton barely two years ago, now fetches less than half that price.[33]

Clearly, the African statesman did not need a policy analyst to advise him on the reality of system overload or its implications for instability and social incoherency.

In the face of heavy demands from the domestic and international environment, the state has three main options, or combinations of options: to resist demands, process demands, or make demands of its own. Such a classification assumes the state to be capable of some degree of self-instigated action irrespective of the option chosen. State actions to resist demands or to process group claims are part of an ongoing activity that includes the promotion of policy alternatives and the implementation of policies. The processing of competing claims involves fine-tuned initiatives to cope with class and ethnic demands, not a mere mechanical reconciling of group claims. And initiatives such as the mediation of group conflict require all the skills of active statesmanship, especially where the situation is complicated by conditions of economic scarcity.

Certainly the act of resisting legitimate public demands is a sign of state frailty. Where state elites close off access to public institutions, they reduce the number of messages received—at a cost in terms of political information. This information gap may place constraints on performance, possibly causing a loss of legitimacy over time. Malawi's peasants reportedly find it difficult to lodge complaints with government or party over such issues as cotton prices or the right to plant tobacco; when their appeals for change bring little response, their range of choices frequently includes little more than adoption of a mental attitude of resignation or a decision to move quietly into food-crop farming—Hirschman's so-called exit option.[34] More formally, regimes may redesign state structures to ban opposition parties or tribal associations (Zaire, 1968; Kenya, 1980) or, as in the case of Gen. I. K. Acheampong's Ghana, to propose a full-blown no-party system, in part at least to depoliticize conflict.[35] Under the 1977 Union Government plan, the Ghana government urged the establishment of a representative political system that would operate without political parties and therefore without an institutionalized opposition. A kind of atomized, issueless participation was envisaged, which sought "to promote national unity" while at the same time stifling conflict. However, the effect of placing limitations on organized partisan activities would clearly have meant the avoidance of conflict—forestalling effective civilian demands for a shift in policies and reducing the strength of powerful class and ethnic appeals for change.[36]

An element of state fragility may also be evident where public authorities process group demands. In practice, the state as processor is not simply a "black box" reacting mechanically to demands from the environment, as some exponents of modernization theory are wont to imply, but a partisan actor taking its own initiatives to defend and advance its own interests. The very act of reconciling demands is neither easy nor disinterested. Hence the state is no mere clearinghouse; rather it actively appeases, puts off, or pays off more or less powerful groups in society. As such, the state is an inextricable part of the African policy process.

Implementing these state initiatives, which occur within a society and represent no challenge to its structure, is complicated by the apparent weakness of African political institutions. In such established contexts, the environment is hard, the choices relatively easy, and the mediatory tasks frequently arduous.[37] Normal day-to-day processing of inputs by state authorities in all systems tends to be an encapsulated process; even so, state-party elites in hegemonical state systems can be said to opt for a narrower range of open conflict among decision makers (in part with an eye to lower decisional costs) than do leaders in exchange state systems.[38] Although I do not want to overstate the differences between hegemonical and exchange state systems in the processing of demands, especially when it comes to the day-to-day activities of policymaking, it nonetheless seems clear that polyarchical systems normally are prepared to accept a greater degree of open conflict among decision elites than is the case in command-type systems. The former allows information to be shared more widely, the avenues of communication to be more accessible, and the state-party elite to display greater responsiveness to group demands.[39] Political exchange occurs in an environment of heightened public participation and preparedness to accept bargaining practices and outcomes, particularly if they come from within the dominant political class. Certainly the diffusion of decision authority raises the costs of decision making; however, if the competing classes and ethnic groups can learn to accept the state's organizing principles and gain experience in the procedures of finding shared interests, the long-term benefits may be seen to outweigh the immediate costs.

If the ways in which demands are resisted or processed are expressive of the state's fragility in Africa, the state as a maker of demands demonstrates a measure of strength and capacity. This is the primary arena for self-generating action: the state acting in its own right to set the terms of political, economic, and social relationships.[40] In fact, however, the fragile state of Africa often finds itself in the position of making extensive demands upon a resistant African society, in particular on those elements living in the rural hinterland. The state's capacity for action is real but limited, and sometimes quite destructive. Thus the African scene is witness to numerous harmful state initiatives, often carried on in conjunction with international lending agencies, that have resulted in the establishment of high-cost settlement and irrigation schemes beneficial mainly to rich farmers and high-status administrators.[41] "Development," whether capitalist or socialist oriented, has invariably been administered from above by a semiautonomous state actor,[42] frequently with the effect of maximizing the interests of the dominant political class itself.

Because of the limits on institutional capacity, the state's active interventions in the productive process or in the mediation of intergroup conflict are necessarily circumscribed. As Goran Hyden contends on the relationship between the state and the peasants: "Officials collect taxes from peasants, thereby forcing them to make at least some contribution to the larger social economy. There is a definite limit, however, to how far enforcement of state policies can go in the context of peasant production."[43] The state can and does tax, but its abilities to implement policies or to alter social attitudes are limited. Similarly, the state is capable of a degree of action in mediating between social classes, economic sectors, and relatively advantaged and disadvantaged subregions. Not surprisingly, the international press has given little attention to those areas where the state has been reasonably effective in setting out and maintaining the terms for interregional relations: Ivory Coast, Cameroun, and, for the most part, Ghana. In such cases, demands for change have remained manageable, and the state has been able to pursue policies of balanced benefit that have channeled conflict along constructive lines, thus enhancing state coherency. More controversial, but still workable, efforts on the part of the state to cope with the ethnic issues are Sierra Leone's and Zimbabwe's provisions on reserved seats in the legislature for traditional and racial interests respectively, Malawi's application of the principle of regional equity in the recruitment of students to secondary schools and universities, Sudan's guarantee of regional autonomy for its south, Nigeria's application of the federal principle to revenue allocation, political recruitment, and the responsibilities assigned to its nineteen states under the 1979 constitution, and so forth. Increasingly the state has participated more openly and actively in the search for new, creative formulas to manage ethnic conflict. The result has been a process of political exchange less structured and more intermittent than "consociational" government is meant to imply, but genuine exchange nonetheless.[44]

But clearly, the state's success as an inter-ethnic mediator must not be overstated. In contemporary Chad, Uganda, and Ethiopia, the state has not succeeded, as of this time, in organizing regularized, restrained, and bounded intercommunity relations. Because formal rules of state-ethnic exchange have yet to gain acceptance, the tasks of decision making and implementation are gravely complicated—adding to existing problems of state legitimacy in these countries. This societal factionalism augments the sense of the state as overloaded and unable to cope and brings on calls for an expansion in coercive powers in order "to increase the price of deviant behavior."[45] In such cases, the gap between basic state principles and the state's managerial abilities has become too great for regularity to emerge in intergroup encounters. *To extricate itself from this situation of potential incoherence, the state must assume the role of an active facilitator.*

Visualizing some scope for political mediations along these lines, Guillermo O'Donnell commented as follows: "The reification of the state in its institutional objectifications obscures its underlying role as guarantor of domination within society; yet—inasmuch as it implies that state and society appear to be separate—it tends to generate various mediations between them through which consensus tends to be created. The state ultimately is based on coercion, but it usually is also based on consensus, which both encompasses and conceals coercion."[46]

The state, then, must attempt to engineer consensus, setting out terms of relationship acceptable over time to key actors in the system. By doing this, it enables the various participants to avoid the zero-sum aspects of class or ethnoregional conflict and rewards political losers as well as winners. The effect is to enlarge choice—providing an arena for the clarification of issues at dispute and for the hammering out of public formulas satisfactory to the conflicting parties.[47] Such an effort to promote mutual-gains formulas is obviously no easy undertaking; this is especially the case under soft state conditions where institutions are ineffective and the distribution of the benefits of modernity brings rival interests into sharp confrontation. It is one thing for Chad's Hissène Habré in 1982 to unite a coalition of forces behind his banner sufficient to defeat his rival Goukouni Oueddei and the Transitional Government of National Unity. It is quite another to use the power of the state to establish regularized relations among the diverse groupings and leaders making up this war-devastated country. The state in such stable and centralized polities as Tanzania, Cameroun, and the Ivory Coast has been relatively successful at managing intermediary mechanisms, but the demands on leadership skills seem more extensive in the bitterly divided and soft state circumstances of Chad or Uganda.

In bringing about the necessary balance between conflict and stability, the active and responsive state rises to one of its most critical challenges. On the one hand, the state as both resister and processor of demands is unable to close the gap between normative principles and action. As a resister of demands, the state avoids dealing with legitimate collective grievances in society; as a processor of demands, it curbs the urge to instigate public initiatives on its own. On the other hand, however, it is the responsive state that most effectively reaches out to receive information on public dissatisfactions and demands and to direct public behavior toward desired goals. As the responsive state pursues an active course, it makes trade-off choices affecting the conflict-stability balance. Such a set of decision-making actions, which entail a ranking of priorities and an implementation of policies, no doubt reflects the preferences (even biases) of the dominant state-party elite regarding the terms of economic and social relations. Thus choice making—even when directed toward mutual gains—may involve an asymmetry of benefits. Nevertheless, to the extent that the regulations of government are in rough conformity with the state's normative principles, they are likely, even despite the inequality of benefits, to garner a measure of political support and legitimacy.

If political exchange is critical to the promotion of coherent social relations, it becomes important to examine some of the ways in which the state, in a largely noncoercive manner, can facilitate reciprocal concessions among group leaders. How can the state coordinate the decisions of group leaders so as to achieve mutually beneficial outcomes?[48] To deal with this question, I will look at this process of political exchange with respect to such issue areas as resource allocation, political recruitment, coalition government, federalism and subregional autonomy, and constitutional protections.

The Issues of Exchange

Because of its pivotal place in the productive process, the African state is well positioned to act as an intermediary mechanism. Not only does it regulate trade and exchange-rate systems and mobilize and distribute public resources, it also carries on a wide variety of commercial, industrial, and administrative activities on its own. As a recent World Bank survey of seven countries showed, the public sector employs 40 to 74 percent of formal wage earners; moreover, public-sector employment, especially in such activities as defense and public administration, has expanded faster than has employment in the private sector.[49] Substantiating the fact that the state in "capitalist" Kenya "now controls a very substantial part of our total economy," Pres. Daniel arap Moi notes that the Kenyan government includes 147 statutory boards, 47 wholly-owned government companies, 36 companies in which government holds a majority of the shares, and 93 other companies in which the government has some direct or indirect interest.[50] The state, by dint of the economic and coercive powers at its disposal, is able to provide an indispensable arena for the adjustment of conflicting interests.

The conditions for the state to function as a mediatory mechanism are outlined by Reuven Kahane:

(1) when the basis of division between particularistic forces and antagonistic principles is universally defined (since such a definition provides a common basis for negotiation); (2) when "mechanical" (primordial) and "organic" (functional) patterns of division of labor overlap and clash in a dialectical way, that is, when primordial affiliations are sporadically utilized as bases for class organizations and for primordial affiliations; and (3) when a special kind of dual actor is available—an agent who dominates the resources relevant to competing (e.g., established and emerging) cultures, and who can therefore interpret and manipulate them.[51]

If one substitutes the looser concept of groups sharing a sense of common fate for Kahane's more rigid "primordial affiliation," the condition he sets for an agent controlling resources and able to interpret the terms of relations fit well with the mediatory role the African state may be able to play. By assuming such a role, the African state—even though constrained by ineffectiveness in formulating and implementing policies—can facilitate the search for mutual-gains formulas, thus holding out the possibility of a reduction in the intensity of conflict.

Before turning to the issues of exchange, two caveats seem pertinent. First, exchange may be just as possible, although perhaps in a different form, in hegemonical as in exchange-type state systems. So long as some intermediary—state, party, or some other actor—is prepared to organize the process of mutual adjustment, political exchanges can occur. Mediation may tend toward indirect or tacit exchanges in a hegemonical system and may include greater use of direct and open bargaining in polyarchies. But regardless of system type, so long as some kind of brokerage mechanism is at hand, the possibilities for implicit or explicit bargaining (1) within the dominant elite, or, less probably, (2) between the state and antagonistic and autonomous subregional actors, are never to be ruled out. With respect to the latter, it is noteworthy that in highly conflict-ridden and authoritarian Ethiopia, Lt. Gen. Aman Andom, the chairman of the Provisional Military Administration, offered in 1974 to discuss redressing Eritrea's old grievances (though not its claims to a federal relationship), thereby raising hopes that the new regime might pursue a conciliatory course on this conflict.[52] If hard-line elements within the Dergue prevented a negotiated settlement in this instance, still the possibilities remain open for new initiatives on the part of state officials once the costs of conflict become unbearable for both state authorities and for other disputant parties, as happened in the Sudan in 1972.

The second caveat is that efforts to facilitate direct bargaining are not without risks. The process of linking disputing groups by means of "amicable agreements" carries its own dangers; well-established practices of "log-rolling" or intraelite "back scratch"[53] can sometimes lead to undesirable mutual concessions.[54] Even where these efforts merely entail an exchange within the dominant political class of existing substantive resources, there is a chance, as Manfred Halpern notes, that "bargaining precludes the building of capacity—at the center and locally—to overcome the underlying incoherence. Time is being bought, but, fundamentally, for no creative purpose."[55] Halpern's point that bargaining may "mask" incoherence, entrenching the status quo, is well taken. Yet even where this is the case bargaining can still have value, provided it contributes to the important process of social learning, through divergent class and ethnic groups coming to expect predictable patterns of behavior from one another over time. Such learned relationships may make an effective coordination of policy feasible, for a sense of community emerges out of a mutual recognition of common expectations, and it is this linkage that allows some margin for policy choice.

I will now look briefly at some of the issues of exchange. My purpose here is not to treat the subject exhaustively, but rather to suggest some of the ways a partially autonomous state might perform a useful intermediary role in class or ethnic conflicts. To be sure, in placing such conflict issues on the agenda, the state may be acting out of its own interests; even so, the effect may still be the promotion of political exchange among divergent groups, and thus social linkage.

In the middle-African countries, conflict and competition occur between elite spokesmen for rival ethnoregional and class interests at the center and in the subregional capitals. Such competition takes place over a variety of issues, but most frequently revolves around questions of public power, the allocation of public resources, and the recruitment of people into state positions. As a consequence of economic scarcity and heightened expectations after independence, particularly on the part of those in the relatively advantaged subregions or socioeconomic classes,[56] demands—sometimes highly intense in character—are made upon an already heavily encumbered state for increased development and welfare expenditures. Although these public demands have, for the most part, been negotiable (i.e., limited claims to rights within the state), occasionally they have amounted to nonnegotiable demands, or claims outside the rules of state (Biafra, Katanga, Eritrea). The state is likely to act as an effective mediatory institution only when dealing with the former, less conflict-laden claims.

How have African state actors used their mediatory powers? To answer this question, it will be necessary to look mainly at the tacit or implied exchanges that mark the one-party authoritarian environment. The limits on effective state power in Africa (i.e., the soft state) require those controlling the central institutions of state to be responsive, even if reluctantly, to some of the demands of group spokesmen. Hence the state enters into a process of "bargaining" on its own with autonomous local and subregional notables at the periphery,[57] as well as reconciling or mediating the claims of spokesmen for other social interests by means of reciprocity.[58] It is this second aspect, the state as mediator of conflict, that concerns us here.

Competition over resources in middle-African societies inevitably takes on some zero-sum implications whenever expectations are relatively high in relation to capacity. To avoid mutually damaging conflicts among ethnoregional interests, the dominant state-party elite must engage in a delicate process of negotiating a consensus around the principle of proportional distribution on the basis of numbers or administrative units. Proportionality, observes Arend Lijphart, "is a method of allocating civil service appointments and scarce financial resources in the form of government subsidies among the different segments. It can be contrasted with the winner-take-all principle of unrestrained majority rule."[59] Proportionality is a principle that state elites can fall back on in their search for relatively low cost and minimally acceptable decisions. By contrast, principles can be described as "nonproportional" when skewed to benefit the relatively advantaged, and they are deemed "extraproportional" when their effect is redistributional (i.e., they benefit relatively disadvantaged social groups).

Largely as a consequence of unequal political power and inherited inequalities (not the least of which is the differentiating impact of colonial policies and practices), middle-African states have, not surprisingly, applied nonproportional allocative principles quite widely in practice. As one example among many, I note that, based on Nigeria's 1973 census figures, capital expenditures on health programs by state governments in the 1970–1974 period showed a wide range of variance, from the £1.47 per capita in relatively advantaged Rivers State to £0.10 per capita in relatively disadvantaged North-Eastern State.[60] Nevertheless, state leaders have, rhetorically, identified themselves fully with proportional and extraproportional allocative principles,[61] and in some cases have gone further, making a conscious effort to put these principles into practice. Thus in oil-rich Nigeria, the federal government has gone to great expense to establish universities in almost all of the subregions; similarly, the Sudanese government has, symbolically, constructed a university at Juba (attended largely by northern students at its outset), and Ghana's former President Limann reportedly spoke in 1981 of government plans to set up a university in the relatively disadvantaged north, "public criticism notwithstanding."[62] The southern Sudan, which was allocated under 5 percent of the state's total revenue in the 1974–1975 and 1975–1976 fiscal years, acquired a fully proportional 20.2 percent in 1980–1981.[63] Proportional principles have also been pursued below the subregional level. It is said to be standard practice for Kenya's District Development Committees to distribute water projects to each division.[64] In all cases, one of the reasons for using proportional principles is to ease suspicions the relatively disadvantaged class-ethnic groups might have that they are being treated inequitably.

Proportional principles are applied from time to time with respect to the location of projects and industries and to the allocation of revenues, and extraproportional principles, though decidedly rarer in scarcity-prone middle Africa, are still not unknown. As I have shown elsewhere, Zambia's priorities shifted during its first plan period, 1966–1970, from the proportional to the extraproportional principle, leading to a deliberate redistribution of capital funds for health and feeder roads away from the line-of-rail to the less advantaged off-line-of-rail provinces. Government health expenditures in 1971 averaged 0.158 Kwacha per person for the three line-of-rail provinces, whereas in the hinterland areas they were as high as 0.614 Kwacha in Western Province and 1.326 Kwacha in North-Western Province. In Ghana, General Acheampong, anxious to expand his regime's base northward, showed a reallocative orientation in capital-fund expenditures on education in the 1975–1976 period. The national average expenditure on secondary-school education during that period was 19.69 Cedi per capita, and expenditures in relatively disadvantaged Brong-Ahafo (₵ 34.76), Northern ₵ 39.31), and Upper Region (₵ 39.60) were well above the country-wide average.[65] The extraproportional principle has also been applied in recent times in the allocative policies of Nigeria and Tanzania, with positive consequences of an integrative nature. Responsiveness on the part of state officials (in practice, the minister of finance and his technical officers in negotiations with their various subregional counterparts) encourages a learning process that supports the growth of coherent social relationships over time.[66]

Table 6.1. "Ethnic Arithmetic" in the Distribution of Key Political and
Administrative Posts in Guinea, 1958–1967

Ethnic Group	Percentage of Total Population	Percentage of Total Key Posts
Foulah	29	26
Malinké	34	37
Soussou	17	18
Forest	18	8
Others	2	11
Total	100	100

Source: Adapted from B. Charles by Ladipo Adamolekun, Sékou Touré's Guinea
(London: Methuen, 1976), p. 131.

State elites also make extensive use of the proportional principle in political recruitment. Again the use of a rule deemed fair by rival interests avoids damaging competition and reinforces confidence in the system and its primary actors. In middle Africa, by contrast with European experience, the application of the proportional principle is an intermittent and largely ad hoc process,[67] yet one finds examples of its application in a wide range of political systems. In Sékou Touré's Guinea, there are indications that the president's own ethnic group, the Malinké, have been somewhat overrepresented while the Forest people have been underrepresented; even so, as shown in Table 6.1, the disproportional distributions are not dramatic, and Touré himself has admitted to practicing "ethnic arithmetic" in distributing key political and administrative posts.[68] Commenting on the application of the proportional principle in the appointment and promotion of Nigerian public officials, Richard A. Joseph concludes: "The military government during the post-civil war years, 1970–79, became very adept at maintaining this 'unofficial' ethnic balance in its ministerial and parastatal appointments. When the Constitution of the Second Republic was promulgated in 1979, it repeatedly prescribed attentiveness to the 'national character' (i.e. multi-ethnic diversity) of Nigeria in the making of public appointments and the disbursement of government funds."[69] And in Ghana, ethnic balancing has figured in the calculations of Flight Lt. Jerry John Rawlings's Provisional National Defense Council (PNDC). An Ewe-led administration (particularly noticeable in the military and police establishments) has shown considerable sensitivity to ethnic sentiments, particularly in the way that it has included two northerners in the seven-member PNDC and has made certain those appointed as secretary of a region hail from that region. Moreover, as an attempt to appease Akan misgivings, a majority of ministerial posts have been given to Akan candidates (although it is significant that within that broad category non-Ashantis have been better treated).[70] These attempts to give life to the proportional principle in recruitment policies represent a form of tacit exchange among the state and ethnic groups that results in indispensable social linkages.

Where the state has overlooked or cavalierly dismissed the proportionality principle in its political recruitment policies, a noticeable rise in intergroup competition and conflict has materialized. François Tombalbaye's heavy reliance upon educated Sara in the Chadian civil service heightened northerners' consciousness of their relative disadvantage in the political process;[71] similarly, the Sudanization policies pursued by a northern-dominated government during the period of self-government and after Lt. Gen. Ibrahim Abboud's seizure of control in 1958 were a key precipitant of the 1955 army mutiny and the subsequent military confrontation. As Dunstan Wai remarks on the mutinies: "The manner in which the Sudanization policy was being implemented was disappointing in the extreme to the Southerners who hoped for a fair share of the posts being vacated by British Government officials."[72] In brief, then, disproportional recruitment policies have contributed to social incoherence—and, in some instances, have led to grave threats to the survival of the state itself.

The proportionality principle is also a factor in a variety of other African issue areas such as coalition formation, federalism and subregional autonomy, and constitutional safeguards. In all these cases, norms of relationship are operational that recognize the legitimate concerns of separate interests and the right of these interests to have a part in the decision-making process. The extent to which these norms have gained acceptance varies widely, from the discriminatory and arbitrary practices of Francisco Macias Nguema in Equatorial Guinea[73] and Idi Amin in Uganda to the more regularized relationships of Nigeria, Senegal, Kenya, Tanzania, and elsewhere. In the artificial state situations in much of Africa, such regularized relationships among groups will not happen automatically over time. Hence the partially autonomous state, acting in conformity with its organizing principles, can perform an indispensable intermediary function—facilitating the acceptance of the proportionality principle, in its own practices as well as in relations between others. Where the state—the key employer in the modern sector—makes use of the proportionality principle in dealing with such issues as coalition formation, political recruitment, and resource allocation, it nurtures a culture of reciprocity and exchange in the society as a whole. Under such circumstances, the state can be said to be a source of social coherence, or to paraphrase the quotation from Harold Laski with which this chapter begins, the basis on which community "security" can be built.

Policy Implications

"Political stability," Claude Ake wrote, "is the regularity of the flow of political exchanges; the more regular the flow, the more stable the polity."[74] I agree with Ake on the critical link between political exchange and stability;

however, I have tried to go further, to ask how the process of political exchange can be facilitated in middle Africa.

The answer, as shown above, lies partly in making more effective use of the state as a mediatory agency. Given a context of overriding resource scarcity, with the aggravated ethnic and class competition that this often entails, state mediation of intergroup conflict is a sometimes unrecognized means for facilitating coherent social relations. As an added benefit, such mediatory practices enhance the state's political capacity at a time of marked fragility of institutions. Mediatory initiatives, which frequently involve only minimal expenditures of scarce fiscal resources, may increase state political capabilities despite limits on bureaucratic effectiveness and reach. The state's political capabilities are broadened mainly through its use of organizing principles in its own activities and its promotion of predictable patterns of relationship among group actors in society. By assisting participants to avoid the zero-sum aspects of ethnic and class conflict, the intermediary state institution helps to reduce the level and intensity of conflict, thereby allowing losers as well as winners to regard politics as a mutual-gains process.

The state, then, is inextricably linked to the process of ethnic and class politics. As Naomi Chazan puts it so well, "The rhythm of ethnic politics . . . is a function of state actions and the fluctuations of state power."[75] As the state sets and enforces the terms of group relations, it helps to foster social coherence, especially when norms regulating the conduct of group competition and conflict gain acceptance. Because the state has interests of its own, it is necessarily a less than neutral actor. The Nigerian bureaucracy's determined opposition to the 1967 Aburi accords, which would have allowed an extensive decentralization of subregional power (John de St. Jorre describes it as a *"de facto* confederation"[76]), revealed central state institutions (i.e., the civil service) acting not only in terms of their country's perceived needs but also in terms of their own organizational imperatives.

The partially autonomous state, then, has interests, power, and resources at its disposal. It can use this power, as in the cases of Nguema's Equatorial Guinea or Amin's Uganda noted above, to invoke nonproportional principles, with the likely effect of intensifying conflict and complicating the process of establishing coherent intergroup relations. Or it can attempt to reduce the costs of group encounters by operating, in direct or tacit transactions, in terms of such widely understood organizing principles as proportionality, and even extraproportionality. The latter, though it may require considerable self-restraint and leadership by the dominant political elite, holds real possibilities for successful state buffering of intergroup differences. What follows in terms of policy implications is the importance of an effort to close the gap between organizing principles and partially autonomous state action in order to establish predictability in relationships. In addition, there is a need to strengthen public institutions, possibly through decentralizing responsibilities, so the state can concentrate its efforts upon such critical functions as mediating between powerful interests within the society. The "domestic foundations of the security problems in Africa" that Ambassador Francis Deng refers to in Chapter 1 are not likely to prove manageable until the soft state becomes both stronger and more responsive.

Notes

1. Harold J. Laski, *The State in Theory and Practice* (New York: Viking Press, 1947), p. 4.

2. R. M. MacIver, *The Modern State* (London: Oxford University Press, 1926), p. 5.

3. Harold D. Lasswell and Abraham Kaplan, *Power and Society* (New Haven, Conn.: Yale University Press, 1950), p. 183.

4. Manfred Halpern, "Changing Connections to Multiple Worlds," in Helen Kitchen, ed., *Africa: From Mystery to Maze* (Lexington, Mass.: D. C. Heath, 1976), p. 13.

5. Gunnar Myrdal, *Asian Drama—An Inquiry into the Poverty of Nations*, vol. 2 (New York: Pantheon, 1968), pp. 895–900.

6. J. Isawa Elaigwu and Victor A. Olorunsola, "Federalism and Politics of Compromise," in Donald Rothchild and Victor A. Olorunsola, eds., *State Versus Ethnic Claims: African Policy Dilemmas* (Boulder, Colo.: Westview Press, 1983), p. 286.

7. Martin R. Doornbos, "Kumanyana and Rwenzururu: Two Responses to Ethnic Inequality," in Robert I. Rotberg and Ali A. Mazrui, eds., *Protest and Power in Black Africa* (New York: Oxford University Press, 1970), p. 1133.

8. David D. Laitin, "The Political Economy of Military Rule in Somalia," *Journal of Modern African Studies* 14, 3 (September 1976):452.

9. Ronald T. Libby, "Further Comments on the Role of the State in Africa and Latin America," prepared for the American Political Science Association Conference Group on Political Economy for the Panel "Theoretical Perspectives on the 'Form of the State' in Africa and Latin America," August 3, 1982, p. 1.

10. Ralph Miliband, *Marxism and Politics* (Oxford: Oxford University Press, 1977), p. 91.

11. Dunstan M. Wai, "Geoethnicity and the Margin of Autonomy in the Sudan," in Rothchild and Olorunsola, *State Versus Ethnic Claims*, ch. 15.

12. See Joseph Lagu, *Decentralization: A Necessity for the Southern Provinces of the Sudan* (Khartoum: Samar P. Press, 1981). Postscript, 1983: Subsequently, Nimeiry did, in fact, decide to redivide the South.

13. Ruth Collier notes that where state norms provided for mass participation in elections—effectively channeled along desired lines by the dominant elite—the effects have been stabilizing. Regime continuity has occurred in two situations: under "one-party plebiscitary" regimes (where, in some French-speaking African states, oppositions have been eliminated around the time of independence by merger or electoral triumph and the legal party has then put forward a list of candidates for public approval) or under the "one-party competitive" regime (where, in some English-speaking African states, a dominant party encountering little electoral opposition has provided for a controlled choice among selected party candidates). "To the extent that a political elite was able to consolidate its position under the electoral system and form a one-party regime according to the norms of that system, that elite was generally able to maintain continuous rule throughout

the post-independence period." *Regimes in Tropical Africa* (Berkeley: University of California Press, 1982), p. 114.

14. Aidan Southall, "State Formation in Africa," in Bernard J. Siegel, ed., *Annual Review of Anthropology*, vol. 3 (Palo Alto, Calif.: Annual Reviews, Inc., 1974), p. 163.

15. On state dominance in the South African context as based on "conformity pressure among a cohesive ethnic group (Afrikaner)," see Heribert Adam, "The Manipulation of Ethnicity: South Africa in Comparative Perspective," in Rothchild and Olorunsola, *State Versus Ethnic Claims*, p. 134.

16. Anne S. Sassoon, *Gramsci's Politics* (New York: St. Martin's Press, 1980), pp. 118–119.

17. Max Weber, *Economy and Society*, ed. Guenther Roth and Claus Wittich (Berkeley: University of California Press, 1978), p. 56.

18. These points are developed further in Donald Rothchild and Michael Foley, "The Implications of Scarcity for Governance in Africa," *International Political Science Review*, 4, 3 (1983): 316–317.

19. J. P. Nettl, "The State as a Conceptual Variable," *World Politics* 20, 4 (July 1968):589.

20. Zaki Ergas, "The State and Economic Deterioration: The Tanzanian Case," *Journal of Commonwealth and Comparative Politics* 20, 3 (November 1982), 287. Also see Michael G. Schatzberg, "The Insecure state in Zaire: Resistance Within, Resistance Without," paper presented to the American Political Science Association, Denver, September 2–5, 1982, p. 5, including his quotations from Theda Skocpol and Anthony Giddens.

21. Miliband, *Marxism and Politics*, pp. 106–107.

22. On this, see Donald Rothchild, *Racial Bargaining in Independent Kenya* (London: Oxford Univeristy Press, 1973), pp. 441–442.

23. For Hamza Alavi, the "bureaucratic-military oligarchy," which has an independence supported by an autonomous material base, performs a mediating role between the rival demands of three propertied social classes. See "The State in Post-Colonial Societies: Pakistan and Bangladesh," *New Left Review* 74 (July—August 1972):72.

24. Crawford Young, *The Politics of Cultural Pluralism* (Madison: University of Wisconsin Press, 1976), p. 212.

25. Nicos Poulantzas, *State, Power, Socialism*, trans. P. Camiller (London: NLB, 1978), p. 14.

26. Youssef Cohen, Brian Brown, and A.F.K. Organski, "The Paradoxical Nature of State Making: The Violent Creation of Order," *American Political Science Review* 75, 4 (December 1981):904.

27. Edmond J. Keller, "Ethiopia: Revolution, Class, and the National Question," *African Affairs* 80, 321 (October 1981):548. By 1974, the Tigreans, Oromos, and others were beginning (inaccurately) to speak of the Dergue as the "Amhara steamroller." Colin Legum, ed., *Africa Contemporary Record 1974–75* (New York: Africana Publishing Co., 1975), p. B183.

28. Young, *The Politics of Cultural Pluralism*, pp. 211–215.

29. Donald Rothchild and John Harbeson, "The Political Economy of Rehabilitation in Uganda," *Current History* 80, 463 (March 1981):119.

30. Miliband, *Marxism and Politics*, p. 84.

31. On continuing, relatively high expectations of central support, particularly among Ghana's disadvantaged peoples, see Donald Rothchild, "Comparative Public Demand and Expectation Patterns: The Ghana Experience," *African Studies Review*

22, 1 (April 1979):135–142; and Fred M. Hayward, "Perceptions of Well-Being in Ghana: 1970 and 1975," ibid., pp. 109–125.

32. Richard Rose, "Overloaded Government: The Problem Outline," paper presented to the International Political Science Association Congress, Edinburgh, August 17, 1976, p. 3.

33. Quoted in *West Africa,* March 16, 1981, p. 592. Also see Maxwell Owusu, "Current Socio-Economic Situation . . . What's To Be Done," *Daily Graphic* (Accra), June 15, 1980, p. 4. On the link between external pressures and political instability in Weimar Germany and Fourth Republic France, see Arend Lijphart, *Democracy in Plural Societies* (New Haven, Conn.: Yale University Press, 1977), p. 116.

34. Albert Hirschman, *Exit, Voice and Loyalty* (Cambridge: Harvard University Press, 1970).

35. On this, see Donald Rothchild, "Military Regime Performance: An Appraisal of the Ghana Experience, 1972–1978," *Comparative Politics* 12, 4 (July 1980):462–466; and Maxwell Owusu, "Politics without Parties: Reflections on the Union Government Proposal in Ghana," *African Studies Review* 22, 1 (April 1979):89–108. On Pres. Kamuzu Banda's enormous discretionary power and the fear this engenders, see T. David Williams, *Malawi: The Politics of Despair* (Ithaca, N.Y.: Cornell University Press, 1978), ch. 7.

36. See, for example, *Report of the Ad Hoc Committee on Union Government, 1977,* Dr. G. Koranteng-Addow, chairman (Accra-Tema: Ghana Publishing Corp., 1977), sec. 330; Col. S. M. Asante, "The Conflict Caused by Parties," *West Africa,* March 20, 1978, p. 547; *Ghanaian Times,* January 31, 1978, p. 1, statement by E. K. Buckman.

37. On the choice environments faced by socialist elites in Africa, see Kenneth Jowitt, "Scientific Socialist Regimes in Africa: Political Differentiation, Avoidance, and Unawareness," in Carl G. Rosberg and Thomas M. Callaghy, eds., *Socialism in Sub-Saharan Africa: A New Assessment* (Berkeley: University of California, Institute of International Studies, 1979), pp. 165–177.

38. See the discussion in Donald Rothchild and Robert L. Curry, Jr., *Scarcity, Choice and Public Policy in Middle Africa* (Berkeley: University of California Press, 1978), p. 48; also Rothchild and Olorunsola, *State Versus Ethnic Claims,* ch. 12.

39. Here one must distinguish between responding to demands as a rational process and responding out of shock or hopelessness. An example of the latter occurred in Guinea, where a highly centralized but fragile state actor was forced to respond to a march of the market women calling for a liberalization of trade practices. With the state unable to function for two days as the women took to the streets to air their grievances, the authoritarian leader, Ahmed Sékou Touré, responded in a conciliatory manner, declaring his government's willingness to tolerate small-scale private trading as well as an opening of trade across state borders. On this, see Aguibou Y. Yansané, "The State, African Socialism and the Cooperative Movement in Western Africa: Case of Guinea," paper presented to the Institute of International Studies Colloquium, Berkeley, Calif., May 14, 1982, p. 40; and Jean Pomonti, "Sékou Touré's dictatorship of the people for the people," *Manchester Guardian Weekly* 127, 5 (August 1, 1982).12.

40. Referred to in Eric A. Nordlinger, *On the Autonomy of the Democratic State* (Cambridge: Harvard University Press, 1981), p. 22.

41. Gavin Williams, "The World Bank and the Peasant Problem," in Judith Heyer, Pepe Roberts, and Gavin Williams, eds., *Rural Development in Tropical Africa* (New York: St. Martin's Press, 1981), p. 40; and Robert H. Bates, *Markets and States in Tropical Africa* (Berkeley: University of California Press, 1981), pp. 91–95.

42. Barrington Moore, *Social Origins of Dictatorship and Democracy* (Boston: Beacon Press, 1967), p. 506.

43. Goran Hyden, *Beyond Ujamaa in Tanzania* (Berkeley: University of California Press, 1980), p. 24.

44. On this, see Brian Barry, "The Consociational Model and Its Dangers," *European Journal of Political Research* 3, 4 (December 1975):411.

45. Claude Ake, "Explaining Political Instability in New States," *Journal of Modern African Studies* 11, 2 (September 1973):350.

46. Guillermo O'Donnell, "Tensions in the Bureaucratic-Authoritarian State and the Question of Democracy," in David Collier, ed., *The New Authoritarianism in Latin America* (Princeton, N.J.: Princeton University Press, 1979), p. 288.

47. See Roger Fisher, "Falklands and the U. N.," *New York Times*, April 20, 1982, p. 31.

48. See Charles E. Lindblom, *The Intelligence of Democracy* (New York: Free Press, 1965), p. 68.

49. World Bank, *Accelerated Development in Sub-Saharan Africa: An Agenda for Action* (Washington, D.C.: World Bank, 1981), pp. 40–41.

50. Quoted in *Weekly Review* (Nairobi), October 22, 1982, p. 21.

51. Reuven Kahane, *Legitimation and Integration in Developing Societies: The Case of India* (Boulder, Colo.: Westview Press, 1982), p. 6.

52. Legum, *Africa Contemporary Record 1974–75*, p. B191. On the Sudanese negotiations, see Dunstan M. Wai, *The African-Arab Conflict in the Sudan* (New York: Africana Publishing Co., 1981), ch. 8; and Kodwe Ankrah, "In Pursuit of Peace in the Sudan," *Study Encounter* 8, 2 (1972):6–11.

53. As used here, intraelite back scratching is a situation in which the various participants expect compensation for refraining from actions that are in society's general interest. Cf. Kenneth A. Oye, "The Domain of Choice," in K. Oye, D. Rothchild, and R. Lieber, eds., *Eagle Entangled* (New York: Longman, 1979), p. 14.

54. Brian Barry, "Political Accommodation and Consociational Democracy," *British Journal of Political Science* 5, 4 (October 1975):484–486.

55. Halpern, "Changing Connections . . . ," p. 15.

56. Donald Rothchild, "Collective Demands for Improved Distributions," in Rothchild and Olorunsola, *State Versus Ethnic Claims*, ch. 10.

57. As Henry Bienen writes on the regime of Leopold Senghor in Senegal: "The national leadership continued to reach local constituencies by bargaining with community leaders." See his chapter, "The State and Ethnicity: Integrative Formulas in Africa," in Rothchild and Olorunsola, *State Versus Ethnic Claims*, p. 113.

58. Robert A. Dahl and Charles E. Lindblom, *Politics, Economics, and Welfare* (New York: Harper and Row, Torchbook Edition, 1963), p. 238.

59. Lijphart, *Democracy in Plural Societies*, pp. 38–39. Also see Eric Nordlinger, *Conflict Regulation in Divided Societies* (Cambridge: Center for International Affairs, Harvard University, 1972), pp. 110–116; Jürg Steiner, "The Principles of Majority and Proportionality," *British Journal of Political Science* 1, 1 (January 1971):63–70; and Milton J. Esman, "The Management of Communal Conflict," *Public Policy* 21, 1 (Winter 1973):49–78.

60. Calculated from *Daily Times*, October 21, 1971, p. 7.

61. For statements of the various Ghanaian regimes supporting a "deliberate policy" of correcting imbalances between different parts of the country, see Donald Rothchild, "Military Regime Performance," pp. 473–474.

62. *Legon Observer* (Accra) 12, 11 (October 23–November 5, 1981):242.

63. I am grateful to Lako Tongun and Judith Geist for help in making these calculations. See *Annual Budget, 1974/75* (Juba: Regional Ministry of Finance and Economic Planning, June 1975), pp. 5–6; Legum, *Africa Contemporary Record 1974–75*, p. B108; Colin Legum, ed., *Africa Contemporary Record 1975–76* (New York: Africana Publishing Co., 1976), p. B132; Pres. J. Nimeiry, *Speech on Main Features and Development Aspects of the Six Year Economic Development Plan, 1977/78–1982/83* (Washington, D.C.: Sudanese Embassy, January 1977), p. 2; "People's Executive Councils' Budgets for FY 80/81," Ministry of Finance; and National Economy, Khartoum, Democratic Republic of Sudan (n.d.), mimeo.

64. Interview, Judith Geist, November 1982. On the economic costs of locating state farms in each electoral district of Nigeria and Ghana, see Bates, *Markets and States in Tropical Africa*, pp. 114–115.

65. Donald Rothchild, "Rural-Urban Inequities and Resource Allocation in Zambia," *Journal of Commonwealth Political Studies* 10, 3 (November 1972):234–236; and his "Military Regime Performance," pp. 472–476.

66. Of course, where expenditures fail to match budgetary allocations by a wide mark, the result may be cynicism and distrust. In the Sudan, where less than £S 400,000 "had actually reached Juba from Khartoum" out of £S 57 million allocated by the Sudan government in the 1973–1974 budget, interviewees did manifest some lack of confidence in central government intentions. The statistics appear in Legum, *Africa Contemporary Record 1974–75*, p. B117.

67. In Belgium, a 1970 constitutional amendment requires that the cabinet consist of an equal number of French-speaking and Dutch-speaking ministers. Arend Lijphart, ed., *Conflict and Coexistence in Belgium* (Berkeley: University of California, Institute of International Studies, 1981), p. 5.

68. Ladipo Adamolekun, *Sékou Touré's Guinea* (London: Methuen, 1976), pp. 130–131.

69. Richard A. Joseph, "Ethnicity and Prebendal Politics in Nigeria: A Theoretical Outline," paper presented at the American Political Science Association, Denver, September 1982, p. 9.

70. Data drawn from interviews and from *Ghana News* (Embassy of Ghana) 2, 3 (March 1982).

71. Virginia Thompson and Richard Adloff, *Conflict in Chad* (Berkeley: University of California, Institute of International Studies, 1981), pp. 23–25.

72. Wai, *The African-Arab Conflict . . .* , pp. 77–78.

73. Although Macias's rule was based largely upon Fang control of the government and bureaucracy, it should be noted that he did not hesitate to turn in a cruel manner against his own community when he encountered resistance there. Robert H. Jackson and Carl G. Rosberg, *Personal Rule in Black Africa* (Berkeley: University of California Press, 1982), pp. 246–247.

74. Ake, "Explaining Political Instability . . . ," p. 356.

75. Naomi Chazan, "Ethnicity and Politics in Ghana," *Political Science Quarterly* 97, 3 (Fall 1982):463.

76. John de St. Jorre, *The Nigerian Civil War* (London: Hodder and Stoughton, 1972), p. 95.

7. Emerging Patterns of Civil-Military Relations in Africa: Radical Coups d'Etat and Political Stability

Claude E. Welch, Jr.

In the quarter century following World War II, military intervention in politics was a common occurrence. Well over two hundred coups d'etat and coup attempts were staged, affecting a substantial portion of independent developing countries.

The factors that impelled officers to seize control naturally varied from country to country. Corporate, resource, and rank-related issues were the major grievances cited in more than 80 percent of the postwar coups d'etat. What Thompson called "strikingly reformist" coups d'etat—seizures of power in which reform was a "primary" phenomenon as contrasted with a verbal pledge overshadowed by other grievances—accounted for less than one-tenth of the instances of successful intervention.[1] In other words, whatever the political coloration of those who seized control, commitment to major social, political, and economic changes constituted the exception rather than the rule.

Looking at the political roles of armed forces in contemporary Africa, one is struck by a relatively new, unusual phenomenon, far removed from the heritages of colonial rule and the initial postindependence roles of the military south of the Sahara. Several recent coups d'etat have given birth to avowedly radical governments, in which sweeping reforms have been pressed by the governing juntas. These newly installed groups claim to govern according to Marxist-Leninist principles of "scientific socialism." They assert a need for profound transformation in the economy, internal political order, and external political alignment. Comparative analysis of regimes of this sort—making allowance, of course, both for their relative newness and for the incomplete nature of information—can yield insights into the preconditions and catalysts of military intervention and can illustrate the extent to which officers who become politicians can effect profound societal changes. In essence, such a study can clarify the extent to which stability in contemporary African states may be affected by political ideology and armed forces' activism.

Why did the governing juntas in the four countries I shall cite Congo-Brazzaville, Ethiopia, and Somalia—turn explicitly to "scientific socialism" as justification for their rule? I shall argue that their adoption of a new political ideology served primarily as a means of differentiating the new military-cum-political elites from their predecessors. Verbal expression has not been matched by substantial policy alteration, however, with the clear exception of Ethiopia. This is not to argue that Marxist-Leninist approaches have been employed solely as smoke screens, veiling markedly different intentions from external scrutiny. A marked disjuncture has existed, nevertheless, between the strong rhetoric for major alteration and the reality of relatively restricted changes in the domestic structures and external relations of these four states. The chief reasons appear to stem from the institutional inheritance of the armed forces and the strength of rural claims for redress. In order first is a survey of scholarly views of the factors influencing policy proclivities of officers, then consideration of the common facets of the four case-study countries.

Obstacles to Radicalism: The Military as Institution

It is common to argue that the military, as an institution, is characterized by political attitudes on the right of the political spectrum. The "military ethic," Huntington proclaimed, is simultaneously "pessimistic, collectivist, historically inclined, power-oriented, nationalistic, militaristic, pacifist, and instrumentalist in its view of the military profession. It is, in brief, realistic and conservative."[2] Though Huntington's portrayal is marred by his near-total reliance on Western examples and despite his claim that the concept of professionalism provides a nonethnocentric means to assess the role of the military across different societies, it represents a widespread view. Armies as institutions embody specific political and social orientations. Paramount among these are desires for order, responsibility, and pursuit of the national interest—as these are perceived by the armed forces. The clear tendency is thus toward conservatism. Why? To quote a provocative assessment, originally published at the height of World War II, "Experience shows that the process of politically sterilizing the rank and file can be carried through, given favourable conditions of service, to an astonishing degree of success."[3] Such political isolation—reducing links between ordinary soldiers and the populace as a whole—protects governments based on domination of a small elite. Officers presumably serve the interests of the system that has selected and promoted them; military discipline means orders will be carried out; favored social strata have customarily provided significant shares of the officer corps; such alliances of interest between government and military leaders, when coupled with effective internal controls within the armed forces, create institutional stability. Only in instances of pronounced breakdown of military norms of structure and hierarchy, as through war, or in instances of extensive boundary fragmentation, might pressures from the armed forces bring revolution.

Instances in which the military has served revolutionary objectives have been few in number and scattered historically. Indeed, many scholars have treated the notion of a "revolutionary" military as a contradiction in terms. Inherent social characteristics of the armed forces prevent a "normal" army from undertaking revolutionary transformation. Wolpin, for example, called the officer corps "privileged social groups which commonly perceive their corporate interests to be threatened by social reforms of an egalitarian character."[4] If the military opens the door for any group, it does so for the middle class, not for the lower classes. Nun,[5] refined subsequently by Huntington and Nordlinger among others,[6] saw officers as playing a "gate-keeper" function for the middle class. Although officers could be dramatic reformers when the upper class dominated politics, they would, when faced with pressures from the lower class, attempt to defend the status quo. The recent history of Peru, examined in several books and chapters, provides evidence for this view.[7]

Rare indeed are the armed forces that academics have cited as having helped effect revolution. The only exceptions come in the rare instances of protracted civil wars eventually won by the insurgents on the basis of new, revolutionary armies built from below. Perlmutter, for example, noted only the Peoples Liberation Army of China and the Zahal of Israel as "revolutionary professional" armies,[8] while Chorley and Ellis, in their historical surveys of armed forces and revolution, drew largely from European examples.[9] It appears as though the time has been too short for the historian to take note of instances in contemporary Africa, the phenomenon too narrow in geographic scope for the comparative sociologist to investigate, and the policy results too uncertain for the political scientist to examine.

The rarity of military-led revolution contrasts with the ubiquity of the coup d'etat as a means of removing governments. As noted at the start of this chapter, the armed forces are prime determinants of political change in most of the world today and historically have frequently intruded into the political process.[10] However, Subsaharan Africa, both during European rule and in the early years of independence, appeared to contrast with this primacy of armed strength in determining political power. Colonial governments, recognizing the military's potential for political involvement, placed extraordinary emphasis on keeping the armed forces apart from "politics" or "nationalist agitation." The conceptions of civil-military relations that were developed by colonial powers in tropical Africa stressed the "nonpolitical" roles of the military: the "theirs not to question why" phenomenon.[11] This nonpolitical (or, perhaps more accurately, apolitical) heritage appears to have made many officers (especially in former British-ruled Africa) initially reluctant to seize control after independence.[12] Civilian presidents and prime ministers, imbued by the idea the armed forces should and would remain on the political sidelines, gave them little attention. Thus, when a series of coups d'etat rocked Africa in 1965–1966, it became abundantly apparent that few governments had heeded lessons drawn from other societies on how to preclude military intervention in politics. For example, following the achievement of independence, only a handful of armed forces in other African states was reconstructed as a means of precluding intervention.[13]

The following points characterized patterns of civil-military relations in tropical Africa, as imposed in the colonial period and as carried on after independence in the majority of states:

1. The major colonial powers used military might to impose and ultimately to sustain their rule.
2. The rank and file were essentially drawn from colonial subjects, but officers came from the metropole, to insure political obedience to the respective European governments.
3. Commissioning of indigenous officers started late in the decolonization process; those selected were inculcated with values of political disengagement.
4. Serious efforts were made during the colonial period to separate the armed forces from their social contexts—that is, to ensure "integral" boundaries of the military as an institution.[14]
5. The relatively peaceful achievement of independence by African states meant the armed forces remained on the political sidelines, neither needed by the metropolitan power to suppress nationalist movements nor countered by guerrilla or liberation armies sponsored by indigenous politicians.
6. In the absence of revolutionary objectives introduced into the armed forces from its command structure, the institutional conservatism characteristic of the colonial period was carried over after self-government was achieved; "localization" of the officer corps generally entailed the promotion of African officers who had served many years under European guidance.
7. Where revolutionary struggle took place, naturally enough, the armed forces inherited from the former colonial regime were eliminated, being replaced by the guerrilla forces of the nationalist movement; under such circumstances, the military would serve direct revolutionary functions.

The possibility that military intervention would become characteristic of tropical Africa was, a score of years back, foreseen by few scholars; that such involvement would lead to the proclamation of Marxism-Leninism was envisaged by even fewer. The chief political problem that analysts grappled with was the single-party state, not causes of coups d'etat. Once students of African politics came to grips with the eruption of the armed forces, they came to question whether the theories developed primarily with respect to Latin America, the Middle East, and South Asia could be applied south of the Sahara. Perhaps ironically, the most important reconceptualization of the role of the military drawn from African evidence stressed the "traditionalizing"[15] as contrasted with the "modernizing" role of the military, an issue to which I shall turn subsequently.

The relative absence of attention to the armed forces as bearers of political change was paralleled by limited analysis of the phenomenon of revolution in immediate postcolonial Africa—perhaps for the obvious reason that there have been few revolutions in postcolonial Africa. Algeria experienced major change as a result of guerrilla warfare. Rwanda and Zanzibar illustrated how ethnically stratified societies could be dramatically altered by revolution based on ethnic awareness. The major struggles for independence leading to radicalism from below occurred in the former Portuguese colonies. In Ethiopia, the governing coalition of officers (the Dergue or "committee") implemented drastic transformations in rural and urban areas, including an effort to move beyond expropriation of the landed elite to collectivization of peasant lands. The unusual circumstances of Ethiopia receive further attention in the following section.

Institutional Conservatism and Radical Adaptation

Radical ideas have been introduced into African military-led states from two chief sources. Deliberate reshaping of political ideology from above has been one cause, transformation of the military from below during the struggle for independence the second. The former resulted primarily from competition for ideological distinctiveness: despite factors of institutional conservatism, governing officers turned to Marxism-Leninism as a basis for justifying their rule. The latter—transformation from below—can be traced in large measure to the conditions of the independence struggle: reshaping postliberation society on the basis of new goals and structures became paramount.

Academic literature dealing with military contributions to "political development" stressed that, under certain conditions, officers could play a modernizing role. For example, twenty years ago Halpern envisaged the "new middle class" of the Middle East and North Africa being propelled into power through the intervention of officers;[16] Pye suggested at the same time that the military could serve as a major means for bringing rapid political development to traditional and transitional societies.[17] In other words, officers represented a vanguard of modernization. Both scholars stopped short, however, of predicting profound *revolutionary* transformation involving widespread peasant participation under military auspices. Well-educated officers might open the way for the emergent bourgeoisie, but they could well slam the door shut when and if lower classes knocked. In this respect, Halpern's and Pye's arguments resemble those of Nun and Huntington cited earlier (Footnotes 5 and 6).

The role of officers as reshapers of domestic politics, in keeping with the Halpern and Pye models just suggested, emerged first in Africa through Nasser and the Revolutionary Command Council (RCC) of Egypt. Such a chronology was historically explicable: Egypt was the first state on the continent (apart from the Union of South Africa) to establish a military academy; the "class of '36" (the first in which large numbers of indigenous Egyptians were permitted to enroll) formed the nucleus of the RCC; specifically; eight of the eleven founding members entered the academy in 1936.[18] Libya was the next African state to manifest an RCC-style military structure. The successful seizure of power by Maj. Muamar Khaddafy in 1969 almost immediately altered what had been a narrow, monarchial system into an Islamic Republic dedicated to the diverse goals of Muslim purification, political populism, and military restructuring.[19] Even more significant, the major rise in Libya's revenues during the 1970s as a result of Organization of Petroleum Exporting Countries (OPEC) price changes both bolstered the government's authority dramatically and permitted Khaddafy to pursue major domestic and international goals. Libya obviously enjoyed a fortunate and unusual position. Wolpin, for example, has suggested that "only unusually well-endowed radical military regimes such as Libya" can provide sufficient resources to the masses to acquire broadly based legitimacy;[20] its revolutionary objectives could be pursued readily because of its petroleum wealth. But to what extent can the RCC model and its attached concept of "Arab Socialism" as contrasted with "scientific socialism" explain *radical* military intervention as a general phenomenon in Africa, and in particular the use of Marxist-Leninist concepts?

The introduction of Marxist-Leninist terminology into African politics, with emphasis on the "toiling masses of workers and peasants," started in Congo-Brazzaville, continued in Somalia, and was further expressed in Dahomey/Benin. Common to these three cases were fragmented political and social arenas. Ethnic polarization had weakened and ultimately destroyed government coalitions. Numerous changes of leadership preceded radical military intervention: Congo-Brazzaville had experienced a so-called revolution in 1963, with the ouster of the president by urban mobs and disgruntled soldiers; Somalia had been governed by several prime ministers in its first nine years of independence and had suffered a presidential assassination immediately prior to the armed forces' seizure of control; Dahomey had been subject to earlier coups d'etat in 1963, 1965, 1967, and 1969. In common with all successful makers of coups d'etat, the three leaders who officially espoused Marxism-Leninism—Alphonse Massamba-Debat, Siad Barre, and Mathieu Kerekou—had to justify their action and provide a rationale for remaining in office. The kaleidoscope of preceding regimes meant almost every means of legitimation had been tried.

"Scientific socialism"—adopted as government policy well after the fact of seizure of control and far more likely left on paper than carried into action—was a means of differentiation. It was a choice made from above, carried out by leaders for largely tactical ends, as brief review will illustrate.

Congo-Brazzaville was proclaimed a people's republic in 1968, after a second coup d'etat. The military seized power in the face of a bewilderingly complex political mosaic of ethnic fragmentation and tension, an urban sector swollen by unemployed but ambitious youth, and an economy dominated by expatriate (largely French) interests. Massamba-Debat's motive, in the eyes of one observer, was simple: "transformed into a Marxist he intervened in the political arena in 1968 essentially to preserve the army's corporate autonomy and—especially—his primacy within the army."[21] General Barre proclaimed Somalia to be a socialist state in 1970, a year following his successful seizure of control; a full six years later, he announced creation of a Socialist party. Ideological statements notwithstanding, it appears clear that "scientific socialism—understood as a *programmatic* ideal for economic and political development—has had little impact on political choice in Somalia."[22] In Dahomey, later rechristened the People's Republic of Benin, the formal adoption of Marxism-Leninism occurred in 1974, more than two years after Kerekou's coup d'etat. Once again, the consequences have been relatively minor. "The leaders of the Benin Revolution," one analyst has written, "have confused or substituted 'paper change' and 'epistemological change' for real socioeconomic change."[23]

A significant source of "radical" military intervention came from the domino effect of intervention itself. Any successful coup d'etat unleashes pressures not only within the society as a whole, but—more important— within the military as an institution as well. Those left out in the political cold have reason to stage their own interventions; after all, it is the first coup d'etat that is the most difficult to carry out, given the inertia of prior arrangements. Seeking to establish foundations for legitimation distinct from those of prior regimes, new juntas naturally claimed new grounds for control. In addition, the outlook of governing officers changed. Second- or third-round coups d'etat brought to the fore men willing to immerse the armed forces extensively in politics. Initial military seizures of control generally had been led by older officers socialized in the mores of the former colonial power and hence accepting of the notion that politics is not for soldiers. For example, leaders as diverse as Abboud (Sudan), Afrifa (Ghana), or Soglo (Dahomey) called for disengagement in almost the same breath as they rationalized their intervention. A return to the barracks thus figured in the plans of the first generation of coup makers—and their anticipated withdrawals helped to legitimate their intervention. But with what Kirk-Greene calls the "encore,"[24] younger officers moved into power. Less socialized into the presumptively apolitical values of the military as an institution, more attuned to the demands of various groups for major societal restructuring, such men formed a "vanguard" of profound change. Kerekou and others of his stripe belong in this category. Military radicalism thus reflected both a need for legitimation and the distinct perspectives of various generations of officers regarding the appropriate level and nature of armed forces' political involvement. Later generations believed the armed forces should commit themselves to long-term, deep-rooted transformation of the political, economic, and social systems—at least rhetorically.

I wish to add a further aspect in the consideration of political ideologies in Africa, however. Studies of radicalism in Africa have concentrated on urban sources. Other potentially more profound sources of radical impulse have been ignored, particularly rural centers of discontent. Radicalism has been perceived as a rhetoric of the cities, as an objective of the university students. Yet, as Weiss illustrated with respect to Kwilu,[25] and as I have suggested with application to other areas,[26] African peasants can advocate social and economic alterations as far reaching as any imagined in a university refectory. If the countryside is the source of profound stability *or* of profound upheaval,[27] it behooves us to be aware of the sources of discontent and the means by which this discontent can become politically prominent.

I contend that a major conduit of such pressure can be the military. Members of the armed forces with close ties to centers of rural discontent may ultimately be the most important source of radicalism in contemporary Africa. They are likely to be found in the ranks of noncommissioned officers or junior commissioned officers, with only short periods during which they might have been socialized into the mores of the military. They can respond, as did Master Sgt. Samuel Doe of Liberia, to upwellings of popular antipathy. Their talk of People's Courts, as in Ghana, mirrors general popular opposition to the self-serving actions of politicians, or indeed of other members of the military who have moved into public office. Second- or third-round coups d'etat, planned and executed by officers low in the command structure, could have far greater chances of radicalization than initial seizures of power conceived and carried out by relatively senior members of the military establishment. The great danger, of course, is that the meteoric rise to the top of such junior officers will disengage them from their rural supporters. Seduced by the material rewards of office, and potentially captured by the bureaucratic elite, these junior officers may soon lose their appetite for profound change. To the extent that long-term stability rests on dramatically altering the structure of *rural* society as a whole, however, certain issues can encourage the armed forces to make such alterations. In particular, severe economic and social strains resulting from shortages of land may lead to revolutionary pressure.

Not surprisingly, given the limited attention to "rural radicalism," the potential impact of peasant longings for social transformation has received equally slight study. The one scholar to examine in detail the impact of rural attitudes on the armed forces has been Mazrui; his conclusions stress the conservative, indeed traditionalistic, consequences of military intervention. Drawing primarily on Idi Amin Dada, Mazrui has sketched an intriguing composite picture of "traditionalizing" soldiers.[28] Such individuals, members of the "military-agrarian complex," manifest a resurgence of the "warrior tradition" and an emergence of the "lumpen militariat" to political power. Though one may disagree with Mazrui's conclusions, his assertions about the "militarization of charisma" and the functions of a "military ethnocracy" give pause. Certainly the glib generalizations of the early 1960s about the military and modernization have not been proven fully accurate guides to the contemporary role of armed forces in Africa.

The bloody policies Amin followed were far removed from both the rational "modernizer" model presented by earlier scholars and the radical perspectives discussed in this chapter.

It is in regard to pressures from below that Ethiopia becomes particularly interesting. Multiple sources of discontent in Ethiopia coalesced and erupted during the "creeping coup" of 1974.[29] Radicalization of the revolution reflected endemic conflict within the officer corps, conflict that was manifested in the execution of sixty senior officers in November 1974, in the competition with radical urban elements for support, and above all, in the attempts to satisfy the aspirations of rural dwellers for land reform. Probably far more than any other society in Africa, Ethiopia has been transformed in the past few years, with the abolition of the feudal land system on which the dominance of the late emperor had been based. One can argue that the struggle for political power in Ethiopia, and the focus of much of the Dergue's attention, was to gain the support of the peasantry. Identification with the plight of rural dwellers, most of whom had been racked by drought, famine, exorbitant rents, and absentee Amhara landlords, provided justification for the profound reshaping of rural society. Although space precludes detailed analysis, the radicalization of Ethiopia bore the mark of rural discontent in its initiation, whereas the problems the Dergue confronted in its attempts to collectivize land indicated the limits to which peasants will accept change.

Emerging Patterns of Civil-Military Relations

Briefly listed, the military radicals of contemporary Africa seek four major policy goals: populism; economic restructuring that couples autarchy with renewed stress on nonalignment; nationalism; and attempts at "spiritual" revival by means of greater use of violence in domestic affairs (especially in suppression of challenges to the dominant policy role of officers) and far stronger assertions of the importance of "progressive" approaches to international relations. Each merits discussion.

All successful makers of coups d'etat claim to have acted in the name of "the people." As a rhetorical device, reference to popular aspirations and concerns is commonplace, as shown in Kirk-Greene's useful documentary collection.[30] But the depth of commitment appears stronger under radical military leaders. They seek to expunge overt evidence of "tribalism." Their vision of society is one of unity—a view that presses them to employ violence against opponents. One should be aware, however, of the considerable gap that exists between rhetoric and reality; countries as fragmented as Benin or Congo-Brazzaville cannot be rapidly or easily transformed into homogeneous societies.

Economic restructuring is sought by radical military governments on two levels. Domestically, and in keeping with the populist stress just noted, emphasis is laid on autarchic policies. "Self-reliance" becomes more than a slogan. Restrictions on imports, notably luxury goods desired by the urban elite, are imposed. Local industry is encouraged, despite inefficiencies caused by restricted scale. Internationally, orthodox remedies for economic development—in particular, deflationary proposals from the International Monetary Fund—are resisted. Deficit financing remains the rule, the benefits being directed toward "the people." However, owing both to lack of resources and to the dominance of capitalist states in the world economy, the fiscal remedies proposed remain far more as slogans than realities. Major disengagement from the Western-dominated international economic system has proven difficult, save in case of full alignment with the USSR— a step taken only by Ethiopia. French aid remains significant for Benin and Congo-Brazzaville; Somalia has been given U.S. drought relief aid and military equipment. Further, despite rhetoric of nationalization, three of the four states have manifested only limited takeovers of externally owned firms, and even in Ethiopia the evidence is mixed.

Strong nationalism motivates the preceding goals of populism and economic restructuring. Military radicals are, in this respect, like officers anywhere. Though they are aware of international trends, they are profoundly attached to their own countries. The revolutionary slogans they employ have far clearer ties to the local setting than to any international— that is to say, Soviet-defined—definition of Marxism-Leninism. (Indeed, the emergency of polycentrism among Communist states has been seen as a necessary precursor to the ideological adjustments cited in this chapter.)[31] Although Marxism-Leninism supposedly is an international ideology, it is interpreted in the four African states far more in light of local circumstances and preferences than of the presumed universalism of the ideology as a whole. In Somalia, for example, "scientific socialism" has been translated as "livestock sharing," while the word for "prosperity" means "the richest grazing grass."[32]

Self-determination for all peoples serves as an international counterpart to such nationalist feelings. A recent example comes from the dispute that has ripped through the Organization of African Unity (OAU). Not unexpectedly, a substantial part of the "Progressive" states that attended the abortive 1982 OAU summit meetings did so on the grounds that citizens of the Sahara Arab Democratic Republic (SADR) should enjoy independence, even though Moroccan troops controlled a substantial portion of the putative state's territory. These sessions witnessed a profound division between supporters and opponents of the SADR's admission to the OAU. Radical military-led states were prominent among the "Progressives": Benin, Congo-Brazzaville, and Ethiopia were all represented at the sessions, which were ultimately adjourned due to lack of quorums; the boycott by Somalia may be explained in large measure by its general opposition to Ethiopia.

Even though spiritual revival, the fourth goal, frequently takes the form of sloganeering, the leaders' deep commitment to a new ideology must not be underestimated. Proponents of "Arab Socialism" provide one example. Khaddafy's "Green Book" combines populism, religion, national awareness, and a commitment to participatory politics. Popular sovereignty lies at the heart of contemporary Libyan practice, at least in the view of one recent observer.[33] However, the attempt at rigorous ideological purity characteristic of classic Marxist-Leninist parties and states cannot be found in the four African radical states examined here. A loose version of populism appears to be the dominant characteristic.

Reliance on violence by military leaders has shocked many outside observers. The most important example comes from Ethiopia—indeed, it appears as though the other self-proclaimed Marxist-Leninist states have not employed significant amounts of domestic coercion in pursuit of their presumed revolutions. In Ethiopia, the cold-blooded execution of senior officers and political leaders of the first military government (July–November 1974) signaled the emergence of Mengistu Haile Mariam from relative obscurity. Subsequent efforts to restore national unity in the face of ethnic and regional challenges (notably in the Haud, Ogaden, and Eritrean regions) and in the face of marked urban dissidence (notably from students and the Ethiopian People's Revolutionary Party) met with severe repression. As Young aptly notes, "From the outset, students considered the soldiers to be the usurpers of the revolution."[34] The Dergue, by contrast, viewed themselves as the only true guides for socialist transformation in Ethiopia— a perspective conditioned by the general desire of intervening officers to impose military models on often recalcitrant peoples.

Finally, military radicals—like most of their fellow officers who seize political control—see the armed forces as paragons for organization of the state and society as a whole. They see little value in clear boundaries between the armed forces and "the people." They reject, in other words, one of the basic distinctions made during the colonial period, the time when the senior officers involved in the initial military seizures of power received their basic socialization. Civil-military relations accordingly are taking on new forms in certain states of Africa. The institutional separation and distinctiveness characteristic of the colonial period have been jettisoned. "Popular sovereignty" as a practical matter means tight direction from the military.

Space limitations of this chapter preclude fuller analysis of internal arrangements. However, if the general tendencies described are correct— the fragmentation of boundaries between the military as an institution and various social forces, the need for intervening officers to carve out distinctive political ideologies, the existence of pressures from competitive urban groups and from increasingly vocal rural interests—there would appear to be strong grounds to believe that radicalism in Africa will be fostered by greater military involvement in politics. The military as radicalizer, not necessarily as modernizer; the military as competitor for support, not necessarily as the agent of the "new middle class"; the military as bearer of major nationalistic changes, not necessarily of attitudes inculcated during the colonial period: such are the implications of this trend. Under these conditions, one should not anticipate that emerging civil-military relations in Africa necessarily will enhance governmental stability.

Notes

1. William R. Thompson, *The Grievances of Military Coup-Makers* (Beverly Hills, Calif.: Sage, 1973), p. 44.

2. Samuel P. Huntington, *The Soldier and the State: Theory and Politics of Civil-Military Relations* (New York: Vintage, 1964; reprint of 1957 edition), p. 79.

3. Katherine Chorley, *Armies and the Art of Revolution* (London: Faber and Faber, 1943), p. 241.

4. Miles D. Wolpin, *Militarism and Social Revolution in the Third World* (Totowa, N.J.: Allanheld, Osmun, 1981), p. 2.

5. Jose Nun, "A Latin American Phenomenon: The Middle Class Coup," in *Trends in Social Science Research in Latin American Studies: A Conference Report* (Berkeley, Calif.: Institute of International Studies, University of California, 1965), pp. 55–99.

6. Samuel P. Huntington, *Political Order in Changing Societies* (New Haven, Conn.: Yale University Press, 1968), pp. 221–223; Eric R. Nordlinger, *Soldiers in Politics* (Englewood Cliffs, N.J.: Prentice Hall, 1978), pp. 79–85.

7. See, for example, David Collier, *Squatters and Oligarchs: Authoritarian Rule and Policy Change in Peru* (Baltimore: Johns Hopkins University Press, 1976); Luigi Einaudi and Alfred Stepan, *Latin American Institutional Development: Changing Military Perspectives in Peru and Brazil* (Santa Monica, Calif.: Rand Corporation, 1971); Howard Handelman, *Struggle in the Andes: Peasant Political Mobilization in Peru* (Austin: University of Texas Press, 1975); Abraham F. Lowenthal, ed., *The Peruvian Experiment: Continuity and Change Under a Military Regime* (Princeton, N.J.: Princeton University Press, 1975); Francisco Moncloa, *Peru: ¿Qué pasó? (1968–1976)* (Lima: Editorial Horizonte, 1977); Henry Pease Garcia and Olga Vernme Insua, *Peru 1968–1973: Cronologia Política* (Lima: Centro de Estudios y Promoción del Desarrollo, 1974); Alfred Stepan, *The State and Society: Peru in Comparative Perspective* (Princeton, N. J.: Princeton University Press, 1978); and Victor Villenueva, *Ejercito Peruano: Del anarquico al miltarismo reformista* (Lima: Libreria Editorial Juan Mejia Baca, 1973). I am currently engaged in a comparative study of military disengagement from politics in West Africa and the Andean states of Latin America.

8. Amos Perlmutter, *The Military and Politics in Modern Times: On Professionals, Praetorians, and Revolutionary Soldiers* (New Haven, Conn.: Yale University Press, 1977), esp. pp. 205–211.

9. Chorley, *Armies and the Art of Revolution;* John Ellis, *Armies in Revolution* (New York: Oxford University Press, 1974).

10. Gaetano Mosca, *The Ruling Class* (New York: McGraw Hill, 1939), p. 228: ". . . history teaches that the class that bears the lance or holds the musket regularly forces its rule upon the class that handles the spade or pushes the shuttle."

11. Claude E. Welch, Jr., "Civil-Military Relations in Commonwealth West Africa: The Transfer and Transformation of Colonial Patterns," *Journal of Developing Areas* 12, 2 (January 1978), pp. 153–170; Claude E. Welch, Jr., "Civil-Military Relations in French-Speaking Africa," in Boniface Obichere, ed., *African States and the Military: Past and Present* (London: Frank Cass, in press). It should not be assumed that colonial armies were indeed "apolitical": in upholding European administration, they served primarily political roles.

12. Robin Luckham, *The Nigerian Military: A Sociological Analysis of Authority and Revolt 1960–67* (Cambridge: Cambridge University Press, 1971), pp. 118–122; Robert M. Price, "A Theoretical Approach to Military Rule in New States: Reference

Group Theory and the Ghanaian Case," *World Politics* 23, 3 (April 1971), pp. 399–430.

13. The chief examples of reconstitution shortly after independence are furnished by Guinea and Tanzania, the former leading to the dismissal of Guinean veterans of French forces, the latter occurring following the January 1964 mutiny. For details, see Victor DuBois, "The Army in Guinea," *Africa Report*, January 1963, pp. 3–5, and Ali Mazrui and Donald Rothchild, "The Soldier and the State in East Africa: Some Theoretical Conclusions on the Army Mutinies of 1964," *Western Political Quarterly* 20, 1 (1967), pp. 82–96.

14. A. R. Luckham, "A Comparative Typology of Civil-Military Relations," *Government and Opposition* 6, 1 (Winter 1971), pp. 25–26.

15. Ali A. Mazrui, "Soldiers as Traditionalizers: Military Rule and the Re-Africanization of Africa," *World Politics* 28, 2 (January 1976), pp. 246–272.

16. Manfred Halpern, *The Politics of Social Change in the Middle East and North Africa* (Princeton, N.J.: Princeton University Press, 1963), p. 253.

17. Lucian Pye, "Armies in the Process of Political Development," in John J. Johnson, ed., *The Role of the Military in Developing Countries* (Princeton, N.J.: Princeton University Press, 1962), pp. 69–89.

18. P. J. Vatikiotis, *The Egyptian Army in Politics: Pattern for New Nations?* (Bloomington: Indiana University Press, 1961), p. 46.

19. Ruth First, *Libya: The Elusive Revolution* (Harmondsworth, England: Penguin, 1974); Sami G. Hajjar, "The Jamahiriya Experiment in Libya: Qadhafi and Rousseau," *Journal of Modern African Studies* 18, 2 (June 1980), pp. 181–200.

20. Wolpin, *Militarism and Social Revolution*, p. 224.

21. Samuel Decalo, "Ideological Rhetoric and Scientific Socialism in Benin and Congo/Brazzaville," in Carl G. Rosberg and Thomas M. Callaghy, eds., *Socialism in Sub-Saharan Africa: A New Assessment* (Berkeley: Institute of International Studies, University of California, 1979), p. 252.

22. David D. Laitin, "Somalia's Military Government and Scientific Socialism," in Rosberg and Callaghy, *Socialism in Sub-Saharan Africa*, p. 174.

23. Decalo, "Ideological Rhetoric," p. 246.

24. A.H.M. Kirk-Greene, *'Stay By Your Radios': Documentation for a Study of Military Government in Tropical Africa* (Leiden, Netherlands: Afrika-Studiecentrum, 1981), pp. 136–151.

25. Herbert F. Weiss, *Political Protest in the Congo: The Parti Solidaire Africain During the Independence Struggle* (Princeton, N.J.: Princeton University Press, 1967), p. 98.

26. Claude E. Welch, Jr., *Anatomy of Rebellion* (Albany: SUNY Press, 1980).

27. Huntington, *Political Order*, p. 292.

28. Ali A. Mazrui, *Soldiers and Kinsmen in Uganda: The Making of a Military Ethnocracy* (Beverly Hills, Calif.: Sage, 1975).

29. For general background to the revolution, see Patrick Gilkes, *The Dying Lion: Feudalism and Modernization in Ethiopia* (New York: St. Martin's, 1975), and John Markakis, *Ethiopia: Anatomy of a Traditional Polity* (Oxford: Clarendon Press, 1974); for the increasing radicalization of the armed forces, see Marina Ottaway and David Ottaway, *Ethiopia: Empire in Revolution* (New York: Africana Publishing Company, 1978).

30. Kirk-Greene, *'Stay By Your Radios,'* pp. 38–100.

31. Kenneth Jowitt argues persuasively regarding the emergence of contending interpretations of Marxism-Leninism: "The absence of an authoritative center of Leninism comparable to the Communist Party of the Soviet Union under Stalin

allows self-designated 'scientific socialist' African elites *to avoid the hard identity choice of bloc alignment internationally and exclusive political choices domestically.*" "Scientific Socialist Regimes in Africa: Political Differentiation, Avoidance, and Unawareness," in Rosberg and Callaghy, *Socialism in Sub-Saharan Africa,* p. 144. Italics in original. A similar point is made in Crawford Young, *Ideology and Development in Africa* (New Haven, Conn.: Yale University Press, 1982), p. 26.

32. Laitin, "Somalia's Military Government," pp. 200-201.

33. Hajjar, "The Jamahiriya Experiment," pp. 193–200.

34. Young, *Ideology and Development in Africa,* p. 76.

8. Security and Stability Implications of Ethnicity and Religious Factors

Victor A. Olorunsola
with Dan Muhwezi

Introduction

The peoples of Subsaharan African states are divided horizontally by language, culture, and religion. In some states, these divisions remained subterranean during the colonial era. On the eve of independence most political leaders viewed political independence as a prerequisite to political and economic development of African states. However, despite these hopes, the postindependence period saw the emergence of internal differences, conflicts, and tensions over the distribution of public goods and services. In some countries, these degenerated into violent repression, widespread massacre of civilian populations, assassinations, and civil wars. Thus, sustaining a viable political environment that could help the authority of the state structures and foster the shared interests of citizens remained a challenge to most African states.

Many factors may contribute to the lack of stability in African states: economic problems and military intervention, to mention only two. Nevertheless, inter-ethnic and sometimes religious conflicts can be seen as major sources of disagreement. These conflicts present a delicate fault line in the distribution of political power and public goods in Africa. Although ethnicity and religion can be effective sources of support for leaders, especially in the context of the politics of decolonization in Africa, both have tended to make state security extremely vulnerable in the postindependence period. It may be that in spite of outward appearances, the trend in African politics is towards a zero-sum game in the midst of heterogeneous and pluralistic political culture. As some actors in the political sphere are eliminated, they are inclined to resort to primordial communal identities and/or seemingly sympathetic foreign governments for redress. This behavior has tended to destabilize a number of countries. Moreover, it may be that the extreme measures used by national governments to eliminate centrifugal tendencies have, in some cases, created conditions that have made dissatisfaction of some groups perpetual and violence and instability almost inevitable.

Throughout this chapter, the term *ethnicity* will be used to connote the defensive and parochial tendencies that arise out of conflict or competitive struggle for scarce resources between ethnic groups.[1]

The Nature of the Problem

Ethnicity has played a salient role in determining the acquisition of political power and the distribution and redistribution of public goods in Africa. Unfortunately, by its very nature ethnicity cannot encompass all the peoples in a heterogeneous state. Ethnic pluralism is a common aspect of modern African states. To the extent that certain groups feel impotent, dispossessed, and neglected in the distribution of power and public goods, they are likely to experience considerable frustration. If such frustrations are not creatively contained or assuaged, they can—and in the case of African countries they tend to—result in crises, violent clashes, or other manifestations of instability.

The pity is that an unstable state cannot pursue development policies systematically and effectively. Furthermore, an unstable country leaves itself open to manipulation by third parties and foreign governments. In short, ethnic and religious conflicts can cause instability that can result in the maximization of state insecurity. In some cases, it can lead to the destruction of political order.

The problem of security in Africa has manifested itself in many levels of instability and in many types of internal strife. Security problems have surfaced in the form of demands for self-determination, territorial claims, and crises in political leadership. The end results in some cases have been civil wars, rebellions, assassinations, military coups, and the attendant large numbers of refugees.

Historical Context

Today no single African state can claim deeply rooted uninterrupted political traditions. All the states are the relatively recent creations of the 1884–1885 Berlin Conference, which partitioned Africa among European nations. Unfortunately, the geopolitical boundaries that resulted from this conference did not take into account traditional boundaries—both social and political—between ethnic groups. To take one example, an agreement was made between Belgium and Britain that the Uganda-Congo (now Zaire) border would be along "Meridian 30."[2] As a result of such straight-line policies, a number of ethnic groups were divided. A few instances will illustrate this point: Somalis were divided between Kenya and Somalia, the Ewe between Togo and Ghana, and the Yoruba between Nigeria and Dahomey. On the other hand, ethnic groups with different values were brought together. In Nigeria, for example, of the three main ethnic groups brought together, the Yorubas cherished a traditional system of government built on principles of limited monarchy, the Ibos had a system of government that could be likened to representative democracy today, and the traditional Hausa-Fulani held theocratic values.[3] In Uganda, the areas of Buganda, Toro, Ankole, Bunyoro, and the territory of Busoga to a large extent held monarchical values, whereas the northern ethnic groups had values that were republican in outlook. These illustrations show the heterogeneity of the colonial states. The values of some ethnic groups were perhaps incompatible.

The main instruments used to maintain civil order in the colonial state were force and indirect rule. The indirect rule, under the guise of protecting the traditional heritage of various ethnic groups, effectively kept such groups separate. As modernization during the colonial period tended to concentrate around the capital city, imbalances in development resulted among different ethnic groups, districts, and regions. For example, the Baganda in Uganda were exposed to better opportunities than any other groups and the South as a whole was more exposed to development opportunities than the North. Furthermore, some ethnic groups in the colonial state were regarded as "warriors" and entrusted with the instruments of defending the colonial state. Similar instances of regional imbalance, differential exposure to westernization, and unequal modernization can be noted in other countries, such as Nigeria and Sudan. These differences, although they helped the colonial administration, created or sustained hostility and suspicion between ethnic groups.

At the time of independence, it became very difficult for politicians to develop organizations that extended beyond ethnic or religious bases. In Zaire, almost every major ethnic group formed its own party.[4] This was also the case in Nigeria. As independence drew nearer, it became absolutely necessary for each group to write into the constitution as many concessions as possible. Later, these concessions and other political arrangements established by the colonial regimes became "critical points of reference or parameters of later struggles."[5] Yet against this background of arbitrary boundaries and heterogeneous ethnic groups in the newly independent states, the Organization of African Unity (OAU) in 1963 agreed to uphold the existing boundaries and defend the sovereignty and territorial integrity of those countries already independent.

Nigeria

The demands for self-determination in Nigeria, which ended in the Biafra war, were not new. There had been considerable rivalry between the Hausa-Fulani in the North, the Ibos in the East, and the Yorubas in the West. As noted earlier, because the colonial administration did not implement its development programs uniformly, at the close of the colonial era the South was better equipped with modern skills than the North. In the South itself, the Ibos were seemingly better equipped with these skills than the Yorubas. When the Ibos began to migrate to other areas in search of better jobs, other ethnic groups, especially the Hausa-Fulani, expressed fears of unequal opportunity. This began a race of ethnic security and intensification of ethnic hostilities.[6]

Ethnic and geoethnic parochialism deepened as elites of various groups competed to inherit political power. In 1950, for example, the northern delegation to the constitutional conference in Ibadan threatened to secede if it was not granted equal representation with the South. In 1953, the Western region made the same threat on issues of revenue and the carving out of Lagos as the federal territory. Despite these parochial tendencies, a precarious balance between the South and the North was maintained: The South controlled economic power, and the North controlled political power in population terms.[7] The North-South tension continued to build up, however, and in 1956 culminated in the Kano riots. These riots happened when delegates of two southern parties—the National Congress of Nigerian Citizens (NCNC) and the Action Group (AG)—were campaigning for self-government in the North.

The alliance between NCNC (predominantly Ibo) and the Northern Peoples Congress (NPC) in the general election of 1959 managed to defeat the western-based AG but failed to narrow the North-South gap. The political influence of the NCNC was gradually eroded, and the conflict on census figures between 1962 and 1963 loosened the bond of the already tenuous alliance. The East and the North turned to the West for alliances and managed to effectuate—or encourage—a split of the AG into two factions. The elections that followed were characterized by extreme violence, especially in the West. Campaign permits were not issued to the opposing parties; arbitrary arrests, wrongful imprisonments, assaults, and killings became campaign strategies. The riots that followed the elections in the West gradually extended to other areas. Interregional disputes at the federal level and internal dissent within the regions led to widespread civil disorder. The politicians were simply not willing to compromise their primordial priorities. However, the North skillfully managed to retain its hold on political power.

The executors of the January 1966 coup were mainly Ibo officers. In their attempt to stamp out ethnicity and regionalism, they were caught in the same trap. The sardauna of Sokoto, the northern secular and religious leader; Tafawa Balewa, the prime minister; Chief Akintola, leader of the western faction that allied with the NPC in 1964; and many senior northern officers were assassinated. Furthermore, decree number 39 of 1966 abolished regions and the federal structure and introduced a provincial system of administration. It seemed clear to the northern elites in particular that this was a blatant attempt by the South to end the northern political influence. The North reacted, and in the northern cities the lives and property of many southerners, especially Ibos, were destroyed.

The July 1966 coup was mainly an attempt by the North to regain the threatened political influence. A very significant number of Ibos living in the North lost their lives and property. This purge caused the Ibo survivors to shift to the Eastern Region, since there was no apparent protection from the government. Finally, the Eastern Region opted to secede and declared itself the Independent State of Biafra.

Attempts to achieve a legitimate government structure had broken down. Inter-ethnic violence to a large extent challenged the validity or existence of the Nigerian state. The East had lost its share of political influence and could not easily trust a negotiated agreement amidst the casualties inflicted on its people. Thus, from the Ibos' perspective, the government as constituted could no longer provide security for their lives and property. Self-preservation became a main driving force of the secession decision of May 30, 1967. It is also important to note that in May 1966 Chief Awolowo had stated that if the Eastern Region was allowed to secede, then the West and Lagos would follow its steps.

Thus it could be argued that the Nigeria-Biafra war resulted from various intentions to provide security, the federal government's intention to protect the territorial integrity of the Nigerian state, and the Ibos' attempt to provide security for people faced with consequences of rampant ethnicity. The execution of the war necessitated the courting of various powers who could supply arms. Although no permanent changes in alliances resulted from the deals dictated by the search for arms, it could be argued that had the Soviet Union been more skillful in its diplomacy and the Nigerian military rulers less skillful, the results might have been different.

The successive Nigerian military administrations took steps to curb the powers of subnational states. One such step was the Murtala Mohammed administration's creation of more states, bringing the total to nineteen. Increasing the number of states or regions worked on the principle of (1) weakening the subnational states (especially in financial matters) and strengthening the federal government to ensure effective control, and (2) suppressing ethnic identity.

This notwithstanding, Nigeria seems to be committed, more than most African states that have had political upheavals, to the politics of compromise and to be more keen to utilize the diversity of its people to the advantage of the state. The Electoral Decree of 1977 and the new Federal Constitution represent a serious attempt to accommodate ethnic diversity and cultural pluralism without allowing them to result in unfair discrimination and to endanger unity and authority of the state. Among steps taken to balance the "tyranny of skills" of the South and the "tyranny of population" of the North is the requirement that political parties and appointments to government positions reflect the "federal character" of the Nigerian state. Party symbols may have no ethnic or religious connotations.

It is conceivable that such a step may help the central government penetrate to the local level, but political cleavages ascribed to such factors as religion and ethnicity cannot be removed by a mere stroke of a pen; much more is required. Indeed, despite the efforts of the central government, the North-South dichotomy still lingers. The South has already expressed concern over the nineteen-regions arrangement that gives it nine; yet an equal number of states would just duplicate the same old barrier in a different fashion. Furthermore, the parties have not yet transcended regional barriers; the Nigerian Peoples Party is seen as the old Ibo-based National Congress of Nigerian Citizens, the National Party of Nigeria as the Hausa-Fulani–based Northern Peoples Congress, and the Unity Party of Nigeria as a replica of the old Yoruba-based Action Group.

Religion is a two-edged sword. On the one hand, in the past it tended to increase the solidarity of various religious groups. On the other hand, recent religious violence in three Nigerian cities in the North—Kano, Kaduna, and Maidugri—shows that sects within one religious group can seriously affect the stability of a region or country. The northern part of Nigeria is predominantly Muslim, but with various distinct sects of Islam. One of these sects, the Maitatsine, has been held responsible for the violence. It is reported that about one thousand people were killed in religious violence in October 1982 in the three cities, following the amnesty of about the same number of Maitatsine followers who had been imprisoned since 1981.[8]

The Sudan

The Sudanese War, another tragic event, affected the African continent for seventeen years. The southern Sudanese have described it as "a struggle against internal colonialism."[9] The causes of this war can be explained in terms of cultural diversity, ethnic mixture, different colonial experience, and geography. The North is predominantly Arab, whereas the South is negroid. Bonds of religion and language have tended to tie the northern part of Sudan to the Arab world; the South is tied to Subsaharan Africa. Arab expansionist attempts are not new, but in precolonial times their cultural assimilationist conquests were inhibited by environmental barriers and armed resistance. With the coming of the British, all forms of Arab culture were suppressed, and the North and the South were administered as separate entities. The system of indirect rule, even though it preserved traditional structures of authority in the South, had little to offer in terms of development, especially in the South. The North's dominance was reinforced with education and other forms of modernity. This created a large elite in the North equipped with political and administrative skills that were lacking in the South. At the time of decolonization the northern political parties were better equipped, and they effectively articulated the politics of one Sudan. The southern party took a defensive stand and worked against unity with the North. On the eve of independence—against the hopes and intentions of the South—Britain, Egypt, and North Sudan decided to incorporate the South into the future independent Sudan. The representatives of the South were ignored at various preindependence conferences. Furthermore, demands for federalism and safeguards against possible tyranny of the North were refused. The protests of the British administrators against this arrangement were not taken into account. Given the modern skill disparity it was not surprising that the "Sudanization" of eight hundred senior administrative jobs netted only six positions for the South.

After independence, a systematic attempt was made to Arabize and Islamize the South. Cultural assimilation and discrimination became the order of the day. The Arabic language was made a requirement in schools, and Christian missionaries were first phased out, then were finally expelled in 1964. To the southern Sudanese the issue became one of self-preservation from a cultural perspective, because they were totally opposed to these attempts. In general, structural reforms hampered political development and limited the southern political influence. This led to the formation of the Anya Nya in 1963 and intensification of guerrilla warfare until 1972.

It has been argued that it was mainly the cultural expansionist tendencies, reinforced by the Sudan government's continued identification of the Sudan as an Arab-Muslim state, that spurred the South to wage guerrilla warfare for seventeen years.[10] The 1972 Addis Ababa Agreement put a stop to the war and recognized the distinctiveness of the South. However, the struggle of the South as a complete entity in independent Sudan seems incomplete. Some northern politicians look at the South's autonomy with envy; some—especially Pan-Arabists—argue that regional autonomy may lead to the Balkanization of the Sudan; others think that the North may be subsidizing eventual South Sudan secession by helping it to become economically viable now. On the other hand, the southerners believe that the northerners have been trying to sabotage the institutionalization of autonomy granted by the Addis Ababa Agreement in 1972. The agreement granted specific powers and functions to the Southern Region, and granted regional autonomy to the South within a united Sudan. Legislative power in the South is exercised by the People's Regional Assembly, charged with such duties as "preservation of public order, internal security, efficient administration and the development of the Southern Region in cultural, economic, and social fields."[11] Its legislation, however, must conform to national plans. National defense, foreign affairs, currency and coinage, communication and telecommunications, customs and foreign trade, nationality and immigration, economic and social planning, educational planning, and public audit are functions of the central government. Amendments to the law that protects the regional government are totally a matter for the South, as it requires a three-quarters affirmative vote in the People's Regional Assembly and a two-thirds majority in a referendum held in the three provinces in the South.

The trend seems to suggest that the South may not hold to its autonomy for long. Article 5 of the Addis Ababa Agreement allows English to be the principal language of the South and Arabic to be the official language of the Sudan. Since 1972, however, Arabic has been widely used in schools at the expense of other languages. Further, Sudan has continued to identify itself as an Arab and Muslim state in spite of explicit provisions in both the Addis Ababa Agreement and the constitution. Arabization and Islamization attempts have surfaced again. The recent merger pact signed with

Egypt leaves no doubt that the Sudan government has moved the state closer to the Arab world.[12] If this pact succeeds, the South may have to accept the terms set by the North, since this pact will increase the military strength of the Sudan government. Alternatively the pact may force the South to renew guerrilla warfare.

In 1980 there were attempts to redraw and alter the North-South boundary. In the new map, first of all, the oil areas of Bentui District were incorporated into the North. The South condemned this move as unconstitutional, and demonstrations followed in the South. The commission of inquiry that was appointed to look into this matter recommended that boundaries be left intact. Secondly, the location of the oil refinery in the North instead of Bentui in the South resulted in student demonstrations and serious protest. The South was made to accept this decision.

There have been attempts to redivide the South itself and to amend the constitution to enable the government to carry out this redivision. A number of groups have petitioned Khartoum to redivide the South. The Blanda and Dogo in particular have asked to have their own regions or to be put with non-Dinka ethnic groups. Lagu in particular has been campaigning to divide the South into two or three regions so as to end the "Dinka domination" in the South.[13] These demands have found support among the northern critics of the southern autonomy and have equally attracted President Nimiery, though most of the demands have been withdrawn from public debate.

There are additional potentially dangerous areas of contention. First, there has been inadequate representation of the South in the national decision-making apparatus. Second, the central bureaucracy is predominantly northern. Third, there is a widespread and growing feeling of economic deprivation relative to those who are in control. Fourth, fears of possible cultural assimilation are increasing. Fifth, the Sudan-Egypt merger may have generated among the southern Sudanese a further loss of bargaining power that they thought the Addis Ababa Agreement provided them.

The growing protests and reported cases of "lawlessness," as well as the alleged rebirth of secession movements by the former Anya Nya fighters in the South, bodes ill for stability and security. One may wonder whether the South will reach a point where its perception of belonging to a state that does not regard the welfare of southerners as equal to that of northerners will lead it to embark upon a desperate course.

It would appear that the Sudanese state is in a precarious position. It remains to be seen whether the 1972 Addis Ababa Agreement will continue to hold legitimacy for both the North and the South. To the extent that the South regards this agreement as its social contract with the state, this is critical. Already some people in the South are asking the old question of whether or not the South is part of Sudan.[14] Futhermore, one could interpret Nimiery's call for assistance from Egypt and the United States as a clear recognition of his and/or the state's vulnerability in the South.

The southerners see their demand for self-determination as necessitated by Arabic-Islamic expansionism. One suspects that the North sees the call for assistance as the state's obligation to protect itself from unwarranted intervention from Libya. To the southerners, Egypt presumably is a foreign and perhaps an unwelcome state. To the North, Libya and Qaddafi are unwelcome. The point is that religion and culture have had destabilizing effects in the Sudan that, more ominously, may increase in the future. If this is the case, either fundamental security problems exist or the potential for such in considerable.

Uganda

Uganda offers examples of how both religion and ethnicity, if not properly contained, can destabilize a country. Uganda is characterized by few—but relatively heterogeneous—ethnic groups. The politics among these groups have been those of competition and intrigue. The South, and Buganda in particular, was exposed more to Western culture. The northern Ugandans were thought to possess great martial abilities; hence they constituted the bulk of the army. Most ethnic issues have tended to be interpreted in terms of the North-South dichotomy. Although there may be a marked distinction between these groups, within each group internal subdivisions exist. For example, in the South all ethnic groups oppose Buganda and have at times allied with the North to defeat Buganda. Within Buganda itself religion has been a dividing factor; at times, Catholic Buganda allied with other Catholics outside Buganda in political issues. Despite similar divisions in the North, it has been able to exploit the North-South cleavage more effectively; this has helped the North maintain political power.

The "Buganda question" has affected Uganda's stability to a large extent. Towards the end of colonial rule the idea of forging a nation in which Buganda would be part was perhaps inconceivable to the local population, particularly because the 1900 agreement between Buganda and Britain made Buganda a state within a state. In addition, Buganda had "traditional enemies." During the process of colonial integration, Buganda had assisted the British to subdue Bunyoro, and as a result, Buganda was awarded part of Bunyoro's territory. This territory—known as the "lost counties"—became a thorny issue in the national politics after independence.[15] Furthermore the Baganda had worked as British agents to spread the colonial gospel in Uganda, a process that has often been called Buganda subimperialism. Thus Buganda felt insecure in an independent Uganda and in 1950 sought unilateral independence. This resulted in the deportation of the Kabaka in 1953.[16]

Although the 1955 Anglo-Buganda Agreement strengthened the Kabaka's position, it did not provide a satisfactory solution to Buganda's feeling of insecurity. In fact, the Kabaka was made a constitutional monarch. Thus, the people of Buganda were hesitant about entrusting the destiny of their country to the hands of inexperienced leaders.[17] This skepticism was further aggravated by the vigorous opposition of the nationalist parties to Buganda's unilateral moves.

The manner in which President Nkrumah dealt with the Ashanti king in Ghana did not make the people of Buganda feel comfortable. Accordingly the Lukiko (Buganda's parliament) submitted a memorandum to Her Majesty the Queen terminating British protection in 1960: "Public announcements made on various occasions by people likely to be leaders of future Uganda are not conducive to unity as Her Majesty's government envisages it. In order to avoid another 'Katanga' in this country immediately after independence, Buganda has decided and is determined to go it alone."[18] These demands were rejected. Although the Lukiko declared Buganda independent on December 31, 1960—to take effect on January 1, 1961—nothing materialized.

In 1961 a predominantly Catholic Democratic party (DP), headed by a Muganda, won the self-government elections. This seemed to be a threat to the Mengo establishment. In a bid to stop DP from forming the independence government, the elites within Buganda and the Uganda People's Congress (UPC) secretariat worked hand in hand to enable Buganda to form its own party—Kabaka Yekka (KY—King alone). Subsequently they formed a UPC-KY alliance that granted Kabaka the presidency of the country.[19] With that arrangement and federal status, Buganda's future position and its Kabaka seemed secure.

The political issues at that time, like those of the "lost counties" between Buganda and Bunyoro, required a neutral central government; yet Kabaka's dual positions as president of Uganda and king of Buganda were irreconcilable. Furthermore, the UPC parliamentary group broke down into factions along the "Bantu-Nilotic" dimension, with each seeking domestic military support. These and other related issues culminated in the 1966 crisis. The steps taken to "contain" centrifugal forces, such as the arrest of the five "Bantu" ministers and the dismissal of Kabaka from the presidency, were labeled unconstitutional and considered a breach of the contract upon which Buganda's future depended. Thus, Buganda's local parliament declared Buganda independent for the second time and requested the central government to remove its capital from "Buganda's soil." The events that followed, such as the attack on Kabaka's palace, were punctuated by extreme violence. The security situation deteriorated, and emergency laws were declared that lasted until the Amin coup in 1971. We should observe that since 1966 Uganda's security situation has been rather precarious.

After the 1966 crisis, Obote attempted to centralize the polity. He abolished kingdoms and federalism, divided Buganda into districts, and sought to remove "Buganda" from the map of Uganda. Although it is difficult to pinpoint the main cause of the coup that brought Amin to power in 1971, both Amin and Obote split the predominantly northern army along ethnic lines. The insecurity ushered in partly by Obote's radical moves led to tightened security measures that clearly carried ethnic connotations. The resulting overreliance on the military created ideal conditions for Amin's coup d'etat.[20] In 1973 the military government increased the number of districts from eighteen to thirty-three, and in 1980 the Binaisa administration changed the names of most districts, presumably because they had ethnic connotations.

Dating back to 1884 when the Muslims and Christian missionaries competed for control of Buganda, religion has been an important political-cleavage pattern in Uganda. In the independence politics, Catholics in Buganda formed a political party—DP. They felt that this would enable them to participate more effectively in the public-goods allocation, hitherto dominated by Protestants. Then the two Protestant parties, UPC and KY (though radically different in other aspects), forged an alliance to counteract the rise of Catholic elites. To the extent that the North and the South formed the bulk of UPC, religion prevailed over ethnicity.

Between 1971 and 1979 the Amin administration, which was predominantly Muslim, seemingly engaged in a systematic liquidation of Christians, especially Protestants, and Langi and Acholi ethnic groups. This culminated in the death of the archbishop of the Church of Uganda. It is not clear whether the motive was ethnic or religious, but it is clear that Amin attempted to Islamize a Christian-dominated country. Uganda was made a member of the Organization of Muslim States purportedly under Qaddafi's design.

A persistent characteristic of politics in Uganda has been the confrontation between Buganda and the central government. It has been argued that one cannot effectively rule Uganda without the tacit consent of Buganda. While this may appear an overstatement and an oversimplification of facts, it is conceivable that if Obote had designed a formula to contain or pacify Buganda, Uganda might not have gone through such a long period of instability. But to the extent that Buganda's political outlook has been largely parochial, sooner or later the confrontation with the central government was inevitable.

The return to civilian rule in Uganda on multi-party principles of democracy raised hope for stability and security in a country that had been ravaged by military intervention. However, current politics in Uganda seem to echo problems of the past. The 1980 elections revived the old parties (UPC and DP) with their old "wounds." The only new parties were the Uganda Patriotic Movement (UPM) and the Conservative party (CP). Although both UPC and DP are "national parties," Buganda voted as a group for DP and DP did not win a single seat in the North. Thus Buganda's subnationalism was to a large extent revived. The UPM contends that UPC rigged elections, then formed a guerrilla wing that has found support within Buganda. This has made the security of the state rather precarious. Once again the security measures being taken, as in the past, are taking on ethnic connotations. The North, and especially the Langi and Acholi ethnic groups, now dominate the army. Buganda and UPM may not radically bring changes in the government, but their dissatisfaction affects the country's stability and perpetuates Obote's dependence on Tanzania[21] for his and the state's security.

The Horn of Africa

Ethiopia is faced with war on two fronts, Eritrea and the Ogaden, and its position is to a large extent legitimized by the OAU principle of territorial integrity. Eritrea is fighting for "self-determination," while the Somalis in East Ethiopia are fighting to join Somalia. This war has attracted the superpowers and Israel for strategic reasons and Arab states for both strategic and religious ones.

Until 1962, Eritrea was in a federal relationship with the Ethiopian Empire. This relationship had been drawn up under the auspices of the United Nations (UN). Ethiopia found a number of the provisions in the federal constitution "unworkable." Furthermore, the constitution had made Tigrinya and Arabic the official languages of Eritrea; this appeared problematic to the Ethiopian government, since it wanted to use Amharic as the main linguistic tool for national integration of its people.[22] Thus, through an allegedly rigged vote by the Eritrean Assembly in 1962, the federal act was dissolved, and Eritrea became the fourteenth province of the Ethiopian Empire.

Eritrea is predominantly Muslim, and there are accounts that Muslims are being harassed by the Christians there. The war between Eritrea and Ethiopia almost became an extension of the Arab-Israel war. Israel helped Ethiopia, largely because a breakaway Eritrea would make it more difficult for Israel to have access to the southern end of the Red Sea. The Eritrean reliance on Arab support is strategically inclined to stress the religious dimension of the war. It should be observed, however, that both Muslim and Christian Eritreans are fighting Ethiopia. After the overthrow of the emperor in 1974, Eritrean liberation fighters expected the new military rulers to accept a negotiated settlement. However, Ethiopian military leaders have convinced themselves that they need, among other things, the Eritrean seaports of Massawa and Assab. So the struggle goes on and the manipulation of ethnicity and religion—and the attendant insecurity and instability—persists.

In addition to Eritrea, Ethiopia has four other major ethnic groups: Amharas, Oromos, Tigres, and Somalis. The Amhara ethnic group has been ruling Ethiopia. The others have each formed a liberation front to work for self-determination. For the purpose of this analysis we shall concentrate on the Somalis in the Ogaden.

Since its independence in 1960, Somalia has pursued irredentist policies and encouraged separatism among Somalis living outside its present boundaries. The Somali nationhood embraces all Somalis living in Somalia, Ethiopia, Kenya, and Djibouti. The Ogaden question, or problem, is essentially an ethnic conflict worsened by "diplomatic mismanagement."[23] Some believe that it began with the British, who allowed Emperor Menelik to make vast territorial claims as they sought favors. After World War II, Bevan, the British foreign secretary, attempted to redraw the boundaries in the Horn but was not able to because of Russia's suspicions.[24]

In 1960, when the Somali state was born, it began to fight for the Somali nation. Somalia began its efforts in the Organization of African Unity. However, OAU's position of respect for boundaries as expressed in Article 3 of its charter and noninterference as expressed in Article 6 favored Ethiopia. Somalia began to build an army with USSR aid in 1969. In 1977 Somalia supported the Western Somalia Liberation Front against Ethiopia. The Soviets, however, then began to support Ethiopia in hope of building a loose socialist confederation in the Horn of Africa. The major powers have managed to deliver weapons for the conflict. Somalia may be unable to sustain the war as the refugee population increases and as tensions between North and South Somalia build up. It may become expedient for Somalia to refashion its policy. Again, the Horn demonstrates the potential of ethnicity and religion as tools of instability.

Central Africa

The Congo of the 1960s offers a classic case of the despicable opportunities that ethnicity offers to the foreign powers interested in destabilization of a country. Almost every major tribe or ethnic group in the Congo had a social organization, which was later converted into a political party. Joseph Kasavubu rose to the post of president through the Bakongo tribal association, and Tshombe's party was equally parochial. Only Lumumba's Mouvement National Congolais could be described to some extent as national or nontribal.

The military mutinies of July 5, 1960, gave Tshombe an opportunity to declare Katanga independent; within a year South Kasai, Kivu, and oriental districts threatened to secede. Belgium seemingly heeded Tshombe's call for aid; thus King Baudouin is said to have declared that: "entire ethnic groups headed by men of honesty and worth . . . ask us to help them construct their independence. . . . It is our duty to respond favorably."[25] It can be argued that Belgium for all intents and purposes was behind the moves taken by Tshombe. It should also be noted that Prime Minister Lumumba's expulsion by President Kasavubu was purportedly under U.S. design. Lumumba was later imprisoned and assassinated; the UN peace-keeping force that he had invited could not provide personal security for such a high official! The tribal rebellions of 1964 ushered anarchy into the whole territory.

In 1965 the military took over the government. It has been argued that the impasse reached in the aftermath of the rebellions appeared to dictate a strategy of cultural demobilization. Accordingly President Mobutu introduced centralized reforms. He attempted to eliminate all social organizations, he redrew the boundaries and reduced the number of provinces from twenty-one to six, and he appointed provincial commissioners outside their areas of origin to reduce the chances of their using the instruments of the state to appeal to their ethnic bases and build power around themselves. He also abolished the post of prime minister, which had been an acute source of instability in 1960 and 1965.[26]

From a religious perspective, President Mobutu tried to deflate the mystique surrounding the Christian faith by making it mandatory to use local names. But religion has not been a serious factor in Zaire politics, so if Mobutu's strategy is to contain the presumed negative impact of religion in the process of national integration or to harness its contribution to instability, the energies may have been unnecessary. However, it could be argued that the strategy is directed at the use of symbols and is aimed at providing the new state and government requisite emotive support.

In Rwanda and Burundi continued ethnic confrontations between Hutu and Tutsi have claimed many lives and destroyed property. Chad, too, has suffered intense conflicts based on ethnic and religious differences, with factional leaders using private armies to compete for power. It remains to be seen whether President Habré can now return peace and security to the country. In Kenya, there are accounts that the Kikuyu have been at loggerheads with the Luos; these are the two dominant ethnic groups there. Political power and influence have immensely rewarded the Kikuyus compared to any other ethnic group in Kenya. The Africanization of civil-service jobs in Kenya came to be termed "Kikuyuization" because of the unbalanced distribution of these jobs among ethnic groups.[27] Like the Nilotic group in Uganda, the Kikuyu-dominated government has at times employed coercive tactics to entrench its political influence. After the assassination of Mboya the enraged Luos went on a rampage, looting and destroying property of the Kikuyu in Luo areas. The Kikuyu retaliated by taking a "maumau" oath, an act that symbolizes Kikuyu solidarity, thus leading to a wave of counterviolence and coercion.[28]

In a nutshell, these acts show the climate in which African politics operate. They show the ethnic jealousies that are easily manipulated by elites who feel economic and political deprivation relative to those in power or in proportion to the population or wealth of their areas. So salient is ethnicity and/or religion in Africa's heterogeneous societies that groups excluded from power and resource allocation feel compelled to utilize ethnicity and religion as power bases for support or survival. In some instances those in power may feel so insecure as to disallow any expression of disapproval (including constitutional ones) by such excluded groups. Alternatively, the ethnic groups not in power may feel uncomfortable within the political order to the extent that they may become refugees and exiles. This is a serious problem in Africa. Needless to say, such a situation is not conducive to state security in the long run (in the short run it may be by virtue of eliminating the most disaffected from the immediate political calculus). In some cases, this has led to invasion attempts, as in Zaire in 1977–1978 and Uganda in 1971 and 1978.

It is largely the blatant attempt of many African leaders—who, aware of the heterogeneous societies they lead, pursue maximum state authority and/or personal rule at all costs—that has put into motion what may well be a vicious cycle of instability or insecurity. The more mobilizational and repressive the state is in the pursuit of domestic security, the more convinced communal groups are likely to be that primordial strategies are the only sensible option available to them.

A number of states have tried to gauge some "ethnic arithmetic" to contain the ethnic factor in politics. After independence, President Mugabe attempted to apply the politics of reconciliation in order to build a stable Zimbabwe. In an attempt to accommodate the existing diversity, the white population was given two cabinet posts and the opposition party (Zimbabwe African People's Union—ZAPU-PF) four seats. However Nkomo, the leader of ZAPU-PF, was sacked from his cabinet post in February 1982 on charges of subversive activities. This has widened the gap between the two factions of the Patriotic Front and is gradually alienating the Ndebele-Kalanga ethnic groups who make up Nkomo's stronghold. The removal of Nkomo may gradually shift Zimbabwe to a one-party state. Mugabe can rule without Nkomo, but—taking into account the circumstances in which Zimbabwe's independence was obtained—Mugabe needs Nkomo for military and political reasons and especially for national stability. If Mugabe can design a formula that would incorporate Nkomo's ethnic political base, the immediate threat to the stability and security of Africa's youngest nation would not be the internal ethnic issues but rather South Africa. In the absence of such a formula, Zimbabwe is extremely vulnerable to the machinations of South Africa.

Conclusion

The intent of this chapter has been to examine religious and ethnic factors as they impact upon the stability and security of African states. On balance, ethnicity appears to be the more manifest. We have tried to show that ethnic heterogeneity in some countries is not conducive to stability. Furthermore, intense competition for power and public goods and the often resulting maldistribution of those scarce resources have created conditions that may easily lead to conflict. However, Tanzania, with over 125 ethnic groups, has managed to maintain relative stability. Tanzania's experience may mean that the multiplicity of ethnic groups and lack of a dominant group in a state can be a blessing and a condition for stability. But the examples of the Baganda in Uganda, Hausa-Fulani in Nigeria, Bakongo in Zaire, and the Kikuyu in Kenya indicate that where major ethnic groups exist, group consciousness becomes strong and may become a destabilizing factor if the groups feel deprived of certain benefits and rights that they believe should accrue to them. Moreover, while the creation of many states may seem to contribute to stability of a nation, caution should be exercised in the redrawing of boundaries in order to avoid creating new minorities and majorities.

The first few years of independence in most states of Africa and the six years after the Addis Ababa Agreement in 1972 between Anya Nya and the Sudan government suggest that what is necessary for stability is not a total suppression of primordial attachments in heterogeneous societies. Rather, creative formulations are needed that are directed at the establishment and enshrining of equity among domestic groups in the distribution of power and public goods.

Sir Arthur Lewis, the Nobel laureate, noted that "the fundamental problem in Africa is neither economic policy nor foreign policy, but the creation of nations out of heterogeneous people."[29] It would be incorrect, nevertheless, to argue that Africa's security and stability problems derive solely from ethnic and religious conflicts. To the extent that ethnicity is ubiquitous and fairly pervasive in Africa's domestic affairs, both ethnic and religious conflicts offer enormous opportunities for those foreign governments bent on destabilizing African governments.

The existence of an Africa plagued by ethnic conflicts and religious skirmishes, in an international system characterized by factionalism and the blind pursuits of selfish interests by first- and second-rate power, is most discomforting. Indeed, it is exceedingly dangerous. African governments, of necessity, must consider this a number-one problem if they intend to keep their independence and lead all their peoples to attain the benefits of development.

Notes

1. B. Hodeler, *Africa Today* (New York: Marathon & Co., 1978), p. 53.

2. Congo-Uganda-Sudan boundary correspondence, Entebbe Archives, Confidential File No. 30. See also Tarsus Kabwegyere, *The Politics of State Formation* (Nairobi, Kenya: East African Bureau, 1974), pp. 55–66.

3. See Victor Olorunsola, *The Politics of Cultural Subnationalism in Africa* (New York: Doubleday and Co., 1972), pp. 10–11.

4. In Zaire, Association des Bakongo pour L'Unification, L'Expansion et la Defense de la Langue Kikongo was the party of the Bakongo through which Joseph Kasavubu rose to eminence as the country's president. The Association des Baluba du Katanga (Balu Bakat) was the party for the Baluba. Tshombe's political party—the Confederation des Associations Tribales du Katanga (CONAKAT)—was equally ethnic bound. Forty-four parties are said to have registered during the 1960 independence elections; see Bob Scott "Another Rescue Operation: Zaire," *Africa Report* (March–April 1979), p. 16.

5. Henry Bienen, "The State and Ethnicity: Integrative Formulas in Africa," in Donald Rothchild and Victor Olorunsola, eds., *State Versus Ethnic Claims: African Policy Dilemma* (Boulder, Colo.: Westview Press, 1983), p. 106.

6. Olorunsola, *The Politics of Cultural Subnationalism*, pp. 22–23.

7. J. Isawa Elaigwu and Victor Olorunsola, "Federalism and the Politics of Compromise in Nigeria," in Rothchild and Olorunsola, *State Versus Ethnic Claims*, p. 285.

8. *Africa News* 19, no. 22 (Nov. 29, 1982). The Maitatsine sect recognizes Malam Marwa, who was killed in the 1980 religious uprising, as the prophet of Allah instead of Mohammed.

9. Dunstan Wai, "Geoethnicity and the Margin of Autonomy in the Sudan," in Rothchild and Olorunsola, *State Versus Ethnic Claims*, p. 306.

10. Ibid., p. 309.

11. Ibid., p. 397.

12. *Africa News* 19, no. 16 (October 18, 1982), p. 10.

13. *Africa Confidential* 22, no. 24 (July 1, 1981).

14. Under this agreement, farmers from Egypt are expected to be allowed to settle in Sudan. Some northern politicians are not in favor of this pact. In the South, southern Sudanese politicians are reported to have strongly resisted the move and petitioned against it to a number of international agencies. See *Africa News* 19, no. 16 (October 18, 1982), p. 10.

15. Nelson Kasfir in Olorunsola, *The Politics of Cultural Subnationalism*, p. 88. See also Kabwagyere, *The Politics of State Formation*, pp. 77–79.

16. Grace Ibingira, *African Upheavals Since Independence* (Boulder, Colo.: Westview Press, 1980), pp. 25–26. See also David Apter, *The Political Kingdom in Uganda* (Princeton, N.J.: Princeton University Press, 1967), pp. 285–300.

17. Ibingira, *African Upheavals Since Independence*, pp. 25–26.

18. David Apter, *The Political Kingdom in Uganda*, p. 485. See also Ibingira, *African Upheavals Since Independence*, p. 26.

19. Ibingira, *African Upheavals Since Independence*, p. 111.

20. Crawford Young, *The Politics of Cultural Pluralism* (Madison: University of Wisconsin Press, 1976), pp. 266–270. See also John Agami, *The Roots of Political Crisis in Uganda* (Copenhagen, Denmark: H. P. Tryk Kastrup, 1977), p. 182.

21. Tanzania assisted Ugandan exiles to overthrow the Amin regime in 1979. Since then Tanzania has been actively involved in the security of Uganda.

22. See Crawford Young "Comparative Claims to Political Sovereignty: Biafra, Katanga, Eritrea," in Rothchild and Olorunsola, *State Versus Ethnic Claims*, p. 213–214.

23. David Laitin, "The Ogaadeen Question and Changes in Somali Identity," in Rothchild and Olorunsola, *State Versus Ethnic Claims*, p. 331.

24. Ibid., p. 332.

25. Quoted in Crawford Young "Comparative Claims to Political Sovereignty," in Rothchild and Olorunsola, *State Versus Ethnic Claims*, p. 202.

26. Thomas Turner "Congo-Kinshasa," in Olorunsola, *The Politics of Cultural Subnationalism*, p. 255.

27. See Donald Rothchild "Ethnic Inequalities in Kenya" in Olorunsola, *The Politics of Cultural Subnationalism*, p. 302.

28. Cas des Villiers, *African Problems and Challenges* (Valiant Publishers, 1976), p. 93.

29. Arthur Lewis, "Beyond African Dictatorship: The Crisis of the One-Party State," *Encounter* (August 1965), p. 50.

9. Cooperation Among African States
John M. Ostheimer

In two decades of independence, African states have not made much headway in constructing continental unity. Old weaknesses still haunt the continent in new and sometimes even more destructive forms, stirred up by the struggles between modern ideologies. Tribal political divisions contributed long ago to colonialist domination. The threat of outside intervention still prevails, largely because Africa, as before, offers a power vacuum for various types of opportunists throughout the world.[1] The African will to remain free is evident; constructive efforts to avoid the outside pressures that reduce Africa's level of real independence are more scattered.

Accompanying this political fractionation, the lives of Africa's peoples since independence have been adversely affected by ongoing economic and technological backwardness, but little progress can be claimed in that realm either. After two decades of varied development policies that must be labeled, by and large, as failures, certain lessons are apparent. Above all, economic growth, educational goals, political machinery, and other crucial aspects of development are all interrelated. They must be carefully dovetailed and articulated so as not to avoid the rural sector. Education should be geared to accomplish a constructive mixture of modern approaches with skills and values that esteem rural, even neotraditional roles. Otherwise, mass rural exodus, with attendant urban overcrowding and unemployment, will foster alienation and instability. Economic policy should recognize the comparative advantages within African agriculture: an emphasis on cash crops at the expense of indigenous food crops should be carefully studied, because local conditions may work against such efforts. In fact, the external orientation of African economies, epitomized by the cash-crop emphasis, has generally been harmful. Experts warn against generalizing about "African" conditions but then regularly proceed with familiar, and accurate, generalizations about the continent's harshness, limited productivity, and physical inflexibility.[2]

Political organizations that focus concern on the needs of the urban elites and ignore the rural masses will contribute to the failure of economic development, a failure that often culminates in intervention by a national military that identifies with the oppressed and ignored. The ensuing cycle of political insecurity, authoritarianism, protestations of humanitarian intentions, and repression has struck the majority of African countries. Sometimes, as Wiseman has pointed out for Gambia, the cycle's worst manifestations set in despite apparent absence of the causal elements.[3] But then for other examples, such as the attempted coup in Kenya, some of the causes seem real enough.[4]

The Need for Cooperation

How are African governments to accomplish development, particularly in the absence of consensus as to what should be done? More modestly, are there ways in which even regimes with contradictory goals can assist each other to common advantage? The answer is that potentials for mutual advantage certainly do exist, and they clearly justify attempts at coordination, particularly in the context of a continent as divided, diverse, and desperate as Africa.

The advantages are usually obvious. First, the black-ruled states would benefit greatly from cooperation in the area of security. Military equipment and organization are expensive and divert resources from the real needs of the continent's peoples. It is becoming ever more clear that too much is being spent on these materials.[5] Manpower that could be devoted to economic and social betterment is being diverted to nonproductive activity.

What does *security* mean in the context of African politics? Without control over their political and economic systems, Africans stand to lose the independence they have—at least formally—achieved. Threats to their political and economic sovereignty must be identified and countered. Disruptive forces within each country are certainly one of the more serious types of challenges to security. "Anti-African" forces located on the continent, such as South African racism, as well as extra-African threats, also pose problems for African security. Such forces might act alone, in alliance with each other, or in intentional or unintended consort with subversive forces within the African states. Cooperation among African states would help greatly to guarantee an adequate and effective level of security.

The logic supporting such cooperation is compelling. The enemies of African security are sometimes physically capable of wreaking real havoc on the fractionated units that currently compose the continent. A significant measure of military cooperation would enable the legitimate authorities to neutralize some of the enemy forces. The indirect benefits of military cooperation are also significant: more efficient regional defense will save resources that are badly needed for non-defense programs.

Second, joint efforts to solve economic and technological problems, although not having such immediate life-and-death urgency as military cooperation, are also of great importance. African countries must try to maximize the complementarity between their economies. They must organize effective communications and transportation links that reduce the old problem of having to travel, call, or send goods or messages from Dakar to Lomé via Paris. They must develop markets that encourage local manufacturing, retaining as much as possible of the value added for African earners and reducing costs to consumers by virtue of the savings in transshipment.

Of course, in spite of the compelling logic supporting efforts to cooperate, the African world is far too complicated to allow the "inevitable" to become the established without a struggle. The very problems that call so loudly for cooperation are the ones that keep it from happening.

Cooperation at the Continental Level

The most impressive sort of political and military cooperation, should African states be able to make progress with it, would be at the continental level. Although there have been encouraging signs from time to time, one must conclude that continental unity has not accounted for many accomplishments in the two decades of independence. In 1982, unity seemed to sink to perhaps its lowest point, with the first peacekeeping force's failure to accomplish its objective in Chad, the Organization of African Unity (OAU) summit's dissension over seating the delegation of the Popular Front for the Liberation of Saguia el Hamra and Rio de Oro (POLISARIO), and the failure to gain a quorum for the annual summit. By more skeptical outside observers, the OAU is referred to as "nonsense."[6] Even to those who believe deeply in the OAU, 1982 was a frustrating year.

The visible failures also have brought out defenders of the vision of African unity, who argue, with considerable justification, that the specific failures should not blind students to the more important survival of the vision's hopes, as well as its structures. As Gruhn wrote about 1982, "This year's disintegrating forces are not the first to have confronted the OAU, and it is worth pausing to ask why the OAU has for almost 20 years survived and commanded both African and international attention, considering it has been ill funded, ill staffed, and constantly confronted with disunity."[7]

To comprehend this situation so full of both hopes and frustrations, one must first understand that the potential of the OAU is reduced by the very suspicions and jealousies that originally limited its jurisdiction. Nkrumah, the great advocate of continental government, was successfully resisted by more cautious voices at the time of the OAU's construction. For years the constraints of the resulting charter made even the boldest African leaders unwilling to intervene in situations that definitely justified intervention. The African leaders seemed to espouse many common principles and aspirations, but their cultural differences and ideological divisions reinforced the limits placed on their actions by the charter.[8] We shall consider the experiences African leaders have encountered in the political, military, and economic realms in an effort to understand the reasons for the lack of solid accomplishments and to assess whether the potential exists for real cooperation.

The OAU has always given the impression to outsiders that Africans had at least a vision of strong unity. No matter how serious the divisions on specific issues, the annual head-of-state summit managed to celebrate the symbols of independent status. But the organization's charter was designed to produce superficial consensus while avoiding messier problems that badly needed attention for the good of all. Inhumane regimes were tolerated, even allowed to be influential, under the constraints of OAU Charter Article 3, by which countries rejected interference in each other's internal affairs.[9] The charter's proscription of interference fails to clearly distinguish between (1) legitimate concern for problems within states that must be countered in the interests of humanitarianism and development, and (2) lingering disruptive (often ethnically based) conditions that exist in most African countries that justify supporting the present regime. For example, some states saw POLISARIO as a guerrilla force not to be encouraged, whereas others saw that movement as a legitimate vehicle for independence. Anti-Western (and anti-Moroccan) sentiment also contributed to the recognition of POLISARIO, and until the continent's states evolve a more sophisticated policy toward each other's internal problems, the intrusion of East-West or neocolonialist ambitions into African vacuums will be inevitable. The 1982 OAU-summit collapse gave the continent a distinct look of ideological confrontation, one important cause of which is the failure of African states to develop a real working policy for coping with collective political disorder. Charter revision may be necessary to clarify that indeed there are legitimate cases of continental interference in the affairs of member states.

To be sure, the OAU's weaknesses were known long before the abortive summit of 1982. Until the late 1970s, the OAU had employed political tactics that earlier had met with some success in reducing tensions. These included (1) establishing presidential commissions for investigation and more-or-less gently prodding, (2) placing most of the blame for African instability on external interference, and (3) just not recognizing conflicts in hopes that they would disappear. By the late 1970s, many African leaders perceived these tactics to be weak. Tanzania, which had played the role of African conscience a decade before by upholding Biafra's right to exist, again triggered intense debate by "interfering" in Uganda's affairs.

As willingness of OAU members to participate in actions beyond collective browbeating increased, the ambiguities inherent in the charter emerged more clearly. Debate over the OAU's role in the Chadian and western Saharan wars centered around the question of whether the organization's efforts had gone too far. Under this pressure, the OAU's 1981 decision to intervene with a referendum to determine the Sahrawi people's fate then gave way to the hasty seating of the Sahara Arab Democratic Republic (SADR), appearing to politicize a previously statesmanlike decision. Quite possibly some OAU votes on this issue were swayed by the knowledge that the referendum would severly tax the OAU's meager capabilities. Perhaps some members had concluded that it was better to admit to the inevitable result without trying to go through the expensive formalities. This vacillation by the OAU resulted in its own worst moment, when the summit failed to meet on schedule in Tripoli.[10]

The Chadian exercise displayed some unfortunate similarities, in that the weakness of the OAU came back to haunt it. The inability to guarantee the February timetable for cease-fire, peace talks, and elections and the uncertainty as to how long the OAU peacekeeping force would (or could) stay were visible weaknesses of the OAU that encouraged the Habré forces to keep trying until they successfully took over by force later in 1982. Thus, a major OAU joint peacekeeping effort ended in frustration and embarrassment. Of course, it should also be pointed out that the Chadian venture had its bright side, in that African states had actually attempted to cope assertively with the Chadian problem. Nevertheless, the mission did fail.

Along with these major catastrophes, more minor irritations have further reduced the faith of member states in the OAU. Particularly crucial are cases that show alienation of key OAU members like Nigeria. The May 1981 border clash with Cameroun, which resulted in five Nigerian soldiers being killed, embittered Nigeria because of the lack of apparent interest or effort by the OAU secretariat to investigate the matter.[11]

For the OAU to be more of a directing force in continental affairs— filling the vacuum that presently invites foreign interference—may require major surgery and resuscitative measures. The organization is poorly staffed and funded, as a number of observers have commented. The secretariat and other executive machinery need more capability for data management and storage capability, more funds for operational expenses, and a strategic planning unit. Funding for these efforts is crucial: The OAU is unable to finance even its more limited present activities, much less deal with expanded functions.[12] The International Peace Academy's 1980 recommendations to the OAU called for greater ties with the Organization of Petroleum Exporting Countries (OPEC), which might solve the funding problem.[13] Past experiences of African-Arab relations, however, offer little optimism about these prospects.[14] Nevertheless, if funding can be found, the improvements mentioned above might succeed, assuming there also evolves a clearer mandate for the organization to take an active role in managing continental affairs. Of course, that assumes greater agreement as to the OAU's essential role than now exists.

The question of the OAU's mandate to be involved in politically disruptive situations within the continent was clarified somewhat in 1979 when the African Commission on Human and People's Rights was established. The commission was approved by the OAU Council of Ministers and by the Assembly and by 1983 had been ratified by about a third of the OAU membership. The commission's role is basically restricted to collecting information and making recommendations to member governments: it has no concrete sanctions. But the commission redresses the moral balance somewhat away from the noninterference doctrine that has created such cynicism about the OAU.[15] Eventually the charter will have to be modified so that the majority of well-meaning African leaders can deal with the Amins and Nguemas in their midst.

Given the need for OAU charter revision and the weakness of the Human Rights Treaty, it seems that outrage over the bloodiest and most repressive aspects of African politics has been growing more rapidly than the structural, legal, and financial abilities of institutions to cope with the expectations for action. One could even argue that the organization's survival up to now has been partly a function of good luck. The collapse that occurred in 1982 might have happened earlier, for example, if Master Sergeant Samuel Doe, Liberia's new head of state, had not chosen to stay away from the 1980 summit but had instead tried to take over the gavel vacated by his assassinated predecessor. On the other hand, given the obviously serious emotional commitment of most responsible Africans to real unity, one would expect the continent's unity structure to bounce back from such reverses. And it seems to do just that.

In the absence of military capability to bring an end to white domination in southern Africa or to external interferences in African affairs, the OAU has found itself limited to protestations that will, so it is hoped, embarrass wrongdoers into more benign behavior. Even cultural issues are sometimes employed for leverage, such as the warnings directed at the United States that the 1984 Los Angeles Olympics will face an African boycott if the Reagan administration fails to pressure South Africa. These tactics may have some subtle effects, particularly given the role politics played in the 1980 Olympic games. Attempts to keep South Africa out of the World Medical Association offer a second example.[16] But in the long pull, there can be no replacement for African actions that demonstrate a willingness to take care of their own problems compassionately, but forcefully if necessary. The more the outside world assumes that Africa's political actions will be only symbolic, the less force those actions will carry. Thus, we must examine more closely the prospects for concerted action of a potentially forceful nature.

Defense Cooperation

The differences that have divided African countries have by no means defeated their desire to cooperate. The fundamental problem is that their weakness causes a power vacuum that will not be ignored by countries eager to use Africa for strategic or economic advantage. Africa's raw materials and strategic position make it a target for great powers, former colonial countries, and smaller powers on the make. The most effective way to fill the vacuum would be to create and maintain credible mobile peacekeeping forces.

Until recently, as we have seen, the OAU structure and mandate did not allow such attempts. Africans had to content themselves with confronting would-be troublemakers with political costs of intervention. Aluko argues that over time such efforts have been gaining effectiveness. His view is that African states have collectively had some success in (1) asserting an African personality in world affairs, (2) making known that external interference would be condemned, and (3) partially defusing some conflicts that would have encouraged interference.[17] But even Aluko's upbeat assessment is replete with admissions that these political and diplomatic accomplishments are really minimal. Only concrete, well-organized cooperation aimed at filling the vacuum will change the situation. In this context, efforts at military unity would represent an important step. However, the prospects for defense cooperation are not bright.

Article 11 of the OAU Charter seems to allow—even encourage—development of an all-African defense-coordinating structure. It charges the OAU with responsibility to defend the member states' sovereignty, territorial integrity, and independence. But little progress has been made. According to Imobighe, the OAU has failed to create the structure of a defense high command because there has been no consensus as to the types of threats the continent faces.[18]

The idea of a high command predates the OAU itself. Nkrumah disliked the way the big powers manipulated the United Nations (UN) Congo force, but his effort to unite African leaders for military cooperation floundered on the conservatism of his contemporaries. The debate during the early 1960s ranged from the Ghanaian view that a high command would actually lead joint forces of a continental union to the view expressed, particularly by Nigeria, that a cooperative military structure would be assigned merely to collect data for member states. The more conservative viewpoint emphasized the United Nations Charter's Article 32, which prohibited armed force against any member state unless self-defense or UN-authorized collective actions were involved. This, the conservatives argued, meant that a joint military command was virtually useless and therefore not a high-priority matter.

By the late 1960s, the Ghanaian initiative was dead, but events combined to remind African leaders of their collective impotence in the face of threats. In 1972, Nigeria, fresh from civil war, suggested a continental "task force" to be stationed in the areas bordering white-ruled southern Africa. A similar idea, for a "collective intervention force," was revived in the 1977 OAU debate, but little was accomplished.

Imobighe's review of African reluctance to consummate a high command points to the many roadblocks: diversity of politics and culture, lack of technical knowledge, and low level of confidence.[19] Further, he implies that there might already be a defense command structure if Africans perceived similar threats to their security. The Nigerian proposal was defeated by arguments of some members that African efforts would have little chance against the technological superiority of North Atlantic Treaty Organization (NATO), Warsaw Pact countries, or even the white-dominated regimes of the continent. Advocates for the task-force idea were not able to convince the doubters that threats from the outside would probably not, in these times, come in the form of high-technology frontal assaults.

Calling for a decentralized force with four zonal commands, Imobighe emphasizes "racist and imperialist threats" that will require rapid mobilizing to potentially far-flung pressure points.[20] But this is only one type of threat Africa faces. In a sense, Imobighe is committing the same oversimplification he believes has limited progress so far: failure to see the broad range of possible threats. One could just as easily argue from recent experience that Africa's most pregnant opportunities for military cooperation come from situations that are indigenous and have been brewing for years. These types of threats to African security are indeed different because they place a more severe challenge on continental cooperation. The Saharan and Chadian efforts, for example, had major indigenous components. In comparison with the challenge of white racism, these cases call for lower levels of military technology but far higher levels of political commitment to finding shared goals that justify intervention in the affairs of member states. The difficult element in these frustrating situations was to arrive at a consensus of goals that would sponsor successful peacekeeping.

Two specific issues, the refugee problem and the question of nuclear-energy development, further illustrate how important it is that Africa establish a higher level of military cooperation. Obviously, failure to remedy Africa's economic ills will intensify the indigenous factors contributing to instability. Refugee-related problems are definitely growing worse. Africa now has the largest concentration of refugees in the world, although no one knows for sure how bad the situation really is. For example, estimates of Somalia's refugee population range from 300,000 to 1.3 million. Either figure represents a severe drain on an already weak economy. Failure to mediate or control political disruptions causes bizarre scenarios such as the Zairian and Angolan "exchange" of refugees who obviously are not contributing anything to either economy but instead are draining both.[21]

Continental peacekeeping forces could have beneficial roles to play in safeguarding minorities until regional autonomy or other solutions could be worked out between the central government and such groups. The example of the Sudan, cited by Deng in Chapter 1, shows that accommodations are possible. Nevertheless, the longer it takes to achieve them, the more openings exist for troublemakers to take advantage of the situations. Chad's trials reflect this sort of cycle. Chad's own problems are certainly real ones, stemming from generations of ethnic hostility. But outsiders, notably Libya and France, have viewed Chad's problems as opportunities to advance or protect their own interests.

Secondly, regarding the level of nuclear development on the continent, African military cooperation must achieve a more advanced state before the continent undergoes a serious level of nuclear proliferation. The desire to obtain nuclear capability is already well underway, spurred by Mazrui's 1979 London lecture advocating an African nuclear presence. Several African countries have the uranium, and Nigeria, at least, seems to have the desire to join the nuclear club. President Shagari has warned that Nigeria's signature under the Nuclear Non-Proliferation Treaty will mean little if other countries, such as South Africa, scorn it. Vocal support for Shagari's position from the director-general of the Nigerian Institute for International Affairs indicates that nuclear power is increasingly seen as a way to reduce what Mazrui called Africa's "diplomatic marginality" in world affairs. At this time, there are still strong arguments being made (1) that other sources of power are cheaper for domestic uses, and (2) that given the size and type of threat represented by the neighbors of those African countries that are approaching nuclear capability, there does not seem to be much point in nuclear investment for military purposes. But the pressures of proliferation are there even though the physical capabilities are still weak, and Africans would be well advised to have their own plan for nuclear control.[22]

Accomplishments in Subregional Cooperation

Obvious progress in international cooperation has been made at the subregional level. Most of the organizations that have emerged are designed to cope with specific problems shared by a few countries. How does one evaluate the significance of such geographically limited and/or functionally specific achievements? How important can they really be? Most recent scholarship on this question doubts the assumption that governments that cooperate for specific technical, economic, or other comparatively narrow purposes will necessarily be willing to extend the cooperative frame of mind to issues that require a real reduction of national sovereignty. Recent critiques of the old hope that functional cooperation will lead to federal union cast doubt on the wisdom of devoting too much attention here to subregional cooperation.[23] Such efforts may have an important place in the overall development effort, but we have suggested that the core problem is that Africa is fundamentally divided by the forces of culture and history. That heritage will only be overcome by a conscious pooling of sovereignty.

West Africa

The West African subregion's experience clearly illustrates how difficult it is to obtain cooperation in key issue-areas. There is progress, but so much still to be done. Subregional organizations range in scope from the sixteen-state Economic Community of West African States (ECOWAS) to the Cape Verde/Guinea-Bissau Free Trade Association. Between these ends of the scale are several other groupings.

Most attention is focused on ECOWAS, which includes nearly all states of the subregion. In economic matters, that grouping has made solid progress, particularly in telecommunications, postal-system development, and progress toward free trade. In May 1981, for example, duties on processed goods originating within ECOWAS were eliminated.[24] There are some grounds for the optimistic view that the rate of progress since the 1975 ECOWAS treaty will eventually lead to a common market at least for West Africa, if not—as Executive Secretary Ouattara claims—for all Africa by the year 2000. But intense debate has accompanied each economic step, and political issues have proven least tractable. 1979's protocol on the free movement of peoples has been difficult to implement. Nigeria and Ivory Coast, targets for immigrants, are most reluctant to embrace the concept. The proposed subregional defense pact, supported by Nigeria but disliked by some smaller states, similarly frustrates consensus. Finally, political actions that are part of a healthy trend toward caring about the sorts of regimes that grace the subregion have a negative impact on short-term cooperation: the rejection of Master Sergeant Doe by the ECOWAS heads of state may be a good long-run omen, but it also meant that no agreement on the defense pact was likely because the absence of one head of state destroyed the chance for the required universal agreement. Eventually, this political floundering is bound to slow the progress in economic realms, because the more advanced and difficult the economic decisions become, the more political consensus will be needed to support them.[25]

Two Francophone groupings exist: the West African Monetary Union (UMOA) and the Economic Community of West Africa (CEAO). The monetary union, composed of Senegal, Togo, Upper Volta, Benin, Ivory Coast, and Niger, can be construed to be a barrier to the success of ECOWAS, to which these states also belong. Their shared Francophone frame of mind adds to their fear, and their suspicion of huge Nigeria and historically ambitious Ghana leads to the expectation that any progress UMOA makes in uniting currencies will mean difficulty for the entire subregion in doing likewise. CEAO, consisting of the above states minus Togo and plus Mali, was even more obviously formed as a reaction to the ECOWAS idea.[26]

These West African Francophone groups have their counterpart at the continental level in the Central African Monetary Organization (OCAM), and similar arguments, that they may weaken the potential for overall integration, could be made.

To contradict the standard view that these smaller Francophone groups will slow ECOWAS down, some argue that for every state like Senegal with its paranoia about the weight of West Africa's anglophone states, there is an Ivory Coast or Togo that has worked very hard to support ECOWAS. ECOWAS's executive secretary argues that these Francophone groups will spur progress for ECOWAS by demonstrating that West African states can reduce commercial and monetary barriers. Nevertheless, most of the Francophone states have close ties to France that may be costly for them to forgo. For example, defense links with France have a measure of reliability that would be hard to replace with inter-African alliances.[27]

Finally, two three-member organizations demonstrate that West Africans are willing and able to cooperate. These are the Mano River Union (MRU), started in 1973 by Sierra Leone, Liberia, and Guinea, and the Gambia River Development Organization (OMVG), composed of Gambia, Senegal, and Guinea. These groupings not only have specific accomplishments to show but also demonstrate that West African states with different historical and cultural heritages can cooperate well for specific purposes. The MRU, for example, boasts the Basin Development Project, major bridge construction, cooperative ventures in agriculture and other economic realms, and cultural cooperation. Customs duties between Sierra Leone and Liberia were eliminated in 1981, and projects are also being undertaken in natural-resources development and joint protection of territorial waters.[28]

The West African subregion has also provided examples of federalist integration. These efforts have usually failed (Mali Federation, Ghana-Guinea-Mali), but the present SeneGambian attempt shows promise. The confederal system drawing together Gambia and Senegal began in February 1982 and proved popular during its first year. Such ways to solve the limited utility of the boundaries inherited from colonialism are praiseworthy, because they require more evident political goodwill than do the activities of functionalist groupings. But the successes, such as Tanzania, are few.

Other Subregions

Other subregions show various levels of accomplishment that are described here in reference to and in comparison with the West African picture. Nearby, eleven central African countries from Angola north to Chad met during 1981–1982 to implement their desire to move from long asserted principles to real structures of cooperation. They face the same sorts of problems as their western colleagues. Economically diverse, they range from the poverty near the Great Lakes to the prospects for oil or uranium-spurred growth. Politically, their postindependence traditions vary from the beneficent strength of an Ahidjo to the horrendous memory of Nguema. Up to 1981, organizational activity was limited to the specific Customs Union of Central African States (UDEAC), the Central African Bank (BEAC), and the Great Lakes Economic Community (CEPGL). It is too early to say whether the eleven-member Economic Community (CEEAC), formed at the December 1981 meeting at Libreville, will amount to much.[29]

The nine-member Southern African Development Coordination Conference (SADCC) overlaps geographically with CEEAC. It includes Angola and Zaire as well as the nine black-ruled states to the south and east. Begun in 1979, this grouping also faces great internal diversity, along with the might of the South African enemy. The member states vary ideologically from Malawi to Mozambique and economically from Lesotho, with its inseparable connection to South Africa, to Tanzania, which is a "frontline" state by choice. Recognizing this diversity, the states have chosen a loose form of coordination, deemphasizing attempts to build any common market or other such sovereignty-reducing structure. Described instead as a sort of subregional think tank, each state will contribute to formulating plans in one of five development-policy areas. For example, Angola is to come up with energy development ideas for the region. Like the South Africa-sponsored "constellation" concept (Constellation of Southern African States—CONSAS) that it was designed to head off, SADCC is not organizationally overambitious, but rather modestly functional in design.[30]

The frustrating collapse of East Africa's unity, after a promising start, serves as a sober reminder to optimists. The high level of functional cooperation reached during the 1950–1965 era centered around the East African Common Services Organization (EACSO), the common organization for harbors, railways, airlines, posts and telegraph, and other infrastructural activities. This first gave way to more ambitious concepts leading to the

East African Community, then to political and economic divisions of the 1970s that brought down the entire edifice. Obote's return to power revived hope, in the early 1980s, that because the leaders were again on speaking terms, progress could be made.[31] One must wonder, however, whether the fundamental economic differences have changed since the first days of tension in the 1960s, when Nyerere argued that the concept of the East African Common Market seemed to mean only that Tanzania was the common market for Kenya.

Nowhere do the prospects for subregional cooperation appear dimmer than on the Horn of Africa. And as Bereket Selassie's analysis shows, the basic stumbling blocks to peace (much less cooperation) come from within the region itself, rather than from the designs of outside powers.[32]

Finally, I must complete this subregional review with the proviso that its enabling assumption—that the continent can logically be subdivided at all—is questionable. Further, the flexible boundaries between "subregions" make it more difficult to build associations along obvious lines of interrelationship. Of course, if one views successful subregional cooperation as a setback for continental unity, groupings like the Kagera River Basin Organization (Uganda, Tanzania, Rwanda, Burundi), which cut across the usual subregions, are cause for cheer.

Conclusion

There are ample ironies and frustrations inherent in the experiences of African states toward cooperation. At the continental level, the desires for coordination and unity are obviously sincere. However, it is difficult to accomplish anything concrete at that level. Subregionally, specific accomplishments are plentiful, but as Anyatonwu points out, "economic integration is dependent upon the political will of the people to integrate."[33] It would be premature to conclude that there is no chance for functional, subregional cooperation to lead eventually to continental unity. Nevertheless, it does look as though it will be difficult for Africa to use the European model of integration. That model is proving hard enough for the Europeans, and the underlying historical and economic linkages in Africa are weaker.[34]

Whether subregional cooperation benefits African unity is a genuinely debatable point. Perhaps too pessimistically, I must side with Cervenka and Legum, who have argued that the 1980s are likely to see prospering alliances of a subcontinental nature, but that such developments will be "to the detriment of continental co-operation."[35] Strong subregional groupings may, in fact, mean trouble for the continent's overall security prospects. To counter this trend, the essential ingredient will be political commitment entailing concessions of sovereignty and drawing on the undeniable reservoir of desire to make "Africa" mean something significant in world affairs.

Notes

1. The present picture differs little from that described many years ago by I. William Zartman, "Africa as a Subordinate State System in International Relations,"

International Organizations 21, no. 3 (1967), pp. 545–564. See, for example, Ali Mazrui, *The African Condition: A Political Diagnosis* (London: Heineman, 1980). Excellent surveys of developments in African alliances and efforts at continental and subregional cooperation are found regularly in *Africa Research Bulletin;* in Roland Oliver and Michael Crowder, "Regional Groupings," *Cambridge Encyclopedia of Africa* (London: Cambridge University Press, 1981), pp. 357–459; and in *Africa South of the Sahara,* 11th ed. (London: Europa Publishers, 1981), pp. 81–129.

2. Recent discussions of these problems are found in David Norman, "Progress or Catastrophe in Africa?" *Africa Report* 26 (July–August, 1981), pp. 4–8. For greater depth, see *Accelerated Development in Sub-Saharan Africa: An Agenda for Action* (Washington, D.C.: The World Bank, 1981); Robert W. Jackman, "Dependence on Foreign Investment and Economic Growth in the Third World," *World Politics* 34, no. 2 (January 1982), pp. 175–196; Richard Sandbrook, "Is Socialism Possible in Africa?" *Journal of Commonwealth and Comparative Politics* 19, no. 2 (July 1982), pp. 197–207; and Adebayo Adedeji, "Africa's Priorities," *International Development Review* no. 4 (1980), pp. 19–22.

3. John A. Wiseman, "Revolt in the Gambia: A Pointless Tragedy," *Round Table* no. 284 (October 1981), pp. 373–380.

4. Jean-Claude Pomonti, "Kenya Moving Right," *Guardian* (August 15, 1982).

5. Ruth Leger Sivard, *World Military and Social Expenditures 1981* (Leesburg, Va.: World Priorities, 1981). See also Frank Barnaby, "Africa at War: The Militarization of the World's Poorest Continent," *Africa Guide* (1981), pp. 28–30.

6. "What African Unity?" *The Economist* (March 13, 1982), pp. 14–15.

7. Isebill V. Gruhn, "Why the Organization of African Unity Survives," *Christian Science Monitor* (Nov. 4, 1982).

8. Zdenek Cervenka and Colin Legum, "The OAU," *Africa Contemporary Record* (1981), p. A58. See also Olajide Aluko, "African Response to External Intervention in Africa since Angola," *African Affairs* 80, no. 319 (April 1981), pp. 159–179.

9. U. O. Umozurike, "The Domestic Jurisdiction Clause in the OAU Charter," *African Affairs* 78 (1979), pp. 197–209.

10. "Threats to the Tripoli Summit," *West Africa* no. 3375 (April 12, 1982), p. 968; and "Bumpy Ride for the OAU," *West Africa* no. 3376 (April 19, 1982), p. 1040.

11. "The Significant Absence," *West Africa* no. 3335 (June 29, 1981), p. 1451.

12. Cervenka and Legum, "The OAU," p. A58

13. "A Role for the OAU in the 1980s," *Africa Currents* no. 24 (July 1981), pp. 6–7.

14. Olusola Ojo, "The Relationship between the Organization of African Unity and the League of Arab States," *Afrika Spectrum* 81, no. 2, pp. 131–141; and E. C. Chibwe, *Afro-Arab Relations in the New World Order* (New York: St. Martin's Press, 1978).

15. Olajide Aluko, "The Organization of African Unity and Human Rights," *Round Table* no. 283 (July 1981), pp. 234–242. See also Claude E. Welch, Jr., "The OAU and Human Rights: Towards a New Definition," *Journal of Modern African Studies* 19, no. 3 (1981), pp. 401–420.

16. *OAU Bulletin* 32 (August—September 1981), pp. 9–10.

17. Aluko, "African Response. . . ."

18. T. A. Imobighe, "An African High Command: The Search for a Feasible Strategy of Continental Defence," *African Affairs,* 79 (1980), pp. 241–254.

19. Ibid.

20. Ibid., p. 252.

21. Colin Legum, "The Year in Perspective," *Africa Contemporary Record 1979–80* (New York: Africana Publishing Co., 1980); Allan Cowell, "Food is Stake in Somalia's Refugee Numbers Game," *New York Times* (September 15, 1981), p. 2; and Aderanti Adepoju, "The Dimensions of the Refugee Problem in Africa," *African Affairs* 81, no. 322 (January 1982), pp. 21–35.

22. For this debate, see E. Iroh, "Nigeria: the Nuclear Debate," *Africa* no. 114 (February 1981), pp. 38–39; Denis Ropa, "Cache-Cache à la Bombe," *Jeune Afrique* no. 1055 (March 25, 1981); and Robert D'A. Henderson, "Nigeria: Future Nuclear Power?" *Orbis* 25, no. 2 (Summer 1981), pp. 409–423.

23. For example, David W. Zeigler, *War, Peace, and International Politics* 2d ed. (Boston: Little, Brown, 1981), ch. 19; and Harold K. Jacobson, *Networks of Interdependence: International Organizations and the Global Political System* (New York: Alfred Knopf, 1979), ch. 4.

24. "ECOWAS Milestone," *West Africa* no. 3381 (May 24, 1982), pp. 1359–1378, and many other articles in *West Africa*. See also "ECOWAS: Tearing Down the Barriers," *Africa* no. 110 (October 1980), pp. 143–145.

25. G. N. Anyatonwu, "ECOWAS: An Approach to Subregional Economic Integration," *Journal of Modern African Studies* 9, no. 1 (Spring 1982), pp. 30–38.

26. The best source for developments involving international cooperation among Francophone states is *Marchés Tropicaux*. See also Sophie Bessis, "CEAO: Ils Rechignent, mais Ils Payent," *Jeune Afrique* no. 1086 (October 28, 1981), pp. 36–37. For specific data on each organization, *Europe Outremer* no. 622 (January 1982), pp. 231–235.

27. "Delicate Problem," *West Africa* no. 3331 (June 1, 1981), p. 1207.

28. "Mano River Union: Breaking Down Barriers," *West Africa* no. 3360 (October 19, 1981), pp. 2451–2452.

29. Mamza Kaidi, "Entraide Exemplaire," *Jeune Afrique* no. 1055 (March 25, 1981), p. 46.

30. Trevor Grundy, "New African Market—The SADCC," *New African* no. 170 (November 1981), p. 74; Gavin Maasdorp, "Reassessing Economic Ties in Southern Africa," *Optima* 3, no. 2. (1981), pp. 113–125; and J. A. Shaw, "Functional Cooperation in Southern Africa: An Experiment in Concensus Decision-Making," *Development Studies Southern Africa* 4, no. 1 (1981), pp. 2–34.

31. John Worrall, "Rebuilding the Community of East Africa," *New African* no. 170 (November 1981), p. 21.

32. Bereket Habte-Selassie, *Conflict and Intervention in the Horn of Africa* (New York: Monthly Review Press, 1980). See also "Horn of Africa: Irredentist Impulses and African Unity," *Afriscope* 11, no. 6 (June 1981), pp. 18–20.

33. G. N. Anyatonwu, "ECOWAS; An approach to Sub-Regional Economic Integration," *Journal of African Studies* 9, no. 1 (Spring 1982), p. 37.

34. Nfumba-Luaba-Lumu, "Quel Modèle d' Intégration pour l' Afrique," *Zaire Afrique* no. 158 (October 1981), pp. 471–481.

35. Cervenka and Legum, "The OAU," p. A58.

10. Playing the Arab Card: Niger and Chad's Ambivalent Relations with Libya

Pearl T. Robinson

Relations between Black Africa and the Arab world have a historical legacy dating back at least twelve centuries. Trade and Islam, sometimes abetted by a military dimension, provided the framework for initial interactions. Although the Arab role in the slave trade and the proselytizing zeal of Islam have given rise to recurring stresses and strains, Black and Arab coreligionists are seen today as an incipient transnational community. The present contours of this community and its special brand of opposition to Western hegemony can be traced to the late nineteenth and early twentieth centuries—the heyday of European colonial rule and a time of unprecedented expansion of Islam in Africa. During that period African Muslims came to be viewed as heirs to a tradition that included long-distance trade, the pilgrimage to Mecca, and intermittent resistance to colonizers.[1] It is this tradition—with its suggestive possibilities for collaboration on ideological, political, economic, and security matters—that provides the basis for the concept of Afro-Arab solidarity as articulated in contemporary global politics.

The focus here will be on the security dimension of Afro-Arab solidarity. I shall argue that security issues, when seen from the perspective of incumbent African regimes, encompass external military and strategic considerations as well as factors that affect internal stability and civil strife. In the context of Afro-Arab relations, these issues translate into calculations of strategic military and political alliances, coupled with the cultivation of Arab sources of aid for economic and social development. According to this formulation, the ideological, political, and economic facets of Afro-Arab solidarity are integral to a broadly defined notion of regime security; but they are made operational as discrete spheres of activity with narrowly conceived policy objectives—often with contradictory implications. The following discussion uses this Afrocentric definition of regime security to examine and explain the erratic relations of Niger and Chad with Arab Libya. In addition to coming to terms with the particularities of these two cases, the analysis offers an explanation of conflict and accommodation between Black Africa and the Arab world that goes beyond a facile elaboration of East-West strategic competition.

Before addressing contemporary affairs, I shall review some of the politically salient aspects of Libya's historical and cultural ties with its neighbors to the south. A summary of the highlights of the 1977 Program of African-Arab Cooperation will then be contrasted with the economic and military implications for Black Africa of strategic competition between militant and moderate Arab states. This background will serve to anchor the case studies, which treat Niger and Chad's dealings with Libya beginning in the early 1970s. After noting the limitations of bilateral Afro-Arab security arrangements, the analysis concludes with a synopsis of the obstacles to a more effective globally oriented strategy.

Libya and the Niger-Chad Region

Niger and Chad are relatively comparable Sahelian states. Both have distinctive population zones inhabited by predominantly sedentary agriculturalists in the south and nomadic pastoralists in the north. As former French territories they share the same colonial legacy, including membership in the franc zone and participation in a series of tightly structured bilateral cooperation accords with France. They have similar border problems with Libya, and in both states the contested territory is in the region of the country known to be mineral rich. On the religious score, however, the two cases diverge. Niger is predominantly Muslim and has no regional religious enclaves, whereas Chad's Islamic population is concentrated in the north. In contrast to Niger's relative calm, Chad has been plagued with repeated clashes between Muslim northerners and non-Muslim southerners.

I shall explore briefly the fundamentals of Niger and Chad's relations with Libya. Ethnoreligious factors, territorial overlap, and a long-standing tradition of economic transactions are the most critical concerns. It is important to understand how these connections from the past are being utilized by contemporary political actors as they plot alliance strategies and cast about for resources to enhance their effective options.

In numerous instances, Libya's Colonel Kaddafi has built barriers rather than bridges to mutually advantageous policy articulation. This tendency is most striking with regard to claims of a special cultural kinship between peoples of the Sahelian and the Saharan ecological zones. The similarity of climate and terrain, the legacy of trade and communications along the trans-Saharan caravan routes, and the movement of nomadic populations across national borders have indeed created a wide range of shared customs and spawned a residue of ethnic communities that straddle territorial lines. Yet a more encompassing formulation of ethnic identity is problematic, and Libyan insistence on this point has generated considerable controversy.

Since many of the non-Arabs resident in northern Chad are bilingual, Kaddafi has proclaimed that "Arab culture is the prevailing culture in

Chad.''[2] But in fact, Arabs are only about 9 percent of Chad's population. In Niger, where Arabs are a negligible presence, the Libyan leader has embraced the Tuaregs, a minority of 10 percent, as his ethnic constituency. The Tuaregs are a Berber people who speak Tamasheq—even though Kaddafi occasionally refers to them as Arabs. While ethnic appeals of this ilk may bear the seeds of their own destruction, in the interim they can prove destabilizing. Such gestures raise the specter of Arab irredentism and weaken the prospects for productive collaboration between Black Africans and Arabs.

Islam offers the potential for a more edifying assertion of commonality among the peoples of the region. It is the faith of the quasi totality of Libyans; Niger's population is about 85 percent Muslim; and northern Chad is thought to be around 95 percent Muslim, with estimates for the country as a whole ranging from 41 percent to 55 percent.[3] However, Tripoli's support for foreign nationals willing to espouse revolutionary Islam and Islamic fundamentalism has had contentious and divisive consequences. In effect, Libya stands accused of manipulating Islam for purposes of territorial annexation and intervention in the affairs of its neighbors. The institutional expression of this thrust is the Islamic Legion, a fighting force of some 7,000 men (including contingents from Chad and Niger) comprised essentially of political dissidents from West African states with Muslim populations. The units are trained by Syrian, Palestinian, and North Korean instructors in about twenty camps scattered around Libya and are armed and equipped from the Libyan arsenal.[4] For the regimes that see themselves as prospective targets,[5] the Islamic Legion is a destabilizing force that belies any rhetoric of a Libyan commitment to Afro-Arab solidarity.

Another bone of contention shared by Niger and Chad is the problem of territorial claims lodged by Libya. This issue has its roots in the imprecisions of colonial frontiers.[6] In 1899, during the heyday of the European scramble for Africa, a Franco-British accord to delimit zones of influence in the Upper Nile region incorporated statements on Libya's borders with the Sudan, Chad, and a portion of Niger. Libya was then a province of the Ottoman Empire, but Turkish protestations at the time were ignored. In 1935 a treaty signed between France and Mussolini's Italy extended the territory of Italian-occupied Libya southward into the French West African Empire. Since the legitimacy of that agreement was called into question after the fall of the Axis powers, a United Nations (UN) resolution just prior to Libya's independence in 1951 directed that the new state's southern boundary be renegotiated with France.[7] A treaty to this effect was finally ratified by Libya and France (acting for Chad and Niger) in 1957.

In theory, Tripoli's claim to "historical rights" over parts of northern Chad and northeastern Niger is a reference to European colonial usurpation of territory that fell within the Ottoman Empire. But the maps used and the borders posited coincide with the Fascist legacy. Moreover, the adjustments called for would cast aside the UN-sanctioned treaty, violate the Organization of African Unity's (OAU) prescription to leave colonial frontiers intact, and transfer to Libyan control strategic regions of Niger and Chad known to be rich in minerals. A decision by Tripoli to turn the matter over to arbitration should go a long way toward easing tensions. There is little doubt, however, that Kaddafi's ten-year campaign to extend his territorial and resource base to portions of Niger and Chad has left a breach that will be difficult to repair.

These repeated attempts to project Libyan power into the domains of its Sahelian neighbors have fostered considerable ill will. Nevertheless, economic transactions have been sustained, modernized, and diversified. To be sure, the nomadic Tuaregs and Tubus based in Niger and Chad continue to cross the borders in their regular cycles of transhumance, while long-distance truckers have replaced camels as the mainstay of trans-Saharan trade. But immensely more important today are the new economic activities spawned by Libya's oil-rich economy. For example, with Libyan financing, Chad has opened up a new market in the export of refrigerated meat by air from N'Djamena to Tripoli and the Middle East.[8] Substantial numbers of Nigeriens have found employment in the Libyan oil fields.[9] And although the government of Niger suspended diplomatic relations with Tripoli between January 1981 and March 1982, it was during this period that Libya emerged second only to France as a market for Niger's uranium.[10]

For political leaders in Niger and Chad, Libya's slow but steady economic penetration poses threats as well as opportunities. They generally try to capitalize on the opportunity side of the equation by evoking the principle of Afro-Arab solidarity. But Libya is just one of many Arab states. As the regimes in question shift from an economic to an ideological to a military sphere of concern, they often find it necessary to seek other Arab partners. The point to be developed below is that the choices they make are directly linked to calculations of internal and external regime security.

Economic Cooperation and Ideological Competition

The protean nature of Afro-Arab solidarity has permitted a wide latitude of applications. Nationalists evoked the principle in their anticolonial struggles. Independent Black and Arab Africa embraced it as a rationale for establishing the OAU. I shall look now at the program of joint economic and diplomatic initiatives fashioned in 1977 by sixty African and Arab states at a Cairo summit as an example of the aggregation of several facets of cooperation.

The 1977 Cairo summit pledged collaboration in all economic and social sectors by the individual signatory states as well as their two regional organizations, the OAU and the League of Arab States.[11] The delegates adopted four declarations of intent—a program of action, instructions for organization and a method of operation, a statement of political goals, and a brief on the principles of economic and financial cooperation. These prescriptions give concrete meaning to the principle of Afro-Arab solidarity in two spheres: political and economic. The political quid pro quo was to be the complete alignment of the regional diplomacies of the African and Arab states on issues pertaining to Israel and the white-minority regimes of southern Africa. Implicit in the economic understanding was an expectation that Arab assurances of preferential oil prices and generous aid to promote economic and social development would ultimately transform the agricultural productivity of the African continent, which in turn could someday supply the growing Arab demand for agricultural commodities.

It should be noted that the Cairo program makes no attempt to coordinate military or security initiatives. The signatories might, for example, have included military options to advance their political objectives with respect to southern Africa and Israel.[12] Or their serious consideration of Afro-Arab security arrangements could have put momentum behind the transition from bipolar to multipolar global strategies. Even within the narrower scope of action adopted, however, adherence to the commitments made has been selective.

Taking 1973 as a benchmark, when the Arab Bank for Economic Development in Africa (known by its French acronym BADEA) and the Arab Technical Assistance Fund were established, we find that Arab aid to Africa through 1979 came to nearly $4 billion—an amount equivalent to total U.S. aid to the continent since World War II. Though massive and unprecedented, these financial transfers tell only part of the story. Africans and Arabs at the Cairo summit had promised to go beyond aid—to facilitate direct trade, to "supply, on a priority basis, as far as possible, their respective markets," and to "take all necessary measures to promote financial cooperation . . . on the most favorable terms possible."[13] To an extent not generally acknowledged, many of Libya's transactions with Niger and Chad have incorporated key aspects of these principles. But in the aggregate the record of Afro-Arab economic cooperation is ambivalent. With the exception of a few sweetheart deals,[14] the Africans never got their dual price structure or preferential access to oil. Arab aid has been programmed through Arab channels to the exclusion, until recently, of African institutions such as the African Development Bank. Most BADEA projects have been cofinanced with other major international financial agencies and implemented by transnational corporations rather than African contractors. And it goes without saying that African agriculture has yet to be transformed—as evidenced by the food crisis that grips the continent.

The Cairo Declaration promised to reorient economic relationships, but the new modalities of Afro-Arab cooperation have been grafted on to the old patterns of dependence on the West. Still, adherence to the economic commitments has far outweighed compliance with the political agreements. For instance, all but four member-states in the OAU had ceased relations with Israel by the end of the 1973 Arab-Israeli war, but ten years later many Black African governments had moved to reopen diplomatic channels even in the face of Israel's settlements policy in the West Bank and the 1982 invasion of Lebanon. The Arab members of the Organization of Petroleum Exporting Countries (OPEC) agreed in 1973 to apply an embargo on oil to South Africa, but Pretoria has been able to obtain Arab oil by paying a premium.[15] And despite the driving role of Nasser's Egypt and Algeria in support of nationalist movements north of the Zambezi River, the Arab bloc has yet to play a major part either diplomatically or militarily in the liberation struggles of southern Africa.[16]

Granted the particular issues I have raised are as intractable as any on the political horizon and cannot be resolved definitively with oil embargoes and diplomatic blackouts. Nevertheless, a more stable Afro-Arab alliance could have significant portent both globally and with respect to specific regional objectives. One factor that imperils such a prospect is the intense ideological rivalry among Arabs and its ramifications in Black Africa.

Libya has mounted a strident bid for leadership of the revolutionary forces in the Arab and Islamic worlds, whereas Saudi Arabia, Morocco, and post-Nasser Egypt are in the vanguard of the Western-allied Arab bloc. A flavor of the antagonism that prevails was conveyed in a resolution adopted in February 1983 by the General Peoples' Congress in Tripoli calling for aggressive action against "the symbols of treason in the Arab arena who follow the imperialist camp headed by the United States."[17]

Colonel Kaddafi's determination to challenge Arab regimes friendly to the West has affected Libya's dealings with states in Black Africa. Thus Libya became more hostile toward the Sudan after President Nimiery backed the late President Sadat's 1979 peace initiative with Israel. In another incident, Saudi Arabia's request for U.S. surveillance planes to monitor the Iraq-Iran war set up a chain of events that resulted in a Libyan boycott of the 1981 Islamic Conference Organization summit, which had included aid to the Sahel on its agenda.[18] At that meeting members set up a special ministerial-level Committee of Islamic Solidarity with the Peoples of the Sahel and pledged a total of $210 million for emergency food assistance and rural development projects in Cape Verde, Chad, Guinea, Guinea-Bissau, The Gambia, Mali, Mauritania, Niger, Senegal, and Upper Volta.[19] As of 1982, contributions to the solidarity committee had come from four donors: Saudi Arabia, Kuwait, Iraq, and the United Arab Emirates. Oil-rich Libya remained aloof, choosing for a time not to express solidarity with the Sahel in this particular forum. This is a prime example of how the Arab ideological schism poses a major obstacle to a broad-based, stable pattern of relations with Black Africa.

Accepting this mercurial climate as a given, let us now turn to an explanation of why regimes in countries such a Niger and Chad are inclined to explore alliance strategies with Libya.

Niger

I shall examine the ways in which political incumbents in Niger manipulate their domestic and foreign policies and cultivate international strategic alliances in order to alleviate internal political pressures. Two critical periods, presided over by different governments, are considered. In both instances, closer ties to Arab countries, including Libya, were deemed essential.

During the early 1970s Niger's first president, Diori Hamani, was confronted with the predicament of a deteriorating domestic situation. This was the height of the 1968–1973 Sahelian drought: Food deficits soared, cash-crop production plummeted, and livestock losses took their toll. Diori's government came under sharp criticism for its mishandling of relief operations, its failure to spur rural development, and its neocolonial relationship with France. In this adverse political climate, Niger's close ties with France became a seious liability for the regime.

Even before the situation reached crisis proportions, Diori attempted to revamp his foreign and domestic policies in ways that would diminish French hegemony. The challenge was staggering because bilateral cooperation accords assured French government and private involvement in the major spheres of national life. In Francophone Africa, aid agreements provide budget subsidies; furnish technical, administrative, and cultural assistance; and buttress security arrangements by stationing French troops on the scene. Diori had personally benefited when French soldiers came to his support in a power struggle in 1963. But in 1972 he publicly criticized France's policies in Africa and confronted President Pompidou with a demand for review of the terms of the cooperation agreements. In moves designed to gain greater economic latitude, Diroi's government called for an upward negotiation of the state's 16.75 percent share in the SOMAIR uranium company and suggested that the members of the franc zone meet to discuss new forms of credit and loans. Signaling the serious implications of these departures, the Nigerien government declared the French ambassador unacceptable and asked for his replacement.

These ruptures with France were combined with a series of steps aimed at diversifying Niger's pattern of external alliances.[20] One of the most promising options was playing the Arab card. Thus in 1971 Diori arranged state visits to solidify relations with Algeria, Libya, and Nigeria—countries that in addition to being Niger's neighbors are also OPEC members and major powers of the Afro-Arab axis. The following year he welcomed King Faisal of Saudi Arabia to Niger. Shortly after Faisal's departure Niger broke relations with Israel. Diori's last major foreign-policy initiative in the field of Afro-Arab diplomacy was a mutual defense treaty signed in 1974 with Tripoli, which promised assistance in case of aggression or a coup attempt.

President Diori was overthrown by a military coup in April 1974, with his policy departures having had no noticeable effect on domestic conditions in Niger. Indeed, even the new security arrangement failed because, unlike France in 1963, Libya did not come to Diori's rescue. General Seyni Kountché was thus spared the onus of a Libyan counterattack in the early days of his rule.

In contrast to Diori's outward-looking orientation, the Kountché government articulated a strategy of national developmentalism as a means to internal stability. Moving cautiously at first, the regime sought a *modus vivendi* with the former metropole. In April 1975 Niger signed an agreement raising the state's share in the capital of the SOMAIR uranium company to 33 percent. France announced greatly increased aid in mineral prospecting, agriculture, higher education, and telecommunications. By improving the terms of economic exchange with France and precipitating a takeoff in the output of the mining sector, these agreements triggered a substantial increase in the state's domestically generated resources for social and economic development. Since 1973 uranium has been the mainstay of the Nigerien economy, accounting for 74 percent of export earnings in 1978 and enabling the government to significantly enhance the rural sector by carefully reinvesting mineral profits in the countryside. Dams for irrigated agriculture and hydroelectric power have been directed toward ending food dependency and reducing energy dependence, and herd reconstitution schemes have helped rebuild the badly depleted livestock population.[21]

While relations with France were returning to a relatively even keel, Niger's ties with the Arab world were faltering. The regime's commitment to an international vocation as an Islamic state is an expression of Afro-Arab solidarity that has not precluded an alliance strategy pitting Morocco against Libya. Accordingly, ground breaking for a West African Islamic University and Niamey's hosting of the 1982 Islamic Conference Organization summit have gone hand in hand with the denunciation of Libya as Niger's number-one enemy. Colonel Kaddafi's aggressive actions provoked this response.

Kaddafi moved troops into the Nigerien border oasis of Toummo and in 1976 had a map published showing the transfer of 19,500 square kilometers of Nigerien territory. Broadcasts from Tripoli in Hausa and Tamasheq have been aimed at recruiting Niger nationals into Kaddafi's Islamic Legion. Niger expelled Libyan diplomats in December 1980 when they transformed their embassy into a "people's bureau," and official relations were frozen the following month. Kountché brandished a January 1981 merger agreement between Libya and Chad as proof that Kaddafi's expansionist intentions had to be checked. But the nadir in relations occurred eight months later with the defection to Libya of a dozen Nigerien Tuareg civil servants, one of whom was a close presidential advisor.

To counter the threat to internal stability Niger turned to Morocco, one of Kaddafi's ideological rivals. Moroccan training and equipment have enabled the Kountché regime to mold a sophisticated, highly efficient secret police operation concerned with quelling dissidents and preventing subversion.[22] The irony is that this stepped-up security response coincided with an upgrading in the importance of economic relations between Niger and Libya.

As I indicated earlier, Niger's carefully calculated rural-development plans depend heavily on uranium revenues, which are vulnerable to fluctuations in the world market. 1981 was a critical year, because a precipitous drop in both world demand and price for uranium severely reduced Niger's development budget and raised the specter of a domestic backlash. From a 1980 tariff of 24,500 CFA francs per kilo uranium fell to 16,500 CFA francs per kilo. France came to Niger's aid by paying 20,000 CFA francs per kilo, but purchased a lesser quantity than originally projected. Libya stepped into the breach. Also paying above the market price, Tripoli acquired 1,212 tons of Nigerien uranium during the first half of 1981—six times more than what it purchased in all of 1980.[23]

Prior to this agreement, the United States had urged Niger to suspend uranium sales to Libya. In the U.S. framework of global East-West strategic rivalry, Niger's hostility toward Soviet-backed Libya dictated the logic of such a course of action. But from the perspective of the Kountché regime, security calculations involve not only the consolidation of external military and strategic alliances but also the acquisition of resources for economic and social development. Since uranium revenues are a key factor in this strategy, the regime was prepared to sell to an otherwise antagonistic Libya at a special "solidarity" price. Perhaps in recognition of this quandary, Niger reestablished diplomatic relations with Libya in March 1982. Such pragmatism intermittently overrides even the most belligerent conflicts between Black Africans and Arabs.

Chad

For Chad's political rulers, regime security has been more fantasy than strategy. Successive incumbents have sought military assistance in fighting a debilitating civil war and economic aid in providing a modicum of social welfare and development. For the first decade of independence, France was the principal source of assistance. In the 1970s Libya began to vie with France for the role of Chad's chief patron. As the struggle intensified, both states became flagrant violators of Chadian sovereignty, but their repeated interventions failed to assure the country's security or stability. One after another the various Chadians who sought external support in their efforts to control the central government lost the initiative in a process that each tried to use as an enhancement tactic.

The process began with Chad's first president, François (later N'garta) Tombalbaye. A southerner and a Christian, he was confronted with the formation in 1966 of the Front de Libération National du Tchad (FROLINAT). This grouping was launched in the Sudan by predominantly Muslim elements from northern Chad who pledged to fight a revolutionary, anti-imperialist war for national liberation. In addition to its Marxist agenda, FROLINAT advocated the official use of Arabic alongside French.[21] Arms and equipment were initially supplied to the combatants by Algiers and Tripoli. Libya recognized FROLINAT as the legitimate government of Chad in 1971.

As the rebellion gained ground in Chad's northernmost prefecture, Tombalbaye asked Paris for combat troops, But in 1972 relations with

France turned sour, and the Chadian president called for the withdrawal of French forces from his army. This move was precipitated by France's refusal to authorize a 4 billion CFA francs loan, conditionally promised earlier that year, on the grounds that Chadian officials had not taken sufficient austerity measures to improve the country's economic predicament. The regime was wrenching under the combined impact of civil war and protracted drought, and it seemed unable to assert control.

Caught in a quandary, Tombalbaye mounted an anti-imperialist barrage and concomitantly reached out to the Arab camp. He announced that Chad would no longer tolerate French interference in its internal affairs and summarily repudiated the bilateral cooperation accords. To reinforce the rupture, he pushed a new directive called "Chaditude"—a return to African authenticity aimed at reversing the effects of French cultural imperialism. On the Arab front, Libya was the prime concern. Hoping to void Kaddafi's support for FROLINAT, in 1972 the Tombalbaye regime signed a pact of friendship with Tripoli, reestablished formal ties, and obtained a promise (unkept) of $92 million in aid. The regime also broke relations with Israel at this juncture.

Taken as a package, these initiatives amounted to a visceral attempt to create an anti-imperialist, internally integrative national identity compatible with the Afro-Arab duality of the Chadian population. But the process of political disintegration in Chad was too far advanced to respond to such crude stratagems. Tombalbaye lost his gamble with Libya, which in 1973 moved troops into the Azou strip along Chad's northwestern border. Two years later President Tombalbaye was killed in a coup that brought Gen. Felix Malloum to power.

Although Malloum's military government announced a policy of national reconciliation and invited all opposition groups to join the new regime, rampant factionalism prevailed. FROLINAT split after Goukouni Oueddei ousted Hissène Habré from its leadership. Goukouni received military backing from Libya and proceeded to capture and occupy territory in northern Chad. Habré, with his own army equipped with help from the Sudan, Egypt, and Saudi Arabia, moved into the south. FROLINAT eventually spawned as many as eight factions, but Goukouni and Habré remained the major players. Chad's national army was the main casualty in this state of affairs. Having suffered numerous routs, General Malloum appealed to both Libya and France in 1978 to halt the hydra-headed rebellion.

What followed was the demise of the state's already fragile civil and military administration.[25] France did not fight with Chad's national army but instead functioned as an independent agent—eventually deciding to back Habré to head a coalition government. Libya vacillated between support for Goukouni and Ahmat Acyl, an Arab Chadian who deserted Goukouni's FROLINAT with his own army. In 1979 the commander of the French forces in Chad allowed Goukouni to move his men into the capital so they could fight alongside Habré against General Malloum's army. Even after their military victory, however, the two forces refused to establish a joint command, and in March 1980 Goukouni and Habré began a nine-month battle for control of N'Djamena. France pulled out of Chad in May, and the stalemate was finally broken in Goukouni's favor when Libya deployed three regiments and an Islamic Legion of 4,500–5,000 troops assisted by East German and Soviet advisors. With Habré soundly defeated and a semblance of order restored, Goukouni traveled to Tripoli in January 1981 and signed an agreement that provided for a merger between Libya and Chad.

The outcry provoked by this move was immediate and widespread. From partners in Goukouni's own coalition government who had not been consulted, to other African states considered targets of Kaddafi's expansionist ambitions, to the OAU with its principle of the inviolability of colonial borders, the merger was condemned as an "impossible marriage." French protests reflected a dual concern with the territorial violation of a former colony and the Libyan challenge to the credibility of the Gaullist protective strategic umbrella in Africa. For the United States, the merger was one more case of Soviet surrogate expansionism in Africa and could not be countenanced. The antagonists eventually prevailed in forcing a Libyan withdrawal, because Kaddafi, who was next in line to take over as president of the OAU at its 1982 Tripoli summit, was concerned with preserving his prospects for continental leadership. France's new Socialist government cooperated with the United States in providing financial and logistical support for an OAU police force to replace the Libyan soldiers garrisoned in Chad, but the power vacuum that ensued precipitated a renewal of hostilities. Deprived of his Libyan firepower and getting no backup from the OAU contingent, Goukouni could not hold his own. By June 1982 Hissène Habré had seized military control of much of the country and installed himself as Chad's president.

Chad's tumultuous experience of war and civil strife reveals the vicissitudes of Afro-Arab relations. Given the ethnoreligious nature of the country's north-south cleavage, ties with Arab states have been sought not only by the central polity but by faction leaders from the north as well. We have seen that Arab ideological and strategic competition further encouraged transnational factional alliances to the detriment of sovereignty. Thus Goukouni gained Libyan backing, whereas Habré received support from the Sudan, Egypt, and Saudi Arabia. This alliance pattern reinforced Chad's internal divisions and at the same time injected intra-Arab rivalries into an already crowded arena of political conflict.

Even as these centrifugal forces were undermining sovereignty and stability, the state received the benefits of Arab largesse from two camps. After announcing the merger agreement, Tripoli assumed responsibility for paying Chad's civil servants and provided budgetary support, technical aid, and famine relief along with military assistance. During this same period Chad received commitments of $4,937,000 in emergency food aid and $20,906,000 for project assistance from the Islamic Conference Organization's Sahel solidarity committee. To the extent that an important element of regime security relates to the availability of resources for economic development and social welfare, Chad and the rest of Black Africa have much to gain from noninterventionist cooperation extended along these lines. The stark contrast between these illustrative approaches to domestic security assistance and the controversial Arab military posture in Chad underscores the contradictory strivings of Afro-Arab solidarity.

Three Levels of Solidarity

This overview of relations between Africans and Arabs combined with the lessons of the Niger and Chad case studies demonstrates the articulation of solidarity as a multitiered concept. Despite the transformative potential of a globally oriented strategic military alliance, no such option has been seriously pursued. More to the point, the proclivity of regimes to manipulate the principle of Afro-Arab solidarity for short-term regional or domestic political objectives has diminished its import in geopolitical terms. It is therefore necessary to note how the parameters of solidarity change as one moves from a global, to a bilateral, to a subnational level of analysis.

Let us begin at the global level. From the perspective of Black African regimes anxious to enhance their security posture, closer ties with the Arab world hold two particularly attractive prospects: The framework offers alliance strategies to counter neocolonial political and military ties, and it promotes Arab aid for development as a way to break out of economic dependence on the East or the West. In international forums such as the United Nations, the Islamic Conference Organization, and the Afro-Arab summit, Africans and Arabs have achieved a considerable degree of rhetorical cohesion with respect to these objectives. Thus, the condemnation of white-minority rule in southern Africa, support for the rights of the Palestinians, and calls for more substantial resource transfers from rich countries to poor countries have been etched on their shared agenda. In practice, however, African and Arab governments have disaggregated these issue areas and treated them as discrete sets of action items. The fact that agencies funded by the Arab members of OPEC have outpaced their Western counterparts in aid transfers to Black Africa is a positive sign of the alliance's import. But the failure of the Afro-Arab bloc to develop sustained, coordinated policy responses with respect to southern African liberation and the Arab-Israeli conflict has caused serious lapses of commitment. Even if the levels of Arab aid remain high, the absence of issue linkage may ultimately undermine Afro-Arab solidarity's political rationale as a vehicle for change in global politics.

At the level of bilateral relations, Afro-Arab solidarity is affected by the ideological and strategic competition within the Arab world. One of the lessons learned from the Niger and Chad cases is that the alliance strategies of Black African regimes make clear distinctions between friendly and hostile Arab powers and vice versa. Solidarity is thus diminished by the fact that one must ask Which Arabs? and Which Africans? It is at the bilateral level that African and Arab states have signed mutual defense agreements and contracted arrangements to provide, train, or equip military and paramilitary forces. The targets of these agreements are frequently neighboring states that are themselves part of the Afro-Arab alliance evoked in global politics.

At the subnational level, the solidarity principle is stood on its head, as in the cases in which ethnoreligious factors were elevated above solidarity between states. In Niger and Chad, Libya manipulated transnational appeals to ethnicity and militant Islam—in the process violating the principle of sovereignty to form alliances with political factions and dissident elements. Such actions are highly destabilizing internally and counterproductive to solidarity goals articulated at the global level.

Relations between Black African and Arab states are subject to the contending thrusts of these subnational, bilateral, and global patterns of solidarity. Clearly, the ambivalence of three uncoordinated levels of policy articulation severely diminishes the prospects for a broadly gauged security alliance of significant import. For the foreseeable future, however, the principle of Afro-Arab solidarity will continue to hold sway in international politics. Indeed, the very failure to consummate an effective challenge to the prevailing world economic, political, and security order perpetuates the conditions that give rise to renewed interest in solidarity.

Notes

1. I. M. Lewis, "Introduction," in *Islam in Tropical Africa*, 2d ed. (Bloomington: Indiana University Press, 1980), pp. 76–83.

2. *Africa Contemporary Record 1980–1981*, (hereafter *ACR 1980–1981*) (New York and London: Africana Publishing Co., 1981), p. 41.

3. Robert Buijtenhuijs, *Le Frolinat et les révoltes populaires du Tchad, 1965–1976* (La Haye: Mouton Editeur, 1978), pp. 38–39.

4. *ACR 1980–1981*, p. B59.

5. The governments of Senegal, The Gambia, Mali, and Niger see themselves as targets of Kaddafi's Islamic Legion. The situation in Chad is complicated by the fact that Libya has at various times supported different Muslim leaders.

6. These border changes are detailed in Bernard Lanne, *Tchad-Libye: La querelle des frontières* (Paris: Editions Karthala, 1982).

7. United Nations, General Assembly, 15 December 1950, Resolution No. 392 (5).

8. *Africa South of the Sahara 1981–1982*, (London: Europa Publications, Ltd., 1981), p. 297.

9. *ACR 1980–1981*, p. B560.

10. *Marchés Tropicaux*, 11 September 1981, p. 2327.

11. My discussion of the 1977 Program of African-Arab Cooperation is based on the analysis by Willard R. Johnson, "Africans and Arabs: Collaboration without Co-operation, Change without Challenge," *International Journal* (Autumn 1980):766–793.

12. Delegates to the Islamic Conference Organization summit meeting in Niamey in August 1982 asked the organization's secretariat to complete arrangements for an Islamic military coordination bureau with Palestine.

13. Johnson, "Africans and Arabs," p. 767.

14. Libya has provided cheap oil under lenient terms to Ghana, Mali, Chad, and Mozambique. Until the outbreak of the Gulf war, Iraq sold oil to Mozambique at a special "solidarity" price.

15. For example, South Africa paid a premium of around $9 a barrel for Kuwaiti oil in late 1979, when the price was $26 a barrel.

16. The liberation movements of southern Africa have received minimal amounts of material and technical assistance from Algeria, Egypt, and Libya. Jordan has provided some financial aid. See François Constantin, "Les difficultés de la coopération militaire afro-arabe," *Annuaire de l'afrique et du moyen-orient, les armées et la défense* (Paris: Jeune Afrique, 1980), pp. 83–85.

17. *New York Times*, 21 February 1983, p. A6.

18. The Saudi request for four U.S. electronic surveillance planes provoked Libya to throw its support behind Iraq and break relations with Saudi Arabia. The Islamic Conference Organization met in Taif (Saudi Arabia) in January 1981.

19. Organization of the Islamic Conference, General Secretariat, *Problems of the Sahel* (ICFM/13-82/SAHEL/D.1), 22–28 August 1982.

20. President Diori's foreign-policy advisor during this period was an Egyptian, Jacques Baulin. Under his tutelage Niger welcomed its first resident ambassador from the Soviet Union, and Diori issued a call for a Marshall Plan for the Sahel to attract new aid donors to a region that was almost exclusively a French domain.

21. Koffi Mamane, "Le paradox nigérien," *Afrique-Asie*, 8 November 1982, pp. 9–10.

22. Koffi Mamane, "Un gant de velours," *Afrique-Asie*, 26 December 1982, pp. 14–15.

23. *Marchés Tropicaux*, 11 September 1981, p. 2327; 17 July 1981, p. 1884; 20 November 1981, p. 2947.

24. Bruno Ver Duzan, "Tensions politiques et éthniques au Sahel: Questions et suggestions," *African Perspectives* 2 (1977):82.

25. *Africa South of the Sahara 1981–1982*, pp. 290–294.

11. South African Liberation: Touchstone of African Solidarity

Annette M. Seegers

Introduction

The purpose of this chapter is to examine the interaction between independent or Black African states and South Africa from the perspective of how this interaction involves, shapes, or changes security issues.[1] This examination will focus on the roots of the conflict between White and Black Africa; African liberation efforts, the collective military arrangements against a possible South African counterattack, and the effects of the liberation struggle on South Africa's internal and external policies during the period 1963–1972; and independent African nations' offensive and defensive measures against South Africa as well as South Africa's reaction to them during the period from 1973 to the present.

The Roots of the Conflict

The reasons for the conflict between South Africa and Black Africa are often taken as self-evident: South Africa is a political system based on inequality, whereas Black Africa is dedicated to equality. Most Black African states, moreover, have a history of colonialism (which by definition is a relationship of political inequality) and accompanying experiences of racial inequality. This background accounts for the consistent and powerful role that anticolonialism plays in African affairs[2] as well as for the desire to rid the continent of political systems based on inequality, colonialism, racism, and the like. Indeed, these historically conditioned concerns are so obvious that Africans themselves have not bothered to develop their political standpoints into full-fledged philosophical statements.[3]

That these issues strike a deep chord in Africans' lives is evident in the rhetoric used against South Africa. The state has been accused of a vast range of transgressions, including racism, violations of human rights, practicing policies similar to colonialism, and being a threat to world peace. Yet this very rhetoric has sometimes clouded the issue. Regardless of whether or not South Africa is guilty of the above, it would be naive to conclude that Black African states are united in support of liberation in Southern Africa because they are united in their commitment to human rights. Many of the states that have been very strong in supporting Southern African liberation, ranging from Amin's Uganda to Sekou Toure's Guinea, are guilty of gross violations of human rights in their own societies. It would be almost as naive to assert that Black African States are committed to the principle of "majority rule," if by that is meant a system of government that allows the majority of the people periodically to choose their own rulers in free elections.[4]

When the principles at the root of the conflict are stripped of their rhetorical excesses, only opposition to racially exclusive political rule remains as the unifying factor. In its negative form, racially exclusive political rule is viewed as "alien" (and as such, "colonial"); in its positive form, it means that political rulers should be racially representative of the majorities of particular societies.[5]

At the time of the creation of the Organization of African Unity (OAU) in 1963 (and subsequently), the African nations expressed their opposition to racially exclusive political rule by stating that it (1) prevents *"national* self-determination" and constitutes a "flagrant violation of the inalienable rights of the *legitimate* [emphasis added] inhabitants of the territories concerned" and (2) inevitably involves racism or "doctrines of human inequality."[6] The logical consequence of these principles was the geopolitical division of Africa into Black and White Africa; and since such a division was also an affront to the principles involved, independent African states, in the words of Article 3 (Sixth Clause) of the OAU Charter, declared their "absolute dedication to the total emancipation of the African territories which are still dependent."[7]

The translation of matters of principle into political practice was, however, problematic. The OAU was forged out of the Casablanca, Monrovia, and Brazzaville groups, and although all agreed that a "White South" in Africa was unacceptable, how the White South affected individual states' security concerns was unclear. Eventually a concensus was reached at the Addis Ababa meeting in 1963. In particular, two areas of agreement emerged that were to structure the OAU and its member states' subsequent interaction with southern Africa. First, even if the powers in southern Africa (Portugal, South Africa, and Britain as the authority in Zimbabwe) were not inherently imperialistic states, the OAU believed that these powers were individually or collectively capable of attacking OAU members. The fear of aggression was especially focused on South Africa as the dominant power in the "White Bastion" and led to proposals for a collective defense arrangement. Second, independent African states would cooperate in offensive moves against southern Africa to effect the liberation of those territories. The OAU would act as a coordinating body in this liberation effort, which would include pressure directed at the colonial powers (Britain and Portugal) to withdraw from the area; aid to the various liberation movements in the form of matériel and moral support; and activities at meetings of international, regional, and other bodies designed to gain support for liberation efforts and isolate the southern African regimes.[8]

The defensive and offensive goals of the African states were formally incorporated in the OAU's structure by the creation of the Defense Commission; as one of the five specialized agencies of the OAU it was charged with the responsibility to "create a security system in Africa."[9] It should be pointed out that this security concern was historically conditioned and, in effect, constituted a declaration of war between White and Black Africa.[10] It was, moreover, not intended to be war-in-speech alone; the independent African states expected to make an actual contribution to the liberation of southern Africa.

The First Ten Years: 1963–1972

At the Addis Ababa meeting in 1963 it was agreed that, although the OAU would have a special role in the liberation of southern Africa, the OAU itself would not be responsible for that liberation. Instead, it would help the various liberation movements by providing aid and would create a united liberation front by coordinating the activities of the movements. To provide aid, a Special Fund was created that would be the repository of voluntary contributions by African (and other) states. To create a united front, an African Liberation Committee (ALC) was created; it would promote unity by, among other things, using its good offices to reconcile rival movements. The ALC would meet biannually, and its budget would be submitted to and approved by the OAU Council of Ministers.[11]

The Liberation Offensive

From the very beginning the liberation offensive was plagued by problems within the OAU and ALC, as well as by the centrifugal effect of unforeseen developments in local and world politics.

With regard to events within the OAU and ALC, there was initial disagreement as to the membership of the ALC. Eventually a compromise was reached whereby not only proximity and experience in liberation struggle were criteria, but also prior contact with the liberation movements (i.e., before 1963) and a geographic balance. Nine states thus became members,[12] but subsequently the ALC has been steadily expanding. One reason for this expanding membership is that states who made financial contributions to the Special Fund have demanded inclusion in the ALC. The financial support by African contributors has been a source of constant criticism. The first report of the ALC indicated that only five states had made contributions, and although this report came shortly after the creation of the OAU in August 1963, the financial condition of the Special Fund since has not shown any marked improvement.[13] The noncontribution by OAU members is commonly attributed to two factors. First, some states have argued that the ALC Executive Secretariat misused or recklessly spent the money allocated to it. Even the liberation movements themselves have expressed dissatisfaction with the ALC's handling of financial matters.[14] Second, other states are simply preoccupied with their domestic financial and other problems and have no surplus resources to make an effective (or indeed any) contribution.

One consequence of the financial woes of the ALC therefore has been that contributing states demand membership. By 1977, for example, there were twenty-one members—a number that turns military planning into a series of political compromises and saps the expenditures of the Special Fund. Another consequence is that most African (and other) contributors prefer either to bypass the ALC altogether or to provide support in nonmonetary forms like providing asylum to political refugees, granting refuge to nonpolitical refugees, and providing political and military facilities.[15] The most likely African contributors are those who are close to southern Africa in a geographic and cultural sense and are ideologically sympathetic to particular movements and whose leader's personality suits such initiatives.[16]

The large role of individual African states in aiding the liberation movements directly complicated the aim of the OAU to unite rival movements within particular territories. In the case of rival movements in South Africa (the ANC and PAC), Zimbabwe (ZANU and ZAPU), Angola (the FNLA, MPLA, and UNITA), Mozambique (COREMO and FRELIMO), and Portuguese Guinea (PAIGC and FLING),[17] the OAU initially called on them to unite. When this failed, the ALC in 1965 appointed several commissions of inquiry to unite the movements, but this also was unsuccessful. Thereupon the OAU decided to support only the most effective or active movements,[18] but this also failed to solve the problem: the movements simply inflated their claims or sent ill-prepared guerrillas into areas without the necessary political preparation.

Besides these problems, several events severely inhibited the liberation struggle. The most severe were the declaration of unilateral independence in Zimbabwe in 1965 by the Smith regime and the Nigerian civil war between 1968 and 1970. With regard to Zimbabwe, the OAU had warned against the possibility of a Unilateral Declaration of Independence (UDI). Unable to prevent it, the OAU also could not persuade a sufficient number of African states to sever diplomatic relations with Britain (for failing to resolve the issue), nor could it effect a prompt and adequate reaction by the United Nations (UN). More than a year after the UDI the UN Security Council determined that the Zimbabwean situation was, as seen by the African states in terms of Article 39 of the UN Charter, a threat to international peace and security. Nevertheless, the Security Council still refused to authorize the use of collective force in terms of Article 42. Sanctions were instituted, but these were broken by many African states. The disenchantment with the UN over the Zimbabwean issue was underscored by the International Court of Justice's initial ruling on Namibia, namely that Ethiopia and Liberia lacked good standing.

The Nigerian civil war also brought divisions: Tanzania, the host of the ALC, was one of the states that recognized Biafra. Nigeria in response withdrew from the ALC.[19] To complicate matters further, a rash of military coups occurred during the 1966–1969 period. This generally prompted a closer attention to domestic affairs; in particular, the overthrow of President Nkrumah and other states' involvement in it caused divisions at the 1966 meeting of the Council of Ministers.

Frustrated by these difficulties, the OAU and ALC in the late 1960s appeared to lose much of their militant character or at least were in a "state of transition" in which socioeconomic matters were stressed.[20] Although many of its initiatives in the 1960s then came to nothing, the OAU did develop the capability to defeat the political and diplomatic initiatives of South Africa. This capability is particularly evident in the defeat of South Africa's "outward," "dialogue," or "detente" policies toward African states in the late 1960s, launched at a time when many African states were frustrated over the initial course of the liberation struggle.

Under the leadership of Prime Minister Vorster, South Africa's foreign policy in the late 1960s started to emphasize a "dialogue" with African states; that is, it expressed a desire for friendship, peaceful coexistence, and increasing contact with African states. In return, aid was suggested.[21] This initiative initially produced a bitter division among African states. Some, such as Ivory Coast and Malawi, argued that since concerted African states' libertion efforts and the liberation movements themselves had failed, diplomatic and political contact with South Africa might prove useful. One possible benefit could be the encouragement of moderate groups and trends within South Africa.[22]

Alerted to the possible schisms in African Solidarity that might result from a response to the Vorster regime's initiatives, several African states met to coordinate their responses. The result of this meeting, the Conference of East and Central African States held in Lusaka in April 1969, was the Lusaka Manifesto, which again outlined the African states' position toward South Africa.[23] The Lusaka Manifesto reiterated the OAU's stress on equality, national self-determination, and racial harmony, but—in a departure regarding how these goals could be achieved—stated that if "peaceful progress to emancipation were possible, or if changed circumstances were to make it possible in the future, we would urge our brothers in the resistance movements to use peaceful methods of struggle even at the cost of some compromise on the timing of change."[24] The implication was thus not only that direct political contact with South Africa was permissible but also that African states would make compromises regarding the ends and means of liberation. The Lusaka Manifesto was nevertheless approved by the OAU Assembly in 1969, as well as by the UN General Assembly in November 1969.[25]

Despite this initial agreement, contact with South Africa continued to be a divisive issue. The Ivory Coast wished to pursue the dialogue question and was supported by Benin, Niger, Togo, Gabon, the Central African Republic, Lesotho, Swaziland, Malawi, and Malagasy. They were opposed by Nigeria, Ethiopia, Kenya, Tanzania, and others. The question of dialogue then came to a head at the OAU meetings of the Assembly and Council of Ministers in Addis Ababa in June 1971, where the OAU reversed the dialogue policy in the Declaration on Dialogue. This declaration reiterated the principles of the OAU Charter, and dialogue was deemphasized, although still an option. Most importantly, the declaration included a formal obligation that any contact with South Africa by individual OAU members could only be undertaken with the OAU's approval. Clearly, the OAU was not prepared to have African Solidarity become a victim of South African Liberation. Thus OAU members did not have the right of independent opinion, and independent foreign policy did not apply in the case of dialogue with the South African government.[26]

Although the Declaration on Dialogue was not unanimously approved, opposition to southern African regimes had produced a formal African Solidarity. Those states who wished to maintain overt contact with South Africa could face charges of undermining the OAU. Accordingly, the members of the Conference of East and Central African States reviewed the issue of dialogue and in the Mogadishu Declaration of 1971 stated that armed struggle was the only possible way to deal with South Africa.[27] The following meeting of the OAU Assembly rode the wave of this solidarity, for the Rabat summit of 1972 was "the finest example of African unity in the history of the OAU."[28]

At the creation of the OAU in 1963 African Solidarity was viewed both as a prerequisite of South African Liberation and as its final result. After ten years it was evident that African Solidarity as a prerequisite for action was more problematic than initially supposed. Solidarity took a decidedly formal form, in that overt contact with South Africa by individual states was formally conditional on OAU approval (i.e., the approval of the majority of OAU members). Thus, while many OAU members maintained covert political and—especially—economic contact with South Africa,[29] only Malawi risked the OAU's disapproval by maintaining overt political contact with South Africa. With regard to the end result, the success of the liberation movements themselves was limited.[30] Yet the African states' actions at the UN and other international and regional organizations, as well as their support of anti-apartheid groups in individual states, did succeed in isolating South Africa from much political and diplomatic contact and drawing attention to the situation in South Africa. This isolation and pressure was exercised by way of discouraging loans to and investment in South Africa; economic and military sanctions; the severance of cultural, diplomatic, and personal contact with South Africa; and a variety of other actions like the limitation of South Africa's sea, air, and telecommunications links with the rest of the world.[31]

Whether these actions aided or impeded progress towards liberation is of course the critical—and controversial—question. Some argue that the African states' actions were counterproductive, in that they led to a South African military buildup[32] and the hardening of a "laager mentality" among white South Africans with no racial reforms in the offing.[33] Others point out that the South African regime was weakened by its isolation in at least the military sphere, because conventional arms procurement would be destabilized by the UN arms embargoes.[34]

Continental Defense

As stated earlier, the OAU Charter created a Defense Commission that, in accordance with Article 2's commitment to the defense of African states' sovereignty, territorial integrity, and independence, was responsible for defensive arrangements against a possible external and probable South African attack. Like much of the OAU Charter, the Defense Commission was the result of compromise: Ghana and—to some extent—Ethiopia wanted to create an African High Command or a centralized collective military system. The idea of a collective military system was, however, not accepted. The more moderate states conceded to the Casablanca group that some continental defense arrangement was necessary, but that it would simply create a fluid, decentralized arrangement by having a Defense Commission that would coordinate member states' defense policies.[35]

Up to the 1970 Council of Ministers meeting in Lagos in the wake of the Portuguese intervention in Guinea, the Defense Commission and the idea of an African High Command was moribund. In fact, the Defense Commission met only twice, in Accra in 1963 and Freetown in 1965; the scheduled third meeting was canceled because a quorum was lacking. At the first meeting Ghana submitted an ambitious proposal for a continental defense arrangement, basically consisting of a centralized military organization with responsibility to the OAU Assembly. The proposal, as later modified, attracted considerable support, but the supporting states still constituted a minority. The 1963 Assembly simply adopted a document entitled "Rationale for an African High Command," which stressed the basic offensive and defensive purposes of the Defense Commission. The Freetown meeting ended with proposals for the unification of military training, including a military academy, but to date this has not been implemented.[36]

There are many reasons for African states' reluctance to create a potent continental defensive system. First, there are purely technical difficulties, such as the standardization of equipment, training, and organizational procedures, as well as scarce resources. Second, some states point out that a high command would result in a loss of sovereignty for member states. Third, the number of coups propelled the African military to political prominence—and political-civil leaders were reluctant to relinquish political control over their military establishments.[37] These problems should be seen, moreover, against the background of African leaders' staggering domestic problems.

In view of these obstacles, a continental defense or a joint military expedition against South Africa was most improbable. Yet the expectation of a South African attack was premised on the actuality of such an expedition.[38] Nigeria indeed pointed out that the possibility of external aggression against any OAU member was remote, but such concerns do raise the question of whether South Africa was disposed to, or capable of, aggression against OAU members.

For the first ten years of the OAU's existence South Africa was ensconced in the White Bastion, and despite the absence of a formal defense agreement among the states in the region, there was cooperation among them regarding counterinsurgent operations. South African police and military equipment were sent to Zimbabwe, and there is evidence of intelligence and other military cooperation between South Africa and Portugal.[39] South Africa's military budget also steadily increased during the 1960s: The total military expenditure as a percentage of the gross national product (GNP) rose from 0.8 percent in 1960 to 2.3 percent in 1973, and actual defense spending amounted to 5 percent of the GNP in 1973.[40] These increases, especially when seen against South Africa's sustained economic growth in the 1960s, have been viewed as an indication of an expansive or "imperial" mood among South African policymakers, but significant evidence to the contrary also exists. Studies on South African foreign policy tend to agree that it has a strong legalistic component, i.e., at least until the 1970s it closely followed international legal guidelines.[41] Moreover, as Grundy has shown,[42] there has always been strong Afrikaner opposition to the employment of troops beyond South Africa's territorial boundaries.

There thus is legitimate doubt as to whether South Africa, alone or as part of the White South, was politically disposed toward aggression against OAU members. The OAU, similarly, had neither the political disposition nor the capability to launch an expedition against South Africa. Indeed, both the defensive and offensive goals of the African nations seemed to exist primarily on a rhetorical level: The liberation-in-speech was well underway, but the prospect for an actual liberation of Southern Africa was gloomy.[43]

The Next Ten Years: 1973–1982

After the 1971 Addis Ababa meeting of the OAU Assembly, African solidarity was guaranteed by the formal OAU prohibition of states' independent courses of action regarding South Africa. At the following Assembly meeting in Rabat, the African nations thus gathered to reaffirm their dedication to South African liberation in a defensive, as well as offensive, sense.

The Liberation Offensive

The Rabat meeting left the goal of liberation intact, but introduced several important changes in the means of liberation. First, it upgraded the status of the liberation movements, allowing them to speak on liberation matters at the Council of Ministers and to attend closed meetings of the Assembly. Second, it attempted to strengthen the ALC by increasing contributions to the Special Fund and enlarging the ALC membership.

Third, it adopted a timetable for African liberation, with the liberation of the Portuguese colonies as a priority. The liberation of South Africa thus was postponed. The OAU also attempted to increase the involvement of individual states by asking that they act as hosts to liberation movements (primarily by providing bases), as well as requesting contributions in the form of equipment and personnel. This would have been a major policy shift, for previously the OAU had not requested troops but simply equipment and money. The proposal for personnel, however, was opposed by the liberation movements, and subsequent OAU directives to the ALC reverted to the view that the liberation movements should supply their own manpower.[44]

The financial end of the ALC did subsequently improve; by 1974 it could provide the Portuguese movements with the aid promised in 1973. The focus on the Portuguese movements, however, was short-lived, as a Portuguese coup in April 1974 toppled the Caetano regime and decolonization became official Portuguese policy. Even so the prospect of independent African states bordering on Namibia, South Africa, and Zimbabwe raised tantalizing possibilities for guerrilla struggle in South Africa. Yet in 1983, ten years after the "spirit of Rabat," the condition of African Solidarity appears deteriorated.

Initially the ALC played an important role in the transfers of power in Mozambique and the former Portuguese Guinea, but at the 1975 meeting in Dar es Salaam the OAU and the ALC were rent by the divisions produced by the Angolan situation. Just as in Zimbabwe, the ALC had failed to unite the rival movements—a situation immensely complicated by the South African intervention of August 1975 and the presence of Cuban troops. Two years after the Portuguese coup, three factors were revealed that were to influence all future events in the area. First, the Front-Line States or presidents replaced the ALC as the OAU's vanguard of liberation. The idea of regular contact between states bordering on liberation targets first surfaced during the Angolan conflict, and the group initially consisted of four members: Presidents Kaunda of Zambia, Machel of Mozambique, Khama of Botswana, and Nyerere of Tanzania. President Neto of Angola and Prime Minister Mugabe of Zimbabwe later joined the group. As host of the ALC, Tanzania became the leading Front-Line State; the ALC and its staff became incorporated with the various policymaking organs of the Front-Line States. The close working relationship with the eastern Front-Line States, Tanzania and to a lesser extent Mozambique, has identified the ALC with these countries' policies and enhanced the position of the ALC within the OAU.[45]

The rise of the ALC–Front-Line States alliance on liberation matters has caused considerable resentment within the OAU. At the 1975 Dar es Salaam meeting there was some criticism of the alliance's "monopoly" of the liberation struggle, as well as its failure to unite rival movements, but the OAU Assembly did eventually endorse the alliance's actions in the Dar es Salaam Declaration. This support continued until the 1977 Assembly meeting in Libreville, where ALC and Front-Line States were again criticized for failing to unite rival movements. At this meeting it became evident that the ALC–Front-Line States alliance was a member of the group of "progressives" in the OAU and that it did not automatically enjoy the support of the majority of OAU members; it needed the support of a powerful patron-state. Although its support base was precarious, the ALC has since undergone further radicalization. It has vigorously supported the cause of the Popular Front for the Liberation of Saguia el Hamra and Rio de Oro (POLISARIO), a stance initially supported by the majority of OAU members, but one that since then has severely divided the organization. In fact, at the August 1982 Assembly meeting, only sixteen heads of state and government attended—fewer than half of the thirty-four needed to form a quorum.[46]

Second, the OAU pays increasing attention to the role of extracontinental powers in southern Africa. One manifestation is the OAU's stress on the contribution that South Africa's main trading partners (the United States, Britain, France, and West Germany) can make to liberation efforts, to the point of viewing these trading links as the critical factor in South Africa's survival.[47] Another manifestation is UN actions, ranging from South Africa's suspension from the General Assembly in 1974 to the mandatory Security Council arms embargo in November 1977. Although the full ramifications of these actions are yet to come and although not all Western nations have severed all their links with South Africa,[48] the supportive Western role can no longer be presumed by South Africa. This was particularly evident in UN-sponsored conferences in Mozambique and Nigeria during 1977.[49] The significance of these changed strategic presumptions can only be gauged when they are combined with the implications of the Cuban presence in Angola and the Soweto disturbances of 1976–1977. As previously noted, sanctions and arms embargoes injected an element of instability into South Africa's conventional arms procurement; the Cuban presence now raised the possibility of an externally supported conventional attack, without Western support for South Africa and with a Soweto-like domestic uprising. For South Africa, clearly a "worst case" strategy scenario was at hand.

Third, although Front-Line States act as hosts of South African liberation movements (particularly Mozambique as host of the ANC), the relationships between South Africa and Botswana, Zimbabwe, and Mozambique to date have not deteriorated to open warfare. The reason is that southern African states are enmeshed in a network of functional—though not political—integration, which renders politically hostile neighbors vulnerable to South African economic pressure. This mediates the political hostility of many Front-Line States, thus limiting their role in liberation efforts.[50] In this regard there has always been a kind of countersolidarity in southern Africa, and although there are indications that the Front-Line States want to reduce their dependence on South Africa, as witnessed in the creation of a Southern African Development Coordination Conference, they are still vulnerable to South African pressure. This pressure could include restrictions on rail and port use, black migration, imports and the movement of nationals, as well as the manipulation of South Africa's exports, technical assistance, and electricity supply and the suspension of the Customs Union Agreement.[51]

Twenty years after the creation of the OAU it is thus clear that solidarity with regard to the goal of South African Liberation still exists, but that African Solidarity as a prerequisite for action or agreement on the means of liberation is improbable or perhaps even unnecessary. The initiative for action resides with the liberation movements in South Africa (and Namibia), the Front-Line States, and increasingly with extracontinental powers. This, again, raises the question of the contribution of African states to African liberation as an end result.

While the White Bastion has been whittled away, it is by no means clear to what extent African Solidarity advanced the decay of the Portuguese empire or the Smith regime in Zimbabwe. It does seem safe to say that neither decay was a *direct* result of African Solidarity.[52] With regard to South Africa, it is of course geopolitically more exposed to guerrilla penetration, but thus far the Front-Line States have been reluctant to encourage such penetration. It could even be argued that African success at isolating South Africa has been counterproductive in that it resulted in the militarization of South African society. This militarization, so the argument goes, is reflected in the rise of the military establishment as a policymaking actor, increases in defense expenditures, the adoption of a "total strategy" since 1977,[53] and the possible development of nuclear weapons.[54] South Africa's estrangement from the West, furthermore, has led to public announcements by the foreign minister and prime minister during 1979 that South Africa would henceforth follow a more neutral course in its external relations. This "neutral option" would be accompanied by increasing economic cooperation with neighboring—and other—African states.[55]

As Gutteridge has remarked, "from the point of view of the Republic, this is normal, prudent contingency planning,"[56] but it has hardly turned South Africa into an impenetrable fortress. Since 1973 the financial position of the South African government has deteriorated, albeit not as a result of disinvestment; it has been calculated that a 40 percent decrease in all foreign investment would result in only a 1.3 percent decrease in total disposable income.[57] Given South Africa's structural vulnerabilities, particularly its reliance on gold exports for foreign exchange and the progressive financial cost of separate development, the nation nevertheless would become increasingly dependent on foreign loans and investment. African nations are unable to control the fluctuations of the world market, but they do have some influence on investment practices of foreign companies and states. This influence, combined with the destabilizing effect of the Soweto and subsequent domestic disturbances, has severely restricted South Africa's ability to attract capital for long-term investments. Many companies have either abandoned their plans for expansion in South Africa or prefer short-term investments with immediate yields. Short-term loans (three to five years) are still available, but at extraordinarily high interest rates.[58]

Although a "strategy for survival" is being pursued and military expenditures have increased, these actions mask several weaknesses of South Africa's military capabilities. One weakness, as already noted, is the difficulty in stable conventional arms procurement; it has indeed been remarked that South Africa's conventional deterrent is presently inadequate.[59] Other problems, such as manpower shortages, inadequate resources, and an exposed defense perimeter and military isolation, are produced by the counterguerrilla operations in Namibia.[60]

In sum, the contribution of African nations to South African liberation is thoroughly ambiguous: they have contributed to both the strengthening and weakening of the South African regime. The situation is nevertheless not hopelessly deadlocked. There is the possibility of reform from above or, failing that, widespread domestic disturbances that would force the Front-Line States and the extracontinental powers to adopt an interventionist political posture. These possibilities are not exhaustive, yet they point out that internal events and problems remain the catalysts of the South African situation.

Continental Defense

The idea of a continental defense against a possible southern African attack could not be actualized during the first ten years of the OAU. Immediately prior to the Rabat summit, however, the Portuguese actions in Guinea gave new urgency to the issue, leading to an emergency meeting of the OAU Council of Ministers in 1970 and the appointment of an executive commission to develop a suitable plan for continental defense in 1971.

At Rabat, the notion of a centralized defense arrangement was abandoned; instead, the idea proposed was that of an interlocking system of defense arrangements, with each region (headed by an executive secretariat) operating under the final authority of the OAU's Defense Commission and its Standing Committee for Defense. This system would be created by bilateral and multilateral defense agreements.[61] However, no agreement could be reached. The proposal was again discussed at the Addis Ababa meeting in 1973, where it met a similar fate. Although the Defense Commission did meet more frequently than in the 1960s, Cervenka remarks that plans for a continental defense arrangement became ritualistic and led to no concrete results.[62]

The inability of the OAU to rise above the level of rhetoric became painfully obvious after the Portuguese coup, as South African and Zimbabwean military forces seemed able to cross borders at will. This was particularly evident in Zimbabwe's frequent raids into Mozambique and South Africa's ventures into Angola and recently into Mozambique. Following the Angola venture, South Africa—which previously had required a soldier's consent for foreign military activities—adopted an amendment to its 1957 Defense Act (retroactive to August 9, 1975), stating that a "member of the South African Defense Force may in a time of war (most broadly defined) be required to perform service against an enemy at any place."[63] Although this was the legal confirmation of the attack the OAU had feared in 1963, it failed to provide a conventional deterrent, just as it failed to come to the aid of those states who were subject to South African and Zimbabwean attacks.[64]

Thus, at present there is a genuine and very delicate security interaction between South Africa and the Front-Line States, especially between South Africa and the states of Angola and Mozambique. They fear a South African attack, not in the form of military/political conquest, but in the form of hot-pursuit raids and other incursions aimed at the liberation movements they host. South Africa, similarly, is threatened by South-West Africa People's Organization (SWAPO) and ANC incursions and is willing to defend its defense perimeter and to punish the liberation movements.

Conclusion

African nations, in the twenty years since the creation of the OAU, have been consistent and united in their goal of South African Liberation. The abandonment of this goal is highly improbable, for its roots lie in a history of colonialism, racism, and inequality; the prevention of a repetition of this history has become Africans' "holy war" in which compromises cannot be tolerated.

Except for the initial period after the creation of the OAU, however, African nations rarely have been in agreement as to how South African Liberation should be achieved. In retrospect the "spirit of Rabat" and the prohibition on African nations' independent actions toward South Africa was only a veneer of solidarity, shattered by the implications of the Portuguese coup. The Front-Line States now select the best means of liberation, but each of these states, enmeshed in a web of economic countersolidarity, has its own *modus vivendi* with the South African government. The actions of the states, taken collectively, have been subject to criticism by OAU members; indeed approval can only be extracted by using Nigeria as a powerbroker. The failure to provide a collective deterrent to possible South African aggression against OAU members is perhaps the most dismal failure of the OAU. This failure, though not as noticeable during the 1960s—there was some muddy logic behind proposals for a collective defense arrangement, and South Africa appeared to be unwilling to launch an attack—became painfully obvious when South Africa and Rhodesia made incursions into the Front-Line States. Deprived of an African security umbrella, the Front-Line States' security can only be guaranteed by a political accommodation with South Africa or the presence of extra-continental forces.

In assessing the contribution of African nations to South African Liberation, it was pointed out that, although the White Bastion has shrunk in geopolitical terms, South Africa today is perhaps less vulnerable to external pressure than in 1963. Its vulnerability, as the Soweto disturbances and other events showed, derives more from the internal workings of the South African system. This internal dynamic of liberation was equally evident in the cases of Zimbabwe and the Portuguese colonies; they primarily decay from within—not from external pressures.

Finally, it should be noted that African Solidarity on South African Liberation has provided African nations with the most powerful unifying impetus in their recent history. It has propelled African nations to power in world affairs, thereby transforming world politics and institutions, and provided them with a useful consensus for socioeconomic—though not military—integration. It has also propelled the ALC–Front-Line group to prominence within the OAU, an exercise in historical irony that may prove to be a divisive factor. As the recent OAU summit showed, adherence to the principles of political liberation is potentially explosive, requiring the liberation not just of states in the White South.

Notes

1. Although South Africa has not been the only target of liberation efforts, this chapter concerns itself mostly with that country and refers to Angola, Mozambique, Zimbabwe, and other states only in passing.

2. Vernon D. McKay, *African Diplomacy: Studies in the Determinants of Foreign Policy* (New York: Praeger, 1966), p. 20.

3. Diallo Telli, "The Organization of African Unity in Historical Perspective," *African Forum* 1 (Fall 1965):18.

4. Ali A. Mazrui and David F. Gordon, "Independent African States and the Struggle for Southern Africa," in John Seiler, ed., *Southern Africa Since the Portuguese Coup* (Boulder, Colo.: Westview Press, 1980), p. 185.

5. Ibid.

6. Moses E. Akpan, "African Goals and Strategies Toward Southern Africa," *African Studies Review* 14 (September 1971):244–246.

7. For the OAU Charter, see Jon Woronoff, *Organizing African Unity* (Metuchen, N.J.: Scarecrow Press, 1970), pp. 642–648.

8. Leonard T. Kapungu, "The OAU's Support for the Liberation of Southern Africa," in Yassin El-Ayouty, ed., *The Organization of African Unity After Ten Years: Comparative Perspectives* (New York: Praeger, 1975), p. 136.

9. Zdenek Cervenka, *The Unfinished Quest for Unity: Africa and the OAU* (London: Julian Friedmann Publishers, 1977), p. 38. The other agencies are the Economic and Social Commission; the Educational and Cultural Commission; the Health, Sanitation, and Nutrition Commission; and the Scientific, Technical, and Research Commission.

10. This dedication to war by a regional organization has been controversial, especially with regard to its international legal ramifications. See Boutros Boutros-Ghali, "The Addis Ababa Charter: A Commentary," *International Conciliation* 546 (January 1964); Ali A. Mazrui, *Toward a Pax Africana: A Study of Ideology and Ambition* (Chicago: University of Chicago Press, 1967); and Ada Bozeman, *Conflict in Africa: Concepts and Realities* (Princeton, N.J.: Princeton University Press, 1976), pp. 23–45.

11. See Cervenka, *The Unfinished Quest for Unity,* pp. 50–52 for the internal organization of the ALC. It has four main organs. The Standing Committee on Information, Administration, and General Policy generally advises the liberation movements, publicizes their activities, and provides OAU members with information. The Standing Committee on Finance receives requests for aid and handles the budget expenditures. The Standing Committee on Defense advises the liberation movements on military matters, acts as a liaison between them and host states and other suppliers, and delivers the movements' financial requests to the Standing Committee on Finance. The fourth body is the Executive Secretariat. The latter's headquarters in Dar es Salaam coordinates the activities of the four organs and acts as a liaison to the liberation movements, thus forming the main link between the ALC and the liberation movements on the one hand and the OAU Secretariat, the Assembly of Heads of State and Government, and the Council of (Foreign) Ministers on the other hand.

12. Algeria, Egypt, Ethiopia, Guinea, Nigeria, Senegal, Tanzania, Uganda, and Zaire.

13. Cervenka, *The Unfinished Quest for Unity,* pp. 59–61, Akpan, "African Goals and Strategies," p. 251; and Kapungu, "The OAU's Support," p. 142.

14. Kapungu, "The OAU's Support," pp. 142–143.

15. For the different types of aid provided, see Vincent B. Khapoya, *The Politics of Decision: A Comparative Study of African Policy Toward the Liberation Movements,* Monograph Series on World Affairs, 12 (Denver: University of Denver, 1974–1975), pp. 26–29.

16. In these terms, West African states tend to be least supportive. Ibid.

17. ANC—African National Congress; PAC—Pan-Africanist Conference; ZANU—Zimbabwe African National Union; ZAPU—Zimbabwe African People's Union; FNLA—Frente Nacional de Libertaçao de Angola; MPLA—Popular Movement for the Liberation of Angola; UNITA—National Union for the Total Independence of Angola; COREMO—Revolutionary Council for Mozambique; FRELIMO—Front for the Liberation of Mozambique; PAIGC—Partido Africano de Independencia da Guiné e Cabo Verde; FLING—Front for the National Liberation of Guiné.

There are several good accounts of the liberation movements in the 1960s. For instance, see Richard Gibson, *African Liberation Movements* (London: Oxford University Press, 1972). For a more recent account of the movements in South Africa and Zimbabwe in the 1970s see, respectively, Gail M. Gerhart, *Black Power in South Africa: The Evolution of an Ideology* (Berkeley: University of California Press, 1978) and Lewis H. Gann and Thomas H. Henrikson, *The Struggle for Zimbabwe: Battle in the Bush* (New York: Praeger, 1981).

18. This policy apparently was reversed later when the ALC fixed its support on ZANU in Zimbabwe, the MPLA in Angola, PAIGC in Guinea, the ANC in South Africa, and FRELIMO in Mozambique. Rival claims were more or less ignored.

19. Zambia, Gabon, and Ivory Coast also recognized Biafra.

20. Zdenek Cervenka, "Major Policy Shifts in the Organization of African Unity, 1963–1973" in K. Ingham, ed., *Foreign Relations of African States* (London: Butterworths, 1974), pp. 332–333.

21. See Robert Molteno, *Africa and South Africa: The Implications of South Africa's "Outward-Looking" Policy* (London: Africa Bureau, 1971) and Sheridan Johns, "The Thrust of Pretoria's African Policy of Dialogue," *South African Quarterly* (Spring 1973).

22. Cervenka, "Major Policy Shifts," p. 335.

23. The manifesto was signed by Burundi, Central African Republic, Chad, Congo, Ethiopia, Kenya, Luanda, Somalia, Sudan, Tanzania, Uganda, Zaire, and Zambia. For the full text, see Kenneth Grundy, *Confrontation and Accommodation in Southern Africa* (Berkeley: University of California Press, 1973), pp. 315–323.

24. Ibid., p. 318.

25. Resolution 2505 (24).

26. Cervenka, *The Unfinished Quest for Unity*, pp. 118–119.

27. Ibid.

28. Ibid., p. 120.

29. Since this contact is covert, it is difficult to gauge its extent and significance. Exports to African states consist mainly of manufactured goods, while South Africa imports light consumer goods and raw materials. See Deon J. Geldenhuys, "Some Strategic Implications of Regional Economic Relationships for the Republic of South Africa," *ISSUP Strategic Review* (University of Pretoria) (January 1981):14–30. Geldenhuys quotes a newspaper report to the effect that Black Africa by 1974 constituted 13.5 percent of South Africa's export market (fn. 42).

30. With the possible exception of PAIGC and FRELIMO.

31. To list all these actions would be impossible. To get a flavor, see the Annual Reports of the Anti-Apartheid Movement (London) and the UN Special Committee on Apartheid.

32. Stockholm International Peace Research Institute (hereafter referred to as SIPRI), *Southern Africa: The Escalation of a Conflict* (Uppsala, Sweden: Almqvist and Wiksell, 1976), pp. 117–150.

33. See, for example, Douglas Brown, *Against the World: Attitudes of White South Africans* (Garden City, N.Y.: Anchor Books, 1969); John Seiler, "South African Perspectives and Responses to External Pressures," *Journal of Modern African Studies* 13 (1975); and F. M. Clifford-Vaughn, *International Pressures and Political Change in South Africa* (Cape Town: Oxford University Press, 1978).

34. This has led to stockpiling and the development of a domestic-arms industry dominated by the South African Armaments Manufacturing Corporation (ARMS-COR).

35. The right to regional collective self-defense prior to Security Council action is recognized by Article 51 of the UN Charter, but it was precisely the role of the UN in the then Congo (Zaire) that led to Nkrumah's suggestion of an African High Command. See T. A. Imobighe, "An African High Command: The Search For A Feasible Strategy of Continental Defence," *African Affairs* 79 (April 1980):241–245.

36. Ibid., p. 242.

37. Ibid., pp. 243, 249–250.

38. A South African attack would come when South Africa was "confronted with the prospect of a showdown with a well-coordinated and determined African force representing the collective moral and material force of all African States." Cervenka, *The Unfinished Quest for Unity*, p. 39.

39. SIPRI, *Southern Africa*, p. 109.

40. Ibid., p. 117.

41. See John E. Spence, *Republic Under Pressure: A Study of South African Foreign Policy* (Oxford: Oxford University Press, 1965); G. C. Olivier, *Suid-Afrika se Buitelandse Beleid* (Pretoria: Academica, 1977); and Edwin S. Munger, *Notes on the Formation of South African Foreign Policy* (Pasadena, Calif.: Castle Press, 1965).

42. Kenneth W. Grundy, *Defense Legislation and Communal Politics: The Evolution of a White South African Nation as Reflected in the Controversy Over the Assignment*

of Armed Forces Abroad 1912–1976, Papers in International Studies, Africa Series, no. 33 (Athens: Ohio University 1978).

43. See Akpan, "African Goals and Strategies," pp. 256–261 and Richard A. Fredland, "The OAU After Ten Years: Can It Survive?" *African Affairs* 72 (July 1973):309–316.

44. Cervenka, *The Unfinished Quest for Unity*, pp. 56–58. These ends and means were later elaborated in the ALC meeting in Accra in 1973. The Accra Declaration on the New Strategy for the Liberation of Africa stressed that liberation was a collective responsibility. This was apparently aimed at the noncontributing members of the OAU (and ALC), urging them to pay their outstanding dues, provide any other assistance (including bases), and be prepared to aid victims of a counterattack that this could inspire. With regard to the liberation movements, only those who were politically united and militantly effective would receive aid, with the largest portion earmarked for the Portuguese movements. Ibid., pp. 58–59.

45. Ibid., pp. 61–62.

46. *Time* (August 16, 1982), p. 34.

47. See, for example, the Resolution on South Africa of the OAU Assembly meeting in Addis Ababa, May 1973; the Resolution on sanctions against the white-minority regimes in Southern Africa of the OAU Assembly meeting in Kampala 1975; and the Resolution on South Africa of the OAU Assembly meeting in Port Louis, July 1976.

48. Western powers' policy options in a conspicuous theme of recent writing on South Africa. See Colin Legum, *The Western Crisis Over South Africa* (New York: Africana, 1979) and Robert I. Rotberg, *Suffer the Future: Policy Choices in Southern Africa* (Cambridge: Harvard University Press, 1980). For an emphasis on internal developments, see Gwendolen M. Calter, *Which Way Is South Africa Going?* (Bloomington: Indiana University Press, 1980).

49. These conferences were "primarily aimed at increasing international support for sanctions against S.A." Legum, *The Western Crisis*, p. 48.

50. See Geldenhuys, "Some Strategic Implications," passim.

51. Ibid. The best discussions of this countersolidarity can be found in Christian P. Potholm and Richard Dale, eds., *Southern Africa in Perspective: Essays in Regional Politics* (New York: Free Press, 1972) and Grundy, *Confrontation and Accommodation in Southern Africa*.

52. Mazrui and Gordon, "Independent African States," p. 183. See also R. M. Fields, *The Portuguese Revolution and the Armed Forces Movement* (New York: Praeger, 1976); Phillip C. Schmitter, "Liberation by Golpe: Retrospective Thoughts on the Demise of Authoritarian Rule in Portugal," *Armed Forces and Society* 2 (Fall 1975):5–33; Douglas Porch, *The Portuguese Armed Forces and the Revolution* (London: Croom Helm, 1977). On Zimbabwe see Gann and Henrikson, *The Struggle for Zimbabwe*; Lawrence Vambe, *From Rhodesia to Zimbabwe*; (London: Heineman, 1978); and Kees Maxey, *The Fight for Zimbabwe: The Armed Conflict in Southern Rhodesia Since UDI* (London: Rex Collings, 1975).

53. The "total strategy" is predicated on the "worst case" scenario, i.e., a combined external attack and domestic uprising, in which all means at the state's disposal would be used. See the Defence White Papers, (Pretoria, Department of Defence, 1977–1982); *ISSUP Strategic Review* (The University of Pretoria), which is devoted to the 1979 Defence White Paper; Legum, *The Western Crisis*, pp. 89–94; Rotberg, *Suffer the Future*, pp. 91–140; and William Gutteridge, "South Africa: Strategy for Survival?" *Conflict Studies* 131 (June 1981):14–21 especially.

54. See R. Walters, *South African Nuclear Development: Political and Strategic Implications* (New York: Social Science Research Center, 1977); Legum, *The Western*

Crisis, pp. 94–95; and Rotberg, *Suffer the Future*, ch. 5 (written in collaboration with Norma Kriger). For the nuclear debate in South Africa, see Mike Hough, "Deterrence and deterrence interaction with reference to the South African situation," and Denis Venter, "South Africa and the International Controversy Surrounding its Nuclear Capability," *Politikon* 5 (June 1978):5–29.

55. For an elaboration, see Wolfgang H. Thomas, "South Africa and Black Africa: The Future of Economic Interaction," and Deon J. Geldenhuys, "Die Regionale Opsie in Suid-Afrika se Buitelandse Beleid: Die moontlikheid van nouer samewerking in die Suid-Afrikaanse subsisteem," *Politikon* 6 (December 1979):103–136.

56. Gutteridge, "South Africa: Strategy for Survival?" p. 17.

57. Tom Wicker, "Should American Business Pull Out of South Africa," *New York Times Magazine* (June 3, 1979), p. 37.

58. Legum, *The Western Crisis*, pp. 48–52. See also Gutteridge, "South Africa: Strategy for Survival?" pp. 16–25; Pauline H. Baker, "South Africa's Strategic Vulnerabilities: The 'Citadel Assumption' Reconsidered," *African Studies Review* 20 (September 1977):89–99; and W. B. Vosloo, "Die Implikasies van Buitelandse Druk op Suid-Afrika," *Politikon* 5 (December 1978):125–141. For a dissenting view see Kenneth L. Adelman, *African Realities* (New York: Crane Russak, 1980), especially ch. 5 entitled "South Africa's Strategy for Survival."

59. Legum, *The Western Crisis*, p. 90.

60. Baker, "South Africa's Strategic Vulnerabilities," pp. 92–94 and Gutteridge, "South Africa: Strategy for Survival?" pp. 18–21.

61. For the details of this plan, see Cervenka, *The Unfinished Quest for Unity*, p. 42.

62. Ibid., p. 43.

63. Grundy, *Defence Legislation and Communal Politics*, p. 47. See also pp. 40–47.

64. Kapungu, "The OAU's Support," pp. 143–144.

12. National Security:
An African Perspective
D. Katete Orwa

Introduction

Concern with national security in Africa is largely a recent development and a consequence of decolonization. Thus most African countries have had fewer than twenty years in which to develop national-security policies. For Africans, national security became a major policy consideration only after the African colonial territories acquired independence and sovereignty. Since indigeneous African leaders began to assume political power in the early 1960s, the difficult tasks of formulating and implementing security policy have fallen into African hands.

National security involves the protection of vital national interests against possible external threat or challenge and entails the extension and promotion of national values—independence, sovereignty, territorial integrity, and a political and economic way of life. In Africa, similar to other developing regions and unlike developed countries, threats to national security may arise from within the nation-state as well as from outside it.

Internal conflicts arise from an uncompromising power struggle among the political elite. Those in power use government institutions to suppress those who are aspiring to supplant them.[1] The "outs" are therefore sometimes forced to resort to illegitimate means of seeking political office, which in turn may lead to civil or guerilla war, with accompanying intrastate and extrastate tensions. The outcome frequently produces political and non-political refugees, which further bear on the national security of the state.

The military seems to be central in this situation. African armies were created by the colonialists to protect the colonizers against internal rebellion by the colonized. After independence, armies were expected to perform two functions: external defense and the maintenance of internal security. In the latter case the military has proved more effective than the traditional security police, so that African leaders tend to rely on the military to help them perpetuate their hold on political offices. The use of the army to suppress political opponents and to thwart and make dysfunctional legitimate institutions for transfer of political power leaves the military as the only major power contender in many African states. The inevitable consequence is intervention in domestic politics. In several African countries such interventions have produced internal instability as well as interstate conflicts. Tanzanian-Ugandan relations during the 1970s and the lingering tension between Ethiopia and Sudan serve as examples. As a result, in some African cases the military intervention in politics has tended to threaten national security rather than to protect it.

National-Security Policymaking

African states frequently lack a clear demarcation between internal and external security in their policymaking. This problem arises because of a lack of trained personnel with long experience in security policymaking and management. The present generation of policymakers emerged with independence in the last twenty or so years (excepting Ethiopia and Liberia). Few of them can claim preindependence experience in the area of national-security policy, let alone in the general field of policymaking.

This situation has given rise to two additional problems, both of which affect national security. The first is that the professional (university-trained) policymakers are often ignored by the nonprofessional political element. This leads to national-security policy management by crisis. The second problem stems from presidential dominance. By and large presidents are nonprofessional policymakers, yet in Africa they tend to dominate and personalize policymaking. Presidents not only make pronouncements on many aspects of security issues, without having consulted with experts, but they also view themselves as competent managers of national-security policy. Consequently, much of security policy in many African countries is a reflection of the personality of their presidents. Policymaking in Uganda under Idi Amin, Libya under Gaddafi, Zaire under Mobutu, and Ghana under Nkrumah can be cited as examples. This situation may at times prove dangerous to the security of the state. The 1977 Egyptian-Libyan military engagement and the 1978–1979 Tanzania-Uganda war are examples of personalized presidential security policymaking and management. In Libya and Uganda the whims of their respective presidents prevailed, threatening the national security of these states.

Unlike the developed world where threats or challenges to national security tend, in large measure, to be external and national-security policies consequently are highly external in orientation, in the developing world the new African states can also face threats and challenges from within the nation-state. African states are experiencing serious economic and social inadequacies,[2] pronounced political deprivation (the monopolization of political power by the very few), and a lingering military weakness.[3] These factors have been made more complex by a dangerous inter-African arms race,[4] unreconcilable ideological divergencies,[5] and growing ethnic refugee problems.[6]

All of this requires that national-security management in Africa be farsighted and carefully thought out, both in short and long terms. An unintelligent policy decision and mismanagement might lead to catastrophic consequences, underscoring the important role of the professional policy-makers and managers. But, as has already been stated, this cadre of professionals has not assumed its proper function in most African countries; the exceptions are Nigeria, Algeria, Egypt since the death of Nasser, and Ethiopia under the present socialist government. Furthermore, the African situation calls for clearly stated strategic doctrines upon which national-security policies can be based. At the moment there are no such doctrines. What exist are some declaratory security statements that have proved quite difficult to put into operation.

Four Policy Statements

Four such declaratory statements are common. The first is the principle of peaceful coexistence, usually known as the good-neighbor policy. This status quo policy with regard to interstate relations among African nations had its origin in the 1961 Monrovia draft charter of African and Malagasy states and was restated in the 1962 Lagos charter of the same group. The principle received its continental legality under Article 2 of the Organization of African Unity (OAU) Charter, which affirmed the independence, sovereignty, and territory integrity of member African states in addition to calling for peaceful resolutions of conflicts between African states.[7]

Second, nonalignment policy evolved with national-security considerations as its main basis. It sought to guarantee the security of the African states by refraining from involvement in either Eastern- or Western-bloc security arrangements and by denying operation of military bases by extracontinental powers, particularly the superpowers. At the founding of the OAU in May 1963, nonalignment was viewed as an essential element of Africa's security posture, one that would ensure the national security of the independent African states themselves. The founding fathers committed themselves to the principle by incorporating it in Article 3 of the OAU Charter.[8] Nonalignment was to provide a way out of the cold-war rivalries of the superpowers. It was founded on "the doctrine of national interest."[9]

The third and fourth declarations seek similar ends to those of non-alignment. The third, the movement to declare the Indian Ocean a "zone of peace," has had as its aim the protection of the continent from superpower conflicts, so that the trade between the Indian Ocean littoral states and the outside world might not be interrupted. Also of concern to the littoral states is the danger to their security should a nuclear confrontation occur between the superpowers in the Indian Ocean.[10] This explains why the littoral states worked hard to get the United Nations (UN) to declare the Indian Ocean a zone of peace. The fourth declaration, an earlier UN resolution to proclaim Africa "a nuclear free zone," came in response to the opposition of African states to French explosion of nuclear devices in the Sahara Desert during the 1960s. Such tests were seen by Africans as threatening their security, and international opinion was brought to bear on the French to cease testing in the region.

Peacekeeping, the OAU, and the UN

In addition to these declarations, the movement for a regional approach to peacekeeping assumed importance in Africa, especially after the failure of the 1960–1964 UN peacekeeping operation in the Congo (Zaire) and the subsequent increase in external intervention in that country.[11] The OAU has, since its inception, attempted to fulfill the role of regional peacekeeper through its Commission of Mediation, Conciliation, and Arbitration. But its efforts have often met with failure, and most recorded successes have left matters in abeyance.[12]

This experience may explain why the OAU has taken eighteen years before it has ventured into the world of international, or regional, peacekeeping, though member states had expected it to do so throughout its existence. It was not until the July 1981 Nairobi summit meeting that the OAU set up the first all-African peacekeeping force as part of a formula to resolve the prolonged Chadian civil war, which appeared to threaten inter-African peace. The force entered Chad early in 1982; in less than three months, its operation had collapsed. With it must have gone the illusion that the OAU would form a basis for inter-African security.

In 1960–1964, African leaders watched the UN betray Zaire's national security. After the Congo experience African countries steered clear of the UN as a source of security assistance, except in social and economic areas. Zaire itself came to depend increasingly on U.S., Belgian, and French direct interventions as an alternative to reliving the UN experience. The deposed Chadian government of Weddeye had turned first to Libya before succumbing to the fateful OAU plan. Angola in 1975 and Ethiopia in 1977 looked to the Soviet Union and Cuba when their security was threatened (Angola by South African invasion and Ethiopia by an external attack from Somalia). These cases underscore the extent to which African states are prepared to go in order to enhance national security and may suggest that in the future African states may shy away from OAU peacekeeping proposals. The inclination is likely to tilt in favor of extracontinental power intervention, with the consequence that the external threat to Africa's security—and, for that matter, to the national security of the continental states—will increase.[13] It is also possible that relatively stronger African states will violate the OAU Charter and intervene in the internal affairs of member states. Libya's intervention in Chad and Senegal's intervention in Gambia may serve as precursors of this trend.

Regional Conflicts

But as is already the case, future threats and challenges to national security of African states will come from within the continent. Many of the threats will continue to arise out of territorial disputes. That this is so is emphasized by the recognition that between 1960 and 1982 there have been two major wars pitting two or more independent African states against each other: the 1977–1978 war between Ethiopia and Somalia and the 1978–1979 Tanzania-Uganda war. The Ogaden war resulted in thirty thousand to fifty thousand deaths on both sides, with the cost for Ethiopia estimated at $500 million, not a little money for that poverty-stricken nation. Idi Amin's invasion and subsequent attempted annexation of the Kagera enclave resulted in the death of approximately forty-one hundred soldiers and civilians on both sides. More than a thousand Tanzanian civilians died during the Amin invasion, and the resulting war cost Tanzania between $375 million and $500 million, thus aggravating further the country's beleaguered economy.[14]

In the early and mid-1960s, a minor clash between Algeria and Morocco (October 1963) and military skirmishes between Kenya and Somalia and between Ethiopia and Somalia (1963–1967) occurred. They, too, involved territorial claims. But the 1977 border war between Egypt and Libya had nothing to do with territorial dispute. It was the consequence of ideological and personality conflicts that were expressed in what might rightly be called a brief power demonstration.

Southern African states face constant threats from the racist regime in South Africa, which accuses such countries as Angola, Mozambique, Zimbabwe, and Zambia of providing sanctuary to those seeking to free Namibia from South African control and to South African blacks opposed to the racist policies in Azania. The white regime in South Africa has therefore built a formidable war machine and has used it repeatedly since 1975 to plunder Angola, Mozambique, and Zimbabwe.

African refugees, the products of internal instability and secessionist movements that result from unresolved ethnic and racial differences, also have a bearing on national security of certain African states. The salient suspicion that exists between Ethiopia, on the one hand, and Egypt and Sudan, on the other, stems from support of refugees and secessionist movements. Egypt and Sudan support the Eritrean liberation fighters against Ethiopia. Sudan has also welcomed Ethiopian refugees opposed to the socialist government. Ethiopia, in retaliation, encourages anti-Numeiry groups living in Ethiopia. As another example, the activities of Ugandan exiles in Tanzania gave Amin a justification to invade Tanzania's Kagera enclave, an invasion that in turn produced a massive Tanzanian invasion of Uganda in late November 1978.

What first becomes evident from these conflicts is that the good-neighbor policy as a national-security doctrine has not received unanimous acceptance. Second, the doctrine of inviolability of territorial integrity of each of the OAU member states has not been adhered to by all, just as nonalignment has proved meaningless when national security is endangered from outside. Finally, the African principle of peaceful resolution of conflicts between African states has not been fulfilled.

National Security and Military Strength

No African state can be sure that each time it asks for external power intervention the request will automatically be acceded to. In recognition of this problem, African states appear to have accepted the cardinal law in international politics—that the national security of each state can only be guaranteed by the state itself and that this means the acquisition and maintenance of military power.[15] Even Kenya, which between 1964 and 1976 had thought that national security could be guaranteed by maintaining its status as a strong and dominant regional economic power, changed course following Idi Amin's claim on western Kenya and the closure of the Kenya-Tanzania border.[16]

The search for military power has therefore made many African states seek massive military assistance from the developed world, especially the Soviet Union and the United States.[17] In addition, African states spend several billion dollars a year to purchase military hardware. For example, in 1980 African countries spent $16 billion on arms. Perhaps because of serious economic problems, the figure dropped to $14 billion in 1981. Still, a large sum of money was used to acquire expensive war matériel that included U.S.-manufactured F5E, F5F, F4, and F16A fighter planes; supersonic French Mirage 2000 fighters as well as Mirage 5SD; Soviet MIG-15s, MIG-17s, MIG-19s, MIG-21s, and MIG-23s. The price of F5s, Mirage 2000, and MIG-23s is about $16 million each.[18] The average annual per capita military expenditure was $30 in 1981. The average cost for keeping one soldier under arms has been estimated at $8,200, with about 3 million people under arms in Africa at any one time. Between 1980 and 1981 seven African countries had a per capita military expenditure of more than $50, and the same number had armies of more than fifty thousand each. These are likely to be larger in the future. So far Egypt, Ethiopia, and Nigeria have forces in excess of one hundred thousand.

Some African countries try to supplement this military armament by entering into security arrangements with other states. Such arrangements have dual functions. For example, in 1963 Kenya and Britain signed a security assistance agreement. Though the details of the agreement are not known, it is believed to provide for British military assistance against both external and internal threats. In 1964 Kenya and Ethiopia signed a military pact against Somalia, when it became apparent that the latter threatened their respective national securities. Sudan and Egypt did the same in 1977 to balance out what Sudan perceived as a threat to its national security stemming from Islamic Fundamentalist Libya and Socialist Ethiopia.

In addition, a number of countries have either given military bases or access to military facilities to the superpowers. Between 1969 and 1977 the Soviet Union enjoyed the complete use of the Berbera air and naval base in Somalia. Since 1980 the same base has been turned over to the United States. Kenya, Sudan, Morocco, and Egypt have granted the United States access to military facilities, while the Soviet Union has treaties of friendship and cooperation with Libya, Angola, Ethiopia, and Mozambique. Soviet warships make calls at the ports in these countries. The underlying reason for this development, the OAU Charter provisions notwithstanding, is national security. Such facilities are given in return for economic and military assistance, either through grant-in-aid or through concessionary sales credit. It is also true that association with one superpower is perceived as protecting the national security of the state against threat or challenge by another superpower. Occasionally such association might be counted on when internal security is threatened from within. During the 1960s France was able to maintain in power its most trusted allies in former French West Africa. France, the United States, and Belgium have enabled Mobutu to become one of the longest-serving presidents in Africa.

If anything can be discerned from this discussion regarding African national security, it is the need for realism. Although African states appear to see their national security as depending on military strength, this reality has yet to be officially declared. What seems to be operating is an unannounced policy based on the assumption that modern and sophisticated weapons and large standing armies can deter potential aggressors. It is clear that in Africa, principles such as nonalignment, the absence of foreign bases, and restraints from entering into alliance with the superpowers must be subordinated to the realities of power politics. Thus armament and military association with the great powers are a reality of inter-African politics. They are the consequences of a desire to maintain, protect, and promote vital national interests.

Development and National Security

Paradoxically, however, the pursuit of power politics bears within it elements that, at times, threaten national security. African countries are held in the grip of underdevelopment, and economic and social indicators suggest no solution to their problems in the immediate future. At the same time that economic development has been slow, Africa has had the world's highest birthrate and population growth remains uncontrolled.[19] In spite of this situation, African states spend large sums of money on military equipment and maintain fairly sizable numbers of troops under arms (including highly trained personnel), instead of directing such crucial resources toward socioeconomic development.

Yet socioeconomic problems are known to cause internal instability. Internal instability, in turn, sometimes leads to interstate conflicts. For example, during the 1963–1965 civil war in Zaire, Zaire's forces and Ugandan troops clashed along their common border. Internal chaos in Uganda also influenced Amin's belligerent behavior during the period preceding the Tanzania-Uganda war. The consequences of this war could have been very grave for Uganda, because Tanzania achieved a capability to undermine Uganda's independence and sovereignty—vital Ugandan security interests.

The African armies, unlike the armies of the industrial countries, constitute power elites that often intervene in politics using their civilian-provided weapons. Once in power, they tend to create insecurity. At worst, the military might bring to power a maniac like Amin, or a fanatic such as Gaddafi, with the consequence that the regional status quo might be disturbed. The growing involvement with the superpowers in security arrangements contains the prospect of future superpower direct confrontation on the continent, as almost happened in Angola in 1975 and earlier in Zaire in 1960–1961.

Finally, the apparent arms race now underway in certain regions of Africa will tend to increase national insecurity. All the violent conflicts that have occurred between one or more groups of independent African states seem to correspond to high levels of armament[20] and have brought with them large numbers of refugees and corresponding internal instability. Insecurity may occur when military expenditures deplete the limited resources available for economic development and social services, in which case further threats will develop from within. Or insecurity may occur when internal conditions force the political leadership to create an external diversion, such as Siad Barre's fateful invasion of Ogaden in 1977 and Idi Amin's Kagera fiasco in 1978.

Conclusions

The national security of African states will continue to be threatened in the future. Their armies will grow larger and stronger and their weapons more deadly, while the sources of interstate conflict will largely remain unresolved. With the growing weakness of the OAU, a regional approach to conflict resolution will most likely be diminished and bilateral conflicts will become more explosive and have the potential to spread throughout the region.

This prospect seems inevitable, unless trained policymaking professionals become involved in solving the problems of Africa national security. Conflict resolution and management demand a sophistication that exceeds that of the nonprofessionals, whose experience and goals fail to account for the long-term and dynamic nature of security issues in the region.

Notes

1. Tom Mboya, *Challenge of Nationhood* (London: Andre Deutsch, 1970), preface.

2. The World Bank, *Accelerated Development in Sub-Saharan Africa* (Washington, D.C.: World Bank, 1981).

3. Kenneth L. Adelman, *African Realities* (New York: Crane and Russak, 1980).

4. See I. William Zartman, "The Foreign and Military Politics of African Boundary Problems," in Carl Widstrand, ed., *African Boundary Problems* (Uppsala: Scandinavian Institute of African Studies, 1969), p. 82; D. Katete Orwa, "Balance of Power Theory and Kenya's Foreign Policy in Eastern Africa," paper presented at the annual conference of the Historical Association of Kenya, August 1981, Nairobi, Kenya, pp. 10–17; and Julius Nyerere, *Ujamaa: Essays on Socialism* (London: Oxford University Press, 1968), p. 295.

5. Vernon D. McKay, ed., *African Diplomacy: Studies in the Determinants of Foreign Policy* (New York: Praeger, 1966), p. 6.

6. Zdenek Cervenka, *The Organization of African Unity and Its Charter* (New York: Praeger, 1969), pp. 94–95.

7. O. Ojo, D. K. Orwa, and C. Utete, *African International Relations* (London: Longman's, 1983), ch. 5.

8. Compare J. W. Burton, *International Relations: A General Theory* (Cambridge: Cambridge University Press, 1967), p. 265; M. S. Rajan, "The Future of Non-Alignment," *Annals* no. 312 (1965), p. 126; Morio Rossi, *The Third World: The Unaligned Countries and the World Revolution* (New York: Funk and Wagnalls, 1963), p. 47; and F. A. Sayegh, ed., *The Dynamics of Neutralism in the Arab World* (San Francisco: Symposium, 1964).

9. McKay, *African Diplomacy*, p. 18.

10. Jeanette Hartman, "Tanzania and the Indian Ocean," *Journal of East Africa Development and Research* 2 (1981).

11. For a critical view of the UN Congo Operation, see D. Katete Orwa, *The Congo Betrayal: UN-US and Lumumba* (Nairobi: Kenya Literature Bureau, forthcoming 1983).

12. K. Mathews, "The Organization of African Unity," *India Quarterly*, 33 (1977); and Ojo, Orwa, and Utete, *African International Relations*, chs. 5 and 9.

13. See Mathews, "The Organization of African Unity," pp. 313–314 and Zdenek Cervenka, "Major Policy Shifts in the Organization of African Unity, 1963–1973," in K. Ingham, ed., *Foreign Relations of African States* (London: Butterworths, 1974), p. 337.

14. See news reports in *Weekly Review* (Nairobi), May 1, 1981 and in *Africa Now*, July 1982.

15. Hans Morgenthau, *Politics Among Nations*, 5th ed. (Calcutta, India: Scientific Book Agency, 1976).

16. Orwa, "Balance of Power Theory. . . ."

17. See David E. Albright, ed., *Africa and International Communism* (London: Macmillan, 1982), p. 3; Ronald Bruce St. John, "The Soviet Penetration of Libya," *The World Today* 37 (April 1982); Mordechai Abir, "The Contentious Horn of Africa," *Conflict Studies* no. 24 (1972), p. 9; A. A. Catagno, "The Horn of Africa: The Competition for Power," in J. S. Cottrell and R. H. Burrell, eds., *The Indian Ocean: Its Political and Military Importance* (New York: Praeger, 1972), p. 162; and Christopher Coker, "Reagan and Africa," *World Today* 37 (April 1982).

18. See Orwa, "Balance of Power Theory. . . ."; International Institute for Strategic Studies, *The Military Balance, 1978–79* and *1979–1980* (London: IISS, 1978 and 1979); and the Stockholm International Peace Research Institute *Yearbooks* for 1979, 1980, and 1981 (Stockholm: SIPRI, 1979, 1980, 1981). Also see relevant news items in *Africa Guide* (1981) and *Africa Now* (July 1982).

19. The World Bank, *Accelerated Development in Sub-Saharan Africa*, pp. 2–4.

20. Ojo, Orwa, and Utete, *African International Relations*, ch. 9.

Abbreviations

AG	Action Group
ALC	African Liberation Committee
ANC	African National Congress
ARMSCOR	South African Armaments Manufacturing Corporation
BADEA	Arab Bank for Economic Development in Africa
Balu Bakat	Association des Baluba du Katanga
BCEAO	Central Bank of West African States
BEAC	Central African Bank
CAE	Central African Empire
CAR	Central African Republic
CEAO	Economic Community of West Africa
CEEAC	Economic Community
CEPGL	Great Lakes Economic Community
CFA	Communauté des Francs Africains
CIA	Central Intelligence Agency
CMEA	Council for Mutual Economic Assistance
CONKAT	Confederation des Associations Tribales du Katanga
CONSAS	Constellation of Southern African States
COREMO	Revolutionary Council for Mozambique
CP	Conservative party
DP	Democratic party
EACSO	East African Common Services Organization
ECOWAS	Economic Community of West African States
EEC	European Economic Community
FLING	Front for the National Liberation of Guiné
FLNC	Congolese National Liberation Front
FNLA	Frente Nacional de Libertação de Angola
FRELIMO	Frente Nacional de Libertação de Mozambique
FROLINAT	Front de Libération National du Tchad
GNP	gross national product
IAF	Inter-African Force
IBRD	International Bank for Reconstruction and Development
IMET	International Military Education and Training Program
KY	Kabaka Yekka
LDCs	less developed countries
MPLA	Popular Movement for the Liberation of Angola

MRU	Mano River Union
NATO	North Atlantic Treaty Organization
NCNC	National Congress of Nigerian Citizens
NPC	Northern Peoples Congress
OAU	Organization of African Unity
OCAM	Central African Monetary Organization
OECD	Organization for Economic Cooperation and Development
OMVG	Gambia River Development Organization
OPEC	Organization of Petroleum Exporting Countries
PAC	Pan-Africanist Conference
PAIGC	Partido Africano da Independencia da Guiné e Cabo Verde
PNDC	Provisional National Defense Council
POLISARIO	Popular Front for the Liberation of Saguia el Hamra and Rio de Oro
RCC	Revolutionary Command Council
RDA	Rassemblement Démocratique Africain
SADCC	Southern Africa Development Coordination Conference
SADR	Sahara Arab Democratic Republic
SATO	South Atlantic Treaty Organization
SWAPO	Southwest Africa People's Organization
TCDC	technical cooperation among developing countries
TOW	tube-launched, optically tracked, wire-guided, antitank guided missile
UDEAC	Customs Union of Central African States
UDI	Unilateral Declaration of Independence
UMOA	West African Monetary Union
UN	United Nations
UNITA	National Union for the Total Independence of Angola (União Nacional para a Independência Total de Angola)
UPC	Uganda People's Congress
UPM	Uganda Patriotic Movement
ZANU	Zimbabwe African National Union
ZAPU	Zimbabwe African People's Union
ZAPU-PF	Zimbabwe African People's Union-Patriotic Front
ZimCORD	Zimbabwe Conference for Reconstruction and Development

About the Contributors

Major **Bruce E. Arlinghaus** is currently a political-military affairs officer serving in the Plans Division of the Office of the Deputy Chief of Staff for Operations, Headquarters, U.S. Army, Europe. In addition to having taught anthropology and political science in the Department of Social Sciences, U.S. Military Academy, West Point (1979–1983), he has taught at Indiana University, the University of Maryland (Europe), and at the U.S. Naval Postgraduate School. He is the editor of *Arms for Africa: Military Assistance and Foreign Policy in the Developing World* and *Industrial Capacity and Defense Planning: Sustained Conflict and Surge Capability* (with Lee D. Olvey and Henry A. Leonard) and author of *Military Development in Africa: The Political and Economic Risks of Arms Transfers.* He is currently coediting (with Pauline H. Baker) *African Armies: Evolution, Impact and Capabilities* (Westview, forthcoming) and (with James R. Golden and Asa A. Clark) *Conventional Deterrence in NATO: Alternatives for European Defense.*

Pauline H. Baker is a research scientist in the Battelle Human Affairs Center's Washington Operations. Prior to her association with Battelle, Dr. Baker was a professional staff member of the Senate Foreign Relations Committee and Staff Director of the Africa Subcommittee. She has held teaching posts at the University of Lagos, Nigeria, and University of California at Los Angeles and is the author of *Urbanization and Political Change: The Politics of Lagos.*

Francis M. Deng is a Sudanese ambassador to Canada. A graduate of Khartoum University and the Yale University Law School, he has been active in both academic and diplomatic pursuits. Before assuming his current post, he was Sudan's ambassador to the United States (1974–1976) and to the Scandinavian countries (1972–1974) and served as the minister of state for foreign affairs (1976–1980). He is the author of numerous books and articles on the Dinka of Sudan, including *The Dinka of the Sudan* and *African of Two Worlds: The Dinka in Afro-Arab Sudan* and has taught both in the Sudan and the United States.

Arthur Jay Klinghoffer is a professor of political science at Rutgers University. He received his bachelor's degree from the University of Michigan and his master's and doctoral degrees from Columbia University. He also received a certificate from the Russian Institute of Columbia University. Dr. Klinghoffer is the author of *Soviet Perspectives on African Socialism, Soviet Oil Politics in the Middle East, Soviet American Relations,* and *The*

Soviet Union and the Angolan War. He contributed to two collections edited by Roger Kanet, *On the Road to Communism* and *The Soviet Union and the Developing Nations,* and one by Della Sheldon, *Dimensions of Detente.* He spent the academic year 1982–1983 as a visiting professor at the Department of Political Science, University of Jerusalem.

Dan Muhwezi is a graduate student in the Department of Political Science at Iowa State University and a research assistant to Dr. Olorunsola.

Victor A. Olorunsola is professor of political science at Iowa State University. A graduate of Indiana University, he has done research in Nigeria, Ghana, and Sierra Leone on grants from the Hoover Institution, Ford Foundation, and the Social Science Research Council. His major publications include *Soldiers and Power: The Development Performance of the Nigerian Military Regime, The Politics of Cultural Subnationalism in Africa,* and most recently, with Donald Rothchild, *State Versus Ethnic Claims: African Policy Dilemmas.*

D. Katete Orwa is a member of the Department of Government at the University of Nairobi. He has studied both in Africa and the United States and is the author of a number of articles and books on African foreign policy and international relations. His latest publications include *African International Relations* (with O. Ojo and C. Utete) and *The Congo Betrayal.*

John M. Ostheimer is professor and chair of Political Science at Northern Arizona University. Author of *Nigerian Politics, Politics of the Western Indian Ocean Islands,* and several articles on African affairs, he earned the doctorate at Yale University and taught at the University of Dar es Salaam.

Pearl T. Robinson is an associate professor of political science at Tufts University. She received a Ph.D. from Columbia University. Professor Robinson is the author of "The Political Context of Regional Development in the West African Sahel" and "Traditional Clientage and Political Change in a Hausa Community" and coeditor of the book *Transformation and Resiliency in Africa.*

Donald Rothchild is a professor of political science at the University of California, Davis, and a visiting fellow at the Institute of International Studies at the University of California, Berkeley. He has lectured at universities in Uganda, Kenya, Zambia, and Ghana. His books include *Racial Bargaining in Independent Kenya;* coauthor, *Scarcity, Choice, and Public Policy in Middle Africa;* and coeditor, *Eagle Entangled, Eagle Defiant* and *State Versus Ethnic Claims: African Policy Dilemmas.*

Annette M. Seegers received her B.A. and M.A. degrees from the University of Pretoria. In 1977 she came to the United States under the Fulbright Hays Exchange Program to pursue doctoral studies in political science at the Loyola University of Chicago. Her dissertation on the outcomes of the revolution in Zimbabwe is expected to be completed in 1983. Among her publications are *Revolutionary Strategy in Mozambique, The Problem of Three Races in America: Majority Tyranny and Its Resolution,* and *Imperialism and Civil-Military Relations: The Portuguese Case.*

Wayne A. Selcher is professor of political science at Elizabethtown College and a prominent writer on Brazil. In addition to many articles and studies, he has authored *The Afro-Asian Dimension of Brazilian Foreign Policy, 1956–72* and *Brazil's Multilateral Relations: Between First and Third Worlds,* as well as edited *Brazil in the International System: The Rise of a Middle Power.*

Claude E. Welch, Jr., is professor and chairman of the Department of Political Science, State University of New York, Buffalo. A graduate of Harvard and Oxford universities, he is the author or editor of nine books, including *Anatomy of Rebellion, Civilian Control of the Military: Theory and Cases from Developing Countries,* and *The Soldier and the State in Africa.* His latest book is *Human Rights and Development in Africa.*

I. William Zartman, director of the African Studies Program at the School for Advanced International Studies of The Johns Hopkins University, is well known among students of comparative politics for his extensive publications on Africa and the Middle East. He has written, edited, or contributed to more than forty books. His most recent publications include *Elites in the Middle East, Africa in the 1980s: A Continent in Crisis, Political Elites in Arab North Africa,* and *The Practical Negotiation.*

Index

Abboud, Ibrahim, 119, 132
Aburi accords (1967), 120
Acheampong, I. K., 110, 117
Acholi, 150
Action Group (AG) (Nigeria), 143, 145
Active Zone, 42–50, 51, 55
Acyl, Ahmat, 180
Addis Ababa Agreement and Self-
    Government Act (1972) (Sudan), 102,
    146, 147, 154
Afars, 107
Afghanistan. *See under* Soviet Union
Africa
    agriculture, 157
    arms purchases, 67–68, 208, 210
    and Belgium, 141, 209
    boundary problems, 10, 16, 21, 141,
        142, 152, 154, 172, 173–174, 207
    and Brazil, 59–74
    and Canada, 37
    and China, 26, 33, 35
    civilian-military relations, 129, 130–131,
        132, 134–136
    and Communism, 20, 21, 22, 26, 31–
        32, 40. *See also* Marxism-Leninism;
        Socialism
    coups d'etat, 126, 128–129, 131, 132,
        133, 177, 189
    and Cuba, 19, 24, 51, 87–88, 193
    development, 4, 7, 19, 20, 111–112, 157,
        158, 209–210
    economies, 105, 157, 158
    education, 90, 112, 117
    egalitarianism, 9, 185
    ethnic groups, 105, 118–119, 153, 173.
        See also Ethnoregional conflict and
        interests
    foreign intervention, 1, 8–9, 10–11, 12,
        44–50, 51
    foreign workers in, 62
    and France, 21, 35, 37, 39–57, 166,
        177, 178, 179, 205, 208, 209

and Great Britain, 21, 35, 37, 43, 51,
    141, 186
internal conflict, 1, 2, 8, 9, 47, 126,
    140, 203, 210. *See also* Class conflict
    and dominance; Ethnoregional conflict
    and interests
and Israel, 175–176, 182
military, 2, 21, 126, 127–130, 132–136,
    203–204, 208, 209–210. *See also*
    African High Command; Inter-African
    Force; Islamic Legion
and military assistance, 2, 8, 9, 20, 21,
    29, 35, 45, 47, 208–209
and national security, 2–4, 12, 16, 99–
    100, 141, 153, 158, 162–165, 203–210.
    See also Organization of African
    Unity
North, 19, 33, 54, 130
and nuclear energy, 164–165, 205
political factionalism, 9, 17, 20, 21, 140,
    157, 203. *See also* Political
    recruitment
presidents, 204
radicalism, 132–133, 134, 135, 136
raw materials, 10, 34, 36, 44, 64. *See
    also specific kinds*
refugees, 9–10, 141, 164, 207, 210
regional defense, 158, 159, 162–165
rural, 133, 134, 157
solidarity, 3, 69, 159–168, 189, 190,
    193, 195, 198. *See also* Libya, and
    Afro-Arab solidarity; Organization of
    African Unity
and Soviet Union, 1, 4, 11, 19, 20, 22,
    24–37, 51, 88, 208, 210
sovereignty, 3, 16, 20, 158
stability, 2, 13, 19, 41, 47–48, 49, 99,
    136, 153, 154–155, 210. *See also*
    Exchange state systems; State,
    concept of
statehood, 1, 7, 11
Subsaharan, 19, 33, 35, 59, 140
and UN, 29, 188, 189, 205, 206

217